Responses to David (

Paradise Incorporated (Presidio, 1982)

"Illuminating … vivid."

> —*The Philadelphia Enquirer*

"Astonishingly objective … captivating, well written."

> —*The Richmond News Leader*

"{The} book is wonderful. I couldn't put it down; and I have been recommending it to all and sundry."

> —Frances FitzGerald, author of *Fire in the Lake*, winner of the Pulitzer Prize and National Book Award

"Meticulously researched."

> —*The San Francisco Chronicle*

"An ambitious and serious book and a real page turner."

> —Mark Kramer, Founding Director, Nieman Program on Narrative Journalism, Harvard University

"The story has been told many times, but rarely with such enlightening objectivity as here."

> —*Publisher's Weekly*

"Rich in detail … remarkably dispassionate. An unusually attentive, shrewd, comprehensive account."

> —*Qualitative Sociology*

The Builder's Guide (Taunton, 1992)

"Gerstel writes with grace and humor."

—*Remodeling*

"Insightful and intelligently written ... a sense of quality and ethics pervade."

—Builders Booksource

"David has achieved the ultimate American dream. For decades he has worked for himself doing something he loves—building good houses."

—*The Master Builder*

"{Gerstel} manages to cover the basics in a way that is both informative and entertaining.... Occasionally the author's confidence in his own methods obscures the usefulness of alternatives, but these flaws are overwhelmed by a great deal of well-considered material."

—Sal Alfano, editor-in-chief of *The Journal of Light Construction*

Running a Successful Construction Company (Taunton; 2002)

"My strongest feelings about you come from all the builders I've known over the years who hold your book in such high esteem."

—Kevin Ireton, editor-in-chief of *Fine Homebuilding*

"The book's awesome, man."

—Matt Sickorez, engineer and aspiring builder

"I've read your book over and over … I find myself doing something right. Later I look through the book, and there's the idea and it's highlighted in yellow."

—Chris Vaughn, general building contractor

"This is a great book. It has helped my company tremendously."

—Jim Paulin, Rubicon Construction, *Amazon Reviews*

"Now, don't get the big head."

—Sandra Gerstel, David's wife

Clients of David Gerstel's company

"What a wonderful job you did. It was a massive undertaking since the house needed so much work. The only problem is, what other builder could I find who would be near your standards?"

—Linda Deaktor, retired postmaster

"When the painters are gone, we all tend to take for granted the builder's work. After four years of reflection, I want to thank you for the great performance in the restoration of our 1905 home. Details were well executed. You understood and embraced suggestions from others. Few have the stature and presence to do that.

—Robert McNeil, Managing Director, Sanderling Ventures

"Thank you for the work you did, the thoughtfulness you gave to the design process, your enthusiasm for your work, and your integrity."

—Pat Graef, project manager

CRAFTING THE CONSIDERATE HOUSE

David Gerstel

Latitude
67

Publisher: Latitude 67

Rights:

Text, drawings, construction process photos © 2010 by David Gerstel
Construction finish photographs © 2010 by Jim Kardos

General Editor: Jackie Callahan Parente jcp@editorial-services.com
Cover Design: Monica Brewer and David Gerstel
Interior Design: David Gerstel

Important Notice—Please Read

Crafting the Considerate House is intended to stimulate and entertain, but it is not intended to serve as a financial, design, or technical guide for other projects. Readers must develop financial strategies, design parameters, and technical specifications tailored to their own locale and circumstance. The author, publisher, and all other persons or entities associated with production of *Crafting the Considerate House* shall have no liability to any person or entity with respect to any liability, loss, or damage caused or alleged to be caused directly or indirectly by information, concepts, strategies, or descriptions of materials , methods, or equipment described herein.

Library of Congress Cataloging-in-Publication Data

Gerstel, David U., 1945–

Crafting the considerate house / David Gerstel   Includes index

ISBN-13: 978-09826709-5-8

1.House construction 2.Sustainable architecture 3.Sustainable buildings— design and construction 4.Ecological houses 5. Real estate development I.Title

TH4811.G47 2010
690.836—dc22

Printed and bound in the United States of America

10 9 8 7 6 5 4 3 2 1 / 14 13 12 11 10

Structured Plumbing is a trademark registered to Advanced Conservation Technology, Inc. DBA as ACT, Inc. D'MAND Systems

www.consideratehouse.com

Please contact us for permissions and bulk purchases

for Sandra, always

Acknowledgements

I am grateful to all of you who have taken an interest in *Considerate House*. A great reward of writing is having readers. I welcome your comments, including criticisms and corrections. Please contact me at ConsiderateHouse.com. If you find the book engaging, you will share my appreciation for the many people who educated and encouraged me, both in the crafting of my considerate house and in writing this book about it.

My wife, Sandra, in her unfailingly candid but kind way, has brought to bear her acute sense of what works or does not in a house and a home, and what works and does not in prose. Much of what is good about the house and the book comes from Sandra. She encouraged important improvements on my initial designs for the house. Readers of the book have been spared a good many corny jokes and overwrought phrases for her having escorted them off the pages.

During construction, I was fortunate to work with outstanding craftspeople including Ron Roberts, Morris Knight, David Haight, Zichao Chang, Ryan Stone, Grant Reading, David Kendall, Greg Steward, Dean Fukawa, and George Nesbitt. The feel of a house derives in large measure from the work of men and women who remain anonymous to the people who eventually make it their home. They have no idea who put in the pipes that unfailingly deliver fresh water for their bath each morning, or who crafted the banister that graces their stairway and keeps them safe. The work of the people with whom I built the considerate house can provide comfort and pleasure to others for a century and more to come. You will get to know many of them in the story that follows. Most of the people who appear in the book go by their own names. A few do not, either for their protection or for the sake of the narrative.

I am grateful as well for the timely suggestions made by fellow builders Fred Blodgett and Randy Hellstern as I was crafting the drawings.

Joyce King's contribution predates even my first hatching of the idea for the house and the book. Her environmental consciousness and activism go far beyond the Johnny-one-note worry about the inconvenience that climate change may cause for our human species, to a deep regard for all living things. Her vision has long inspired me. Joyce not only contributed to the design of the house. She read my entire manuscript with care and gently pointed out many instances of unclear thinking and awkward writing even while encouraging me to push *Considerate House* to completion.

Jim Kardos, who is both a skilled carpenter and a gifted photographer, created the photos of the completed house at 19th Street. His work speaks for itself. Both Jim and I are grateful to Nan Phelps for her suggestions. Nan's wonderful portraiture can be viewed at www.nanphelps.com.

Curt Burbick and Tony Rinella, two able architects, coached me in drafting and redrafting my line illustrations. Carol Staswick did an efficient and thorough job of copy editing my manuscript, removing left-over grammatical errors and correcting weak syntax. Nancy Adess, Janet Smith, and Peter Masterson, author of the invaluable *Book Design and Production,* consulted expertly on the layout and production of my book. Carolyn Crampton steered me in the right direction as I set about learning book design, and Monica Brewer provided key design ideas for the cover. Judy Hardin has been a source of inspiration and helped me to keep abreast of the rapidly changing world of publishing. Stephen Denney aided me greatly in penetrating the mysteries of the copyright page. Tom Hassett carefully proofed the entire book the reliable old-fashioned way, with a sharp red pencil in hand. As the reader will see in Chapter Eight, Chris Kelley and Dean Fukawa contributed greatly to analyzing the strengths and shortcomings of the house once it was completed and became a home.

From the beginning to the end, my skilled and astute general editor, Jackie Callahan Parente, coached me in the writing and production of the book with patience and utter reliability. Writers understand how crucial good editors are to the success of their books. Jackie is so good an editor she makes you wish you had someone equally observant and candid to advise you in every aspect of your life. Jackie can be reached at www.editorial-services.com.

David Gerstel
Kensington, California
February, 2010

CONTENTS

FOUNDATIONS

The site where my crew and I awaited our first load of concrete one sunny morning in early June 2006 was labeled in the public records as, "Parcel Number 413280026-0, Andrade Rose" tract. It had no mailing address. None would be conferred until a building inspector deemed the house we would build on the parcel safe for human habitation. The site would then be named, "2768 19th Street, San Pablo, California." A town of 20,000 near the northern end of the San Francisco Bay, San Pablo had once been best known for its bikers and meth labs. Now it was rapidly changing as first and second generation American families of Asian, Indian, Persian, Mexican, and Salvadoran origins bought and renewed its bungalows, adding second stories, wrought iron gates, arched porticoes, and coats of richly hued paint.

"Nineteenth Street," as we named first our parcel and later the house we built on it, was the last open lot on a long street of reviving bungalows. My wife, Sandra, and I had acquired it in 2003. I had decided to construct a house on the lot as a way of exploring certain concerns I had developed during my nearly forty years of building and renovating houses: How can we provide people who are not wealthy with houses they will love and can afford? How can we build those homes so that they are healthy to live in? Can we learn to build without consuming

1

resources so greedily that we wreck our larger environment? But the house would not attempt to answer the questions with any headline-winning technological innovation. It would try to solve problems not with "a single silver bullet but with 100 silver B-Bs," as a fellow builder who is also interested in keeping things simple says about his own efforts. We'd fire the first of our B-Bs during construction of the foundation. And we would bag a few successes.

An engineer in suspenders, a builder in suspense

There are many ways to build a house foundation. Insulating concrete forms (ICFs)—large, dense, hollow foam blocks, which are stacked to form a wall, laced with bars of reinforcing steel, and then filled with concrete—have come into use for foundation construction in recent years. Wood set directly on the ground, but so saturated with chemicals that termites and other agents of decay want nothing to do with it, serves as the foundation for hundreds of thousands of houses in the United States. In the housing tracts of the western United States, millions of homes have been stood up on slabs of concrete reinforced with grids of steel bar or with cable that is tightened after the concrete is poured.

Along 19th Street in San Pablo, homes are built both on slabs and on another type of foundation. That's the T-footing, so named because in section (the view you have when you slice through a structure as if it were a loaf of bread) it has the shape of an upside-down "T," typically extending one to two feet into the ground and about eight inches above it. Each of the foundation types has its time and place, its pros and cons. ICFs are easy to assemble and offer energy efficiency...*maybe*. One energy efficiency expert reports that the claimed insulating value of certain ICFs is based on measurements before concrete and steel are installed, and that with steel and concrete in place, that value drops by two-thirds, to around that of medium-performance windows. Such suspect or disputed claims for building products are, as we shall see, one of many obstacles we must navigate around in our attempts to build more considerate houses.

As for slabs, they can be inexpensive. Artisans have invented wonderful ways of scoring, staining, and waxing them, enabling the slabs to perform double duty, to serve both as structure and as beautiful finish flooring. But walking on concrete can be unpleasant and hard on the legs. Insulating slabs properly is costly, and if they are not insulated they will drive up heating costs. And slabs crack and eventually fail. So do all foundations. Replacing slabs, however, is particularly difficult and expensive, requiring that the living space above be emptied and risking destruction of other elements of the house along with the foundation.

For 19th Street, I had in mind a foundation that would be economical to build and also relatively easy to replace when its useful life expired. The choice of foundation type had not, however, been entirely mine to make. In fact, it was largely dictated by Peter Murphy, whom I had hired when the house was barely imagined, amounting to only preliminary sketches on sheets of grid paper. Peter's letterhead describes him as an "Earth Science Consultant" and "Geological and Foundation Engineer." He is, in other words, what construction people call a "soils engineer." A report from a soils engineer is required by San Francisco Bay Area building departments for any substantial construction. He analyzes the composition and geological history of the earth below the surface of the proposed structure (is it stable, is it sliding, how has it responded to earthquakes) and then mandates guidelines for securely attaching a building to it.

Soils guys typically arrive for work at a building site in a good looking SUV and bring along motor driven augers to probe the earth. Peter Murphy arrived in a worn, faded blue pickup truck loaded with sectioned tubes, sledgehammers, and five men with whom he conversed in Portuguese. He sported bright yellow suspenders that seemed exhausted, allowing his baggy brown canvas trousers to droop low at the back, revealing more than one would normally expect to see of a licensed geological consultant. Peter's relaxed, low-tech style may help to limit his overhead. He does charge highly competitive rates. His fellow professionals speak of his work with respect for its rigor; builders and developers sometimes speak of the rigor with bitterness and anger over the costs it imposes on their projects.

At four points along the perimeter of the house, Peter marked the soil and his men began sledgehammering the tubes into the ground, screwing a new three foot section of tube into the previous one just before it reached ground level. After the tubes had been driven nine feet down in two locations and eighteen feet in two others, Peter signaled his satisfaction.

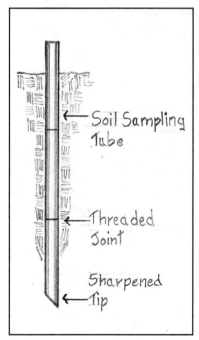

Soil Sampling Tube

Threaded Joint

Sharpened Tip

The men attached crossbars to the tubes, set jacks under the crossbars, and began cranking the tubes upward and out of the ground a section at a time. Peter seated himself on a stack of my lumber, pulled a manual from worn briefcase, and commenced reading.

Because their analysis of the earth beneath a site determines the type of foundation that may be used at the site, and the type determines the cost, soils engineers have great power in the lives of Bay Area builders. Though the cost can be relatively low or high, at best it starts around painful and extends upward to brutal. You are lucky if the foundation takes only one dollar out of every ten you have to spend on your building. In difficult soils, the foundation can consume a quarter or more of a construction budget.

Edgy but hopeful, I walked over to Peter to lobby him a bit. Admiringly, I pointed out the neighboring houses, emphasizing that their foundations were fifty and more years old, likely made of lousy concrete, barely reinforced, and shallow; and that the houses were nevertheless quite stable, as indicated by the level lines of their siding, eaves, and sills. "Good soil," I enthused. Peter pointed directly across the street at a garage. It slumped sadly to the left. "You wouldn't want that happening to your work, would you?" "It couldn't possibly," I countered. The problem with the garage was surely not the foundation but a lack of lateral shear resistance (what you'd call "bracing" if you were not trying to impress an engineer with your knowledge of building structure), and I would be installing plenty of that, I assured him. Peter was not impressed. The houses we were looking at had not yet experienced a severe earthquake, he said. They had not been tested, but would be eventually, and probably soon. The fact that they were still upright and intact at this point did not reassure him.

Peter opened a book of soil-stained and much-fingered maps, pointing out the lines drawn jaggedly across the familiar topography of the Bay Area. The lines marked zones of contact, or faults, between gigantic sections of the earth's crust. From time to time, those sections, or tectonic plates, abruptly move in order to release tension built up over years as they slide slowly in opposing directions. One particularly fearsome line marked the San Andreas Fault, whose last major movement had occurred just two months shy of a century before the day Peter came out to 19th Street. Somewhere west of San Francisco, miles beneath the Pacific Ocean, the San Andreas plates had slipped merely the length of a small truck. The slippage expressed itself at ground level with such force that men and women in the city were flung against the walls of their homes and work places; the masonry skin of buildings rattled loose and piled atop people on the sidewalks below; and poorly constructed houses tumbled from their foundations and into the street.

The 19th Street site is located eighteen miles from the San Andreas, not right up against it like San Francisco. Some consolation there? Enough to mollify Peter? Well, no. In 1989, an earthquake mild in comparison with the 1906 San Andreas episode, and originating not eighteen but some seventy miles from 19th Street, had opened a fifty foot hole in the roadbed of a nearby five lane bridge over the Bay and collapsed a mile and a half long section of an elevated freeway. In short, Peter emphasized, at eighteen miles' distance, the San Andreas easily threatened 19th Street. And nearer by lay the Hayward Fault. Its last major slippage, in 1868, had collapsed virtually every building in small towns nearby.

The geological record suggests that the Hayward Fault adjusts forcefully about every 150 years. On the day Peter and I talked at the 19th Street lot, the Hayward was, therefore, just about due for another slip. And it lay, at its northern extremity, not seventy miles from the 19th Street site, or even eighteen miles, but a leisurely five minute walk away—within a few feet of the hot dog hut, junior college, ice cream parlor, and Salvadoran restaurant that grace San Pablo's downtown. Of course, San Pablo might get lucky. The Hayward might slip not right below its commercial hub but much further south, as it had in 1868. Nevertheless, Peter emphasized, our site was at risk for assault by a very violent earthquake—one at the upper end of the five-step scale used to characterize earthquake force—during the useful life of the house we proposed to construct. And no telling how often it would have to stay upright and protect its inhabitants during mild, strong, very strong, and violent earthquakes before or after the Big One struck.

As his crew jacked the tubes to the surface and laid them in rows on the ground, Peter opened a few, revealing thin cylinders of soil—samples of the vertically stacked layers of earth that extended to a depth of eighteen feet below us, now displayed horizontally. "Not so bad," he hinted. I smiled. "And not too good either," he continued. I grimaced. "Expansive clays," he told me. Different compositions at different depths, but generally silty.

Another geological torment for Bay Area builders. Swelling into a sticky, black, dense goop during the rainy season, then shrinking into a gray, fissured, rock-hard mass during the dry summers, the stuff tortures house foundations. When it swells in the rain, it shoves foundations upward. When it shrinks away, it leaves them insufficiently supported so that they slump downward. The alternation of up and down movement cracks concrete foundations, sometimes all the way through, breaking them into a series of large chunks.

Expansive clays! Now I was done with hopeful and way into tense, feeling my wallet deflate as I crouched to study the soil samples. To give a house a chance of holding out against a very violent earthquake and expansive clay, what sort of foundation would Peter be dictating? He gave me a tentative answer as he and his crew began packing up: a T-footing foundation, probably. One with the footing dug four feet into the ground, the first three feet of soil being of such low quality that it was useless, in his opinion, for bearing the weight of the house. The footing itself would need to be maybe a foot thick and two feet wide, and the vertical stem about a foot wide. Or, should I choose to go with a slab. . . . "Never mind the slab," I said. As far as I was concerned, houses built on slabs were virtually throwaway houses. I would not build one. As for a

T-footing foundation, the costs would be up in the punishing range, so steep they'd kill the project. San Pablo was a modest town. A financially reasonable project there could not accommodate massive foundation costs. The T-footing that Peter was suggesting would require excavating a trench four feet deep and two feet wide around the perimeter of the house. The excavation would produce a dozen large dump trucks' worth of dirt. Almost all of it would have to be hauled to the landfill. Building forms for the foundation in that deep trench would be hazardous. Protecting workers against the hazard would require costly shoring of the sides of the trench. Building the forms would require much lumber, and when the forms were complete they would gobble up huge quantities of concrete. A deep T-footing foundation was just not financially feasible.

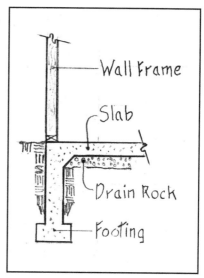

I countered Peter with another idea. How about an entirely different type of foundation, a pier and grade beam system, I suggested. Yes, I knew they were typically specified for steep hillside lots. I had installed them on hillsides but also on nearly flat lots. Why not install a pier and grade beam system here? It would, relative to a deep T foundation, greatly reduce the volumes of excavation, formwork, and concrete. Peter gave me a look that might have been a mixture of startled, puzzled, and intrigued, muttered something that sounded like a combination of "hmm" and "goodbye," and drove away, the engine of the faded blue pickup accelerating smoothly.

Piers and grade beams

Peter Murphy's written report and requirements arrived in my office neatly bound between thick black covers, containing news so good I hardly winced at the invoice for $2,000 accompanying it. The report firmly ruled out, as if no one would ever consider such an absurd idea, the use of a T foundation. Instead, it dictated exactly the pier and grade beam that I had proposed.

A pier and grade beam foundation can be visualized as comparable to the post and beam construction, a series of posts with a beam across their tops, which you have seen in structures from garden fences to the roof supports of big-box stores. The piers, however, are not wood or steel, as the posts for walls and roofs usually are, and they are not visible above ground. Instead, they are constructed of concrete poured into shafts drilled in the earth. The beams, too, are cast from concrete, which is poured into forms built at ground level across the tops of the piers.

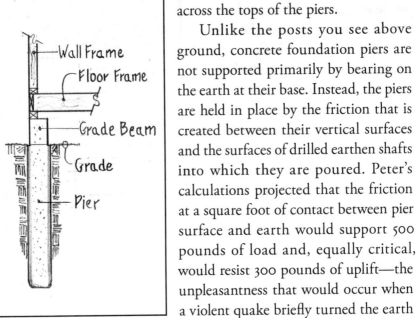

Unlike the posts you see above ground, concrete foundation piers are not supported primarily by bearing on the earth at their base. Instead, the piers are held in place by the friction that is created between their vertical surfaces and the surfaces of drilled earthen shafts into which they are poured. Peter's calculations projected that the friction at a square foot of contact between pier surface and earth would support 500 pounds of load and, equally critical, would resist 300 pounds of uplift—the unpleasantness that would occur when a violent quake briefly turned the earth upon which San Pablo is built into a trampoline.

Wood frame houses are not very heavy. The load imposed by the house we would stand up on the foundation at 19th Street, even allowing for furnishings and a crowd of guests at a New Year's party, is generously stipulated in standard building codes to max out at about forty tons. Four piers could hold up the forty tons in everyday conditions. However, they also had to support their own weight and the weight of the grade beam. They had to be numerous enough so that a reasonably sized grade beam could span piers without sagging or breaking. And they needed to be able to sustain the house through the momentary but extreme loads that would occur during earthquakes. We would end up installing twenty-one piers—enough, it was calculated, to hold the house in place and keep the occupants safe during even a major jolt from slippage along the Hayward Fault.

The chances that 19th Street with twenty-one piers anchoring it to the ground would handle a major (if not every conceivable) earthquake were good. Often lost in the tragic, dramatic accounts of the building collapses and loss of life in San Francisco during the 1906 San Andreas quake is the fact that wood frame houses well built on solid ground (as opposed to manmade fill) survived the quake. It was the fires the quake started that consumed the houses. During the 1989 quake, which brought down a section of the bridge over the San Francisco Bay as well as a mile and a half of elevated freeway, several nearby homes I had built or remodeled and retrofitted to modern standards had merely swayed a bit and then settled back into place with no damage done, not even a door askew and sticking in its frame or a crack appearing in wall surfaces. We Californians are not crazy to live in earthquake country. We are just nuts to let weak buildings go up or remain unstrengthened.

Even with twenty-one piers, the pier and grade beam foundation was, financially speaking, an attractive option. It would require excavation of merely a tenth as much soil as the T-footing foundation, so little that all of it could be used for landscaping right on the site. It would eliminate the dangerous work down deep in a trench. It would require only a fifth as much concrete and lumber as the T. Using less material would, of course, result in lower labor costs as well (the fewer the planks to be put in place, the less time needed to do it). Skilled construction labor imposes not only high costs for wages but also multiple layers of additional cost for insurance, taxes, equipment, and supervision.

Hand in hand with reduced material and labor cost associated with the pier and grade beam option would come reduced environmental impact. Virtually all construction, as we do it today, results in severe damage to the environment. For all the congratulatory noise about it in the media, there is no such thing in our modern society as a "green" way of building—one that is actually symbiotic with plant, animal, and human life. We are not even close. The best shot we can now take aims only to lower the impacts. At 19th Street, the pier and grade beam did lower impacts. Less excavation meant no particulate-spewing diesel trucks hauling earth to the dump. Less concrete meant less production of CO_2 and of toxic substances during mining, manufacture, transport, and installation. And less lumber use meant diminished assault on forests. By greatly reducing materials for the foundation at 19th Street, we'd manage to be a little more considerate of the larger world.

Concrete maestro

The machines needed for installation of our piers rolled up one by one. A concrete pump riding behind a pickup truck loaded with a heavy black hose pulled to the curb first. A large tractor pulled a trailer cautiously around the corner and onto 19th from Lake Street. Atop the trailer rode a cranelike machine, its boom neatly folded against its cab, and an earth auger, a giant version of a spiraled wood-boring bit, strapped alongside. Dead on schedule the concrete truck arrived, its huge drum rotating with a slow rumble. A faded sign on the door declared that it had been dispatched from Sugar City, the concrete batching plant located a few miles to the north.

The machine operators were burly men with huge forearms and heavy bellies. Each shook my hand and said hello to the crew. They were relaxed, looking forward to an easy morning's work and easy money on our flat site. They worked by the hour. If things went badly, the cost would be mine. For them, it would mean a fatter check. But they did not loaf. They were interested in repeat business, not padded charges. "Not trying to get rich in a day, just eventually," the pump operator said to me, invoking an old work site mantra. Efficiently they deployed their machines. The drill rig was off the truck, parked in the middle of our site, its boom unfolded with the auger bolted in place and dangling down, ready to bite into the earth. The concrete truck was backed up to the pump with its chute extending over the pump's hopper. Hooked to the pump's outlet pipe, the black hose looped across the earth between the markers for our twenty-one piers.

Just as preparations were complete, a clean green Ford Ranger coasted to the curb. Dave Kendall stepped out and instructed the big black dog that had been sitting next to him to settle into the bed of the truck. A stocky man with the sure-footed walk of someone who has lived much of his life navigating through debris, across open trenches, and between men wielding hammers, shovels, saws, and other deadly weaponry, Dave plucked a pair of rubber gloves from his tool box and exchanged good mornings all around. The machine operators welcomed him, though his arrival meant they would have little chance for a fattened check. With Dave on site and in the lead, the likelihood of problems and delays dropped precipitously. Dave had been working concrete for forty years, since he was a small child cleaning trowels at his dad's jobs. When the question arises among construction people in my part of the world as to who is tops at placing and finishing concrete, who can best coax the massively heavy and harsh stuff into graceful and strong shapes, Dave has a lock on number one. There are admirers who feel he is so good that no one else should be ranked closer than tenth.

When Dave is done with the intense, sometimes ferocious, push he makes to execute a concrete installation and he can then ease back, Dave will treat you to an exposition of his world view. It includes affection and admiration for capable builders who pay his bill on time, for his dog, and for his wife and their son (in that order, going up the ladder). It includes dismay at people who "won't work for a living," and for architects and, worse yet, government bureaucrats who "tell you how to do your job, which they know nothing about." Dave looks forward to someday building a home well beyond the reach of bureaucrats on his land in the mountains. Meanwhile, when he is not consumed with the work of properly placing concrete, he devotes himself to doing volunteer maintenance at a homeless shelter and at his son's school, partly from concern that if he did not, the place would fall into decrepitude due to the bureaucrats not getting their job done.

Dave has a passion for the orchestration of a concrete pour like the passion good artists have for the deploying of their materials into compelling form, line, color, and texture. Once, as we cleaned the shovels and trowels at the end of a workday, Dave quietly compared concrete work to the performance of a piece of classical music. He gestured at the graceful bends and sharply tooled borders of the wall and walkways we had just installed. Like a musical composition, it was a creation of several distinct movements, he explained, from initial pour through the screeding, floating, and final tight troweling, with each note within each movement needing to be struck just so and at just the

right instant. If you were entrusted with concrete, said Dave, you should treat it with the same attention and care exercised by a symphony orchestra entrusted with a Mozart composition.

Dave nods his head and twirls a finger in the air. Bob, the owner and operator of the drill rig, picks up the time-honored signal and then proves his right to the name, "Bull's Eye," painted on his rig. Sighting from twenty feet away in his cab, he drops the point of his huge auger within an inch of an orange stub of steel marking the center of the first pier hole, and with a blast of his engine drives the auger down into the earth.

In less than a minute, Bob has bored a shaft eleven feet deep, reversed the spin on the big bit, and is withdrawing it. Watching the auger come up, I am holding my breath, anxious to see what the first shaft will tell us about the prospects of the next twenty. When you drill piers, there is always a danger of collapse. When a pier collapses, the sides must be lined and held back with cylindrical steel casings at great cost in material and labor. The dollars stay in the ground. The builder does not get them back. No realtor has yet figured out how to lure customers with an ad that boasts, "Oak flooring, granite countertops, luxurious tiled baths, and steel-cased piers hidden from view below grade."

Together with Dave, I gaze down the first drill hole. Tension eases away. Beautiful. A clean, straight, tight, black shaft. But even as we look, a pool of water begins to form at the bottom and the sheen of seepage begins to show on the black clay, threatening the erosion that could collapse the hole. But Dave is ahead of the water. He has already instructed the crew to stand up one of the rebar cages—five-eighths inch bars of reinforcing steel wired tightly into twelve foot long skeletal tubes, which had been delivered to the site a week earlier. Now he tells the crew to lower the cage into the shaft, and down it slides, held off from the sides by small concrete bumper blocks wired at intervals around its perimeter. Dave and I feed the black pump hose down the center of the steel cage all the way to the bottom of the shaft. He twirls a finger in the air once more. The pump operator catches the signal and nods to the concrete truck driver. Concrete flows down the truck's chute into the pump's hopper. The pump drives concrete through the hose. It surges into the shaft, pushing the hose up and out. With a sharp slash of his hand through the air, Dave signals to cut the flow just before the concrete reaches ground level. Now Dave is looking content. He is thinking that this will be a good day, the drilled shafts are going to hold, and Sugar City has delivered sweet mud indeed.

These days, getting just the right concrete to your job site can be a challenge. Hundreds of different chemicals, fibers, compounds, or liquids can be mixed, matched, and proportioned to suit every above-ground, in-ground, and underwater application as well as any weather condition. Structural members of a skyscraper extending a third of a mile above the desert in Dubai are made of concrete. So are the countertops in kitchens I have built. The concrete we are installing at 19th Street is, however, a basic mix of gravel, sand, and cement—with just one twist. Only three-quarters of the cement in our mix is the traditional portland cement. For the last quarter we have substituted fly ash.

Fly ash, a powdery residue scrubbed from the stacks of coal fired power plants, has become a staple of the so-called "green" building movement. It is much loved for several reasons: It is a waste product. It is toxic and is thought to be best entombed in concrete rather than dumped in landfills from which it seeps into streams, lakes, and oceans. It can be used directly, with no further energy input other than for transport to concrete batch plants and from there to job sites. The portland cement displaced by the fly ash is, by contrast, produced at staggering environmental cost in extremely high-heat kilns, contributing roughly a *tenth*—yes, 10 percent or even more—of the atmospheric carbonization thought to be a major cause of global climate change. Lastly, fly ash concrete, if properly cured, can be more durable than the portland cement product.

Properly handled fly ash product is far less permeable (with permeability in the range of granite's) than its portland cement based counterpart, and, due to the particulars of the chemistry by which it cures, it is less prone to cracking. In fact, it can be crack free, laying to rest a line that an old-time builder once taught me to invoke in order to fend off disgruntled customers. "If it ain't cracked, ma'am, it

ain't concrete." Fly ash based concrete is, therefore, far less prone to admit water, which leaches away cement and weakens the concrete, causes steel reinforcing to rust, and freezes and expands, thereby causing the concrete to fracture and fail. It also cures to higher strengths. As a result of all its superior qualities, concrete made with fly ash may need less frequent replacement, thereby eliminating a whole new generation of impacts.

With the first pier installed, we are on the move. Bull's Eye drills a shaft. Down drops a rebar cage. In goes the hose. The concrete flows. The hose leaps out of the shaft. "Cut!" signals Dave. On to the next pier. "Watch out," he warns. Don't crimp the hose. If you do, when the concrete surges through, the hose will straighten with a violent snap that can break your leg or tear your shoulder loose from its socket. Grab a shovel; break up any concrete spillage before it can harden; toss it onto a plastic sheet so it does not poison the soil. Don't allow yourself to become dehydrated; drink some water, *now*. How much mud left in the truck, Mister Sugar City driver? Great! We might make it with one truckload. Things are going *real* good today!

After drilling each shaft, while the concrete is pumped in, Bull's Eye rotates his cab and crane until the auger, now encased in a spiral of sticky clay, dangles above a spot fifteen feet behind the back line of the house. He accelerates the auger to a rapid spin, then stops it abruptly. The clay breaks loose and drops into a tidy pile, where it will await use in landscaping months later. A few hours after Bull's Eye drilled the first hole, all twenty-one piers are installed. Sugar City, the pump truck, and Bull's Eye have folded up their rigs and rolled away. Dave, the crew, and I are raking the site, sweeping and hosing the street, and bagging remnants of concrete (a hazardous substance) for safe disposal. As we work, we muse about ways to build an environment considerate, good-looking, and affordable driveway into the mountain redoubt that Dave intends to build far from the reach of the bureaucrats.

Massive beauty

The following morning, Dave is back to lead construction of the wooden forms for a grade beam atop the piers. Using a laser, we set the forms at dead level. We align them exactly with the nylon layout lines stretched earlier to define the outside perimeter of the house. For a fourth and fifth time, we check that all corners are precisely square, exactly ninety degrees. Any variation from level and square will cause frustration when it comes time, months away, to set cabinets, lay flooring, and set baseboards around the perimeters of rooms. If the foundation is not true, not level or not square, and therefore the frame we will build atop it is not true, we will find ourselves cutting finish flooring to taper along slanted walls, shimming the backsides of cabinets, and fussing with baseboard to join it cleanly at out-of-square corners. Our carpenter pals would see the problems when they stopped by. They would say, "Who the heck did you sub out the foundation and frame to on this job?" When we admitted we had done the work ourselves, they would admonish us, "Finish work begins at the foundation." Since I had trained some of them as apprentices and coined the phrase as a slogan for my construction company, I would be particularly embarrassed. The grade beam forms have to be spot on.

Grade beams got their name during the time when they were built right on the surface of the ground, "at grade." Our beam, though it retains the name, is not actually built on the ground. Improbably enough, it is built atop rows of cardboard boxes—each four inches high, a foot wide, and three feet long—which we place end to end in a four inch deep trench neatly cut between piers. The boxes are not ordinary boxes, however. Their interior consists of a dense waffle pattern of cardboard ribs. Their exterior is heavily waxed. The wax waterproofs the boxes. The ribs give them great strength. Cardboard *can* be assembled into strong structures. After all, it is made of trees, just like lumber. As an apprentice carpenter, I worked briefly with a man who made sturdy furniture from cardboard. A heavy person can stand on our grade beam boxes and they will not bend or buckle. They will support the weight of the concrete we will pour on top of them.

The boxes are called "void forms." As the name suggests, the purpose of the boxes is to form a void under the grade beam. After the grade beam is installed, the boxes will weaken and decay, leaving a four inch space beneath the beam. When that damnable "expansive clay" at our site swells and thrusts upward during winter rains, it will expand into the space rather than heaving right against the grade beam and causing it to rise and crack. The void forms are the first of three protections incorporated into the grade beam to protect our house against the tumultuous landscape upon which we are building it.

As a second protection, inside the wooden concrete forms we set horizontal cages made of the five-eighths inch rods of reinforcing steel, and wire them tightly to the vertical cages protruding from the piers. Many years ago, house foundations in the Bay Area were built without reinforcing steel, or "rebar" as it is called. My construction company has demolished the fragmented remains of several unreinforced foundations. They are vulnerable to earth movement. They crack apart. Concrete and rebar together, however, form a strong foundation. They are ideal partners. They need each other. The concrete can resist great compression but has virtually no reisistance to tension. The steel can resist tension but sags under compression. Together, concrete and steel can resist tension and compression both, and powerfully. With reinforcing steel and concrete collaborating, the grade beam we are constructing, though it is merely twelve inches wide and sixteen inches high and will be supported only at eight foot intervals by the piers once the void forms decay, will easily carry the house we will build on top of it.

With the steel cages set, the interior side of the forms is installed, and the forms are braced in place. At corners and every two feet along the length of the grade beams, threaded steel anchoring rods or bolts, a third protection against earthquake, are hung down into the forms. They will be captured at their lower ends by the concrete. Their upper ends will be bolted to the floor and wall frame, attaching the house securely so that an earthquake will not throw it off its foundation. Now that the void forms, rebar, and anchors are in place, we have made a good start toward guarding our house against the expanding clay and the seismic events sure to come, and also against powerful storms that come off the Pacific, gaining velocity as they are funneled toward a narrowing canyon at the east end of San Pablo. We will add further protection all the way to the roof as we frame the house.

When we had finished construction of the forms, I offered Dave Kendall a five gallon bucket of "green" release agent. Intent on making my project environment considerate from the ground up, I had mail ordered the stuff to be used in place of the toxic petroleum products traditionally sprayed on form boards so that they will readily separate from the concrete after a pour. Dave waved off the bucket. "Won't need it," he told me. "Not if you cure the concrete properly."

The next day, the pumper and a Sugar City truck rolled up again. We pumped a load of concrete into the forms, stabbing it every two feet with an electric vibrator to make sure it settled in snugly around the steel rods and bolts. Dave worked the top surface of the concrete with his trowels, performing his Mozart. He was pleased. Sugar City was living up to its name again, sending us sweet mud indeed. So much better than the stuff we got from a certain plant we had no choice but to rely on for jobs outside Sugar's range, stuff so "hot," so quick to set up, so poorly batched that it could be crafted into clean surfaces and precise joints only with body bruising effort. How could anyone do that to concrete? Dave could not fathom it. But Sugar City, now they could batch just right. Dave smiled as he rhythmically tooled the concrete to a tight, smooth, perfectly flat finish that would support our floor frame continuously, without gaps between the concrete and the lumber that would rest on it.

For the following week, the grade beam was mine to pamper. I covered it with wet canvas tarps and covered the tarps with plastic sheeting to protect the concrete from overheating by the sun. Concrete cures slowly, gaining strength for years, not by evaporation of the water but by the process of hydration, a chemical reaction between the binding ingredients and the water. The amount of water placed in the concrete should be calculated to provide maximum strength. You do not

want too much water in your mix. And you do not want the water that has been added to be cooked off too quickly by the sun. The critical curing occurs in the first week. If the curing is short circuited by immediate stripping of the forms and subjecting of the concrete to direct sunlight, it will fall far short of its potential strength.

Construction is a time-crazed business, with interest on loans mounting, with clients pushing impatiently to occupy their building, with weather threatening to halt progress. The pressure is relentless: Get it done for less money. Get it done faster. Builders feel the pressure and give in. I have seen foundations poured in the morning, stripped of their forms by noon, and subjected to carpenters nailing floor frames in place before the day is done. With portland cement based concrete, you might get away with rushing. The resulting weakness in the foundation may not show, at least not immediately, perhaps not until it is subjected to the pressures of expanding soil and the assault of an earthquake.

With fly ash concrete, you can't get away with cutting corners. You will get extremely strong concrete if you handle the material with respect, but you must give it the initial curing time it needs. The Pantheon and other structures of ancient Rome were constructed from concrete made with fly ash—though from volcanoes, not power plants. Now that we are using fly ash again, we understand more clearly why Rome was not built in a day. Fly ash demands patience.

When the crew returned, we pulled the stakes and steel ties holding the form boards in place. With a slight tug, the boards separated cleanly from the concrete, coming away straight, unwarped, needing only a light wire brushing to be ready for use in wall frames and leaving the grade beam unblemished, just as Dave Kendall had promised when he turned away my expensive bucket of green form release.

After a foundation is completed, visitors to the site often think that a small house is going up, even though the house will actually be quite large. Clients of mine, seeing the foundation of their new home or addition going in, have expressed fear that they have severely undersized it and will not be able to squeeze in. As the job moves along and floors, walls, roof, and interior finish are added, their size calculation changes, bouncing back and forth between "too small" and "good-sized place."

I wondered what my wife would think when she saw my latest foundation. As my drawings for 19th Street House had evolved, she worried that my desire to use resources frugally, to build a house that was not so big, had led me to design a house that would be not big enough. But when Sandra and a friend stopped by the site, they said nothing about the size of the house. They just gazed at the foundation and said, "It's beautiful." I thought so too. The massive gray beams on the raked brown earth, clearly revealed in sunlight, casting crisp shadows, seemed to me to have a beauty detached entirely from the function they would serve.

HOPES FOR THE 19TH STREET HOUSE

I have enjoyed remarkably good luck along the life path that led me to 19th Street. I was raised in a small city in North Carolina in a family of scholars. My dad was a scientist, my mother a sociologist, my little sister a university professor in the making, my grandfather a retired judge. Building was the last line of work they would have imagined for me. It was too far from our family's experience or sense of where opportunity lay. We knew only one builder. He constructed a hideous shopping mall, went bankrupt, and got tossed in prison for fraud.

Yet the seeds of my future as a builder were planted at an early age. I began studying design under the aptly named Miss Cross, a strict to the point of terrifying fifth grade teacher who required her students to write a history of architecture. Mine, running about forty pages in length, included drawings of the Parthenon, the Taj Mahal, Gothic cathedrals, and my favorite, the Blue Mosque in Istanbul. About the same time, I began building as well, though not with great initial success. My friend Tommy and I built a tree house. We did not understand safety specifications. Tommy fell out of the tree house and ruptured his spleen. The doctors sewed him up, saving him for a successful career as an insurance broker, but his mother would not allow him to play with me for a year. So I started hanging out with Galen, later to become a used car dealer in Cleveland. Using scraps from his uncle's wood pile, we built a fort at the top of the grassy hill behind Galen's house. We did not understand structure. Our first night in the fort, it collapsed and slid down the hill with Galen and me inside.

Fortunately, I had a neighbor who could show me how to build things right. Mr. Bazemore crafted cedar boxes and chests in a woodshop in his basement. He spoke of the wood, joinery, and his well-kept tools with reverence. I loved to assist him in his shop, breathing in the sweet scent of cedar shavings, and felt honored when he supervised my construction of a cedar box for my family. Mr. Bazemore was not only a builder. He was an author, the editor of a Baptist magazine. Fifty years after helping out in his shop, I realized that he was my first role model for the path I would eventually take.

After high school I went off to college at Brandeis University near Boston and at University College in London, England. When I got my first apartment, I fixed it up, patching and painting walls, nailing together shelving, and decorating with a passion greater than I brought to anything else during college excepting tennis, basketball, and serving as editor-in-chief of the student newspaper. Perhaps that's when I began to understand that I did not want the sort of career my family traditionally embraced. I wanted to do physical work and to write.

After college, I had the good fortune to meet two builders of surpassing talent. I loved the forms, surfaces, and textures of the structures they created, was taken with the athleticism with which they performed their craft, and was inspired by their celebration of work done well. I was discovering, also, that I craved freedom. A regular job would not suit me. I needed an independent career that would allow me freedom of expression and control over my own time. I noticed that many people I met working in the world of construction enjoyed uncommon freedom—working at their trade when they needed, and pursuing other interests when they wished. Some were mountaineers, others surfers; a number were artists. I imagined a life of building and writing on my own schedule, and so I set out to become a carpenter.

Luck struck again, though at first it did not look like luck. In the mid-1970s the construction industry collapsed during a deep recession. Carpentry jobs with the large companies that had employed me evaporated; I was forced to go on my own. I did small projects for friends that led to jobs with their friends. Soon I had a network of clients who referred me to others. As economic conditions improved, I found myself with my own thriving operation. I discovered I had a gift for organization. My company ran efficiently and afforded me much free time. I used it to write. I published my first book; wrote articles about my company's projects, publishing them in *Fine Homebuilding* magazine; and then spent six years researching and writing a book about running a construction business. Emphasizing careful craftsmanship, collaborative work arrangements with designers and clients, rigorous financial controls, respect for the abilities and needs of employees, and profit sharing and flexible work schedules, the book sold by the thousands year after year. Its success lent a bit of cachet to the Gerstel brand. Ever more and bigger projects flowed to my company.

But at the same time, the socioeconomic terrain we operated in was moving under our feet in ways that made me uneasy. The digital age arrived. With it came a huge shift in wealth. Most people in the Bay Area, as across the country, lost ground economically. A minority greatly increased their earning power. A few became stupendously wealthy. Gradually, as a result, our work changed. We found ourselves building ever grander accommodations for people with already ample or very large homes. I took the jobs, at first proud to have been chosen for such coveted projects, and then because without them I would not have been able to provide my crew with work. The wealthy clients were the ones who could afford to hire a construction company with highly skilled, well-paid employees.

My pride soon diminished. I saw that even as we built posh accommodations for our well-to-do clients, increasing numbers of people were appearing on the streets begging for handouts. I saw that our projects gouged materials from the environment for negligible social benefit. I grew embarrassed to be doing our big jobs. Finally, I could no longer stomach them. I felt like a predator. I gradually rolled up my company, helping my employees start their own construction firms.

In the following years I found great satisfaction working again as a carpenter and building small, necessary projects. I became ambitious to write about building in a socially and environmentally responsible way, and I imagined crafting a house that incorporated those values as best I understood them and chronicling the experience in a book. The idea for 19th Street House was born. I severely underestimated the challenge. I had been spoiled by my years of upscale building with its huge budgets. To build for people of moderate means, I had to pare building costs by half. I had to rethink every step in the conceptualization of the form, function, structure, and finish of houses and in their fabrication. And, along with reimagining those traditional concerns, I had to come to terms with what "environment considerate building," as I came to call it, was really all about.

Building scientists, Babel of voices, builder's pyramid

As I explored so-called "green" building, I began to understand that it was not simply a matter of recycling job site waste, choosing products advertised as "earth friendly," and placing elaborate devices atop roofs to capture solar power. On the contrary, I saw that measures heralded as "green" could, at times, actually be counterproductive. Sometimes they consumed more energy than they saved. Sometimes they consumed resources that could have been used to achieve much more environmental benefit had they been deployed in other ways. Being green, it turned out, was much harder than cultivating a few virtuous-sounding habits and adding groovy gadgetry and products to one's buildings. I learned, also, that a number of very smart people had been working for decades to understand how environment consideration might really be achieved. They wrote and spoke with deep knowledge about energy efficiency and resource conservation and a host of related strategies whose very names, "optimal value engineered framing," "thermal boundaries," "blower door testing," threw me at first, but that I would come to believe were the real guts of environment considerate construction.

Their work was described as "building science," a discipline I had never heard of, though as it turned out there were even professors of building science at universities. They analyzed the relative strength of various construction materials, such as fly ash vs. portland cement concrete. They ran controlled experiments to compare the performance of building products such as windows and water heaters to their manufacturers' claims. They analyzed and compared the energy efficiency, cost-effectiveness, and toxicity of structural, waterproofing, and insulating systems.

As I read books and attended seminars by building scientists, the magnitude of learning that lay before me became clear, and so did one other thing. As good as the building scientists were, none offered a comprehensive overview of the complex challenge that builders now face: melding effective functionality with pleasing form, putting up durable buildings, staying within owners' budgets while maintaining a sound business, and at the same time doing the new "green" thing. In other words, putting up a sturdy house that works well, feels good, and costs a reasonable amount even while it spares the planet.

One of the best known of the building scientists referred to his colleagues in the construction industry as a "dysfunctional family." Each focused on his or her specialty to the exclusion of other issues. Sometimes listening to the scientists along with advocates for other building priorities was like listening to a dozen people at once, with each speaking a different language.

To sort out the input from building scientists, architects, house designers, construction rating agencies, healthy house experts (and the list goes on), I created a simple diagram. It's an equilateral pyramid with

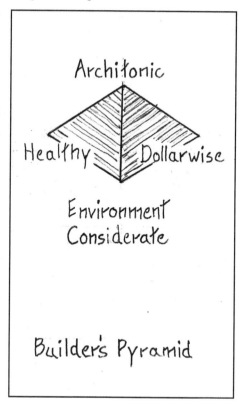

one of the four principal building challenges named at each of the four points. A couple of the names I invented myself for lack of existing words that I felt would do the job. The pyramid is easy to keep in mind, and I referred to it constantly in the crafting of 19th Street House, from the initial sketching through planting the garden. It did duty as a compact mission statement. I used it to remind myself, as I navigated through the thickets of decisions that go into making a house, not to focus so intently on one of the values that I neglected others.

Such tunnel vision is a constant hazard in building. An architect enthralled with the sculptural qualities of her concept loses sight of the costs of building it. She ends up with her design filed away in a drawer. She leaves behind clients enraged at the charges for drawings of a structure they cannot afford to build. On the other hand, a builder who focuses too passionately on the dollar cost or environmental impacts of his project will neglect form and function. He ends up creating an ugly, awkward box that offends its neighbors, would be unpleasant to live in, and is difficult to sell.

Environment considerate

Naming the points of my pyramid, I decided against using the word "green" even though the word is likely here to stay. Its meaning has been diluted. Thoughtful building scientists, builders, and designers concerned about environmental issues are rightly uneasy with the often opportunistic way "green" is affixed to products and projects, giving reassurance and serving as a badge of pride where none is due. For example, a window company ballyhoos its insulated replacement windows as "green," but glosses over the fact that the windows will never save nearly as much energy as goes into making and installing them.

Even ardent nature lovers may commit "greenwashing" when it suits them, as in the case of a certain biologist who has set up shop as a designer and installer of "green roofs," namely roofs that support a garden of ground covers, shrubs, and even trees atop a waterproof membrane. At a presentation sponsored by a green building organization, the biologist explained the benefits of his roofs. They provided habitat for wildlife. They slowed release of rainwater that might otherwise run off too quickly, carrying pollutants into streams and rivers. They offered spiritual uplift for the people who came to relax in the rooftop gardens. They even contributed a bit to insulating the space below, and thereby lowered the use of energy for heating and cooling.

As the biologist showed off photos of his roofs, I found myself wondering about his claims. His roofs sat atop large, luxurious homes, each registering considerable environmental impact in order to pamper a very few people. The houses raised obvious questions: Should such buildings ever be labeled environment considerate? Should they be honored simply because they sported purportedly green features like the biologist's roof? When a lavish project roofed with the biologist's garden won an award for its greenness, was the roof in actuality functioning merely as a green veil to disguise the predatory character of the building beneath it?

I had already learned from my explorations of the green building world what the answer to these questions would likely be: The rich will always be with us. They will always build palaces. Better that they should be encouraged to incorporate green features than be left to ignore environmental concerns altogether. Perhaps. But another question provoked me even more. After the presentation, I approached the biologist to ask him that question. Pointing to a nearby old warehouse, I asked him whether he would like to put a green roof on top of it. "Oh yes," he replied. I explained that as a builder I saw a potential consequence that might not come immediately to his biologist's mind. Putting a garden atop the warehouse would require that it be heavily strengthened. Constructing the concrete footings, columns, trusses, and steel connections required for that strengthening, not to mention all the components of the green roof itself—the waterproof membrane, protection for the membrane, drainage mats, irrigation systems, soil, and plants—would register a series of substantial environmental impacts. They included: Extracting raw material from the earth for every component. Processing it. Manufacturing it. Transporting it. Transporting workers back and forth to the site to reconstruct the building and install the green roof. Disposing of or recycling of waste.

And then more impacts from extraction through transport and disposal for year after year of maintenance.

"Oh yes," the biologist assured me, he knew about all of that.

"Well, in that case," I asked him, "was it possible the environmental benefits that a garden atop the warehouse roof would deliver might be outweighed by environmental hits it left in its wake?" Before he embarked on one of his roof projects, did he figure those costs along with tallying the benefits? And if the cost seemed to exceed the benefits—if, in fact, it appeared that the roof would result in net environmental damage—would he advise against the green roof?

He told me his answer was going to surprise me. He was right. It did. He said he did not care about cost/benefit analysis. "I'm not a numbers guy," he said. "Building roof gardens is not just what I do for a living. It's more than that. Providing wildlife habitat is my spiritual life. I'm a birds-and-bees guy. It's who I am."

If his answer startled me, it outraged a friend who has devoted much of her life to protecting plant and animal habitat. "The hubris of it," she exclaimed. "To create a small patch of artificial habitat, he is willing to destroy who knows how much natural habitat. And he calls himself a biologist!"

I decided against using "green" not only because it's overused and abused but because it is inaccurate as a description of virtually any building construction we do now. With its overtones of "organic," the word "green" suggests a building process integrated with the biological cycles of living things (including ourselves) rather than disruptive of them. There are, for practical purposes, no such processes in building, at least not in the industrialized world. Not yet. Every step in the sequence from resource extraction through maintenance of structure and finish results in negative environmental impacts, including habitat destruction and poisoning of the earth, water, and air. We are not yet capable of green. The best we can do now is try to lower the impacts of building in the habitat we share with the plants and animals, to give them a bit more *consideration.*

How, then, could I achieve my hope of being environment considerate at 19th Street? How could I assess possibilities and make the right choices?

Would it be just a matter of guesswork? Deduction? Induction? Or, could I also employ measurement and calculation; and if so, would the numbers be more useful than intuition and logic? To arrive at an answer, I started with a reconsideration of practices long promoted by the environmental movement.

Reuse—recycle—reduce

Environment consideration in building began with seemingly straightforward prescriptions: Take this measure (build near public transport). Add this ingredient to your project (kitchen countertops made of recycled glass). Eliminate that ingredient (decking milled from thousand year old redwood trees). Moving beyond such specific prescriptions, builders concerned about the environment adopted the overarching prescription contained in the environmentalist mantra, "reduce—reuse—recycle." In everyday usage the three mandates are now often given equal weight. Or their order of importance is even reversed, with so much attention given to "recycle" that "reduce" is nearly lost sight of. They should not be given equal importance, much less reversed, certainly not in building.

Consider *the prescription to reuse.* It is now an established part of the construction economy, with thousands of small businesses selling salvaged materials ranging from pedestal sinks pulled out of defunct hotels to wood flooring manufactured from antique timbers. Re-use, we sometimes naively assume, spares the environment entirely. "Save a tree," we say. Use an old beam from a dismantled building instead of cutting a new beam from a freshly harvested log. But in fact, re-use registers a sequence of impacts nearly identical to new-use, and sometimes even more intense. For a beam to be reused it must be *extracted*, though from an old building rather than a forest. It must be *transported*. It must be *manufactured*, not from a log but from an old timber, which like a freshly cut tree requires stripping and cleaning, sawing, and planing. In addition, the old timber may be coated or saturated with toxic substances. Removing them will register environmental impacts that will not occur at all with a fresh tree. Like a new beam, the beam salvaged for re-use must be *stored*, likely in a barn or in a yard shorn of plant life and covered with gravel or asphalt, construction of which engendered its own set of impacts. And a crew and equipment must be brought to a site to *install* the salvaged beam. It may require *maintenance*—repeated cleaning and sealing or painting. Additionally, it may burden the environment with *marketing*, just like its newly made counterpart. When the companies that sell wood products manufactured from salvaged timbers post quarter page ads for a year in a certain admired construction magazine, each of them consumes over half a million pages of inked paper annually.

Whether the impacts of re-use are of greater or less magnitude than new-use in any given situation is a difficult question. Determining a reliable answer will likely not be easy. But as I came to understand, when I salvaged posts and planks from an aging deck for re-use in 19th Street House, the benefits to the environment (as well as to the pocketbook) can be marginal or nonexistent.

I was in the earlier stages of imagining 19th Street when I took a job renovating a home built around 1915 by Julia Morgan, most famed as designer of the Hearst Castle in San Simeon, California. The renovation included removal of a hideous, crumbling 400 square foot deck that had been attached to the house around 1960. I decided to salvage what I could of the Douglas fir lumber from the deck for re-use at 19th Street. Having been imbued with the reuse-recycle-reduce mantra, I assumed that salvaging was the environment considerate thing to do, and I looked forward to all the pats on the back I would get for being a good green guy.

Here, then, is what was required to salvage the lumber: Each morning for several days, three laborers and I drove (in separate cars) to the house to dismantle the deck, pull thousands of nails from the lumber, cut away rot, and transport the salvaged material to my storage area, from where it would eventually need to be transported to San Pablo. At 19th Street, the old deck boards were sawn to length and planed with power tools for use in the front porch. Because of mismatches in size and other defects, the boards and timbers from the 400 square foot deck provided just barely enough material for 19th Street's sixty square foot porch. The remnants were transported back to storage once again. There they still sit five years after salvaging while I contemplate somehow using them in a future project. The material that did go into the porch was coated twice with clear sealer. Now, two years later, it needs sealing again. And it will need further coats at least a dozen more times over the course of its useful life.

Had I used a new decking—which was available in just the right lengths from a supplier just blocks away from 19th Street—less transport, negligible sawing and planing, and no sealing (*ever!*) would have been necessary. Moreover, the new decking, a composite product made from discarded plastic grocery bags and hardwood sawdust, would likely have outlasted the reused lumber by decades.

The folks who now live in the 19th Street House like the patina of the reused lumber, the orange-golden color of the old fir. It *is* beautiful. And we *did* save a tree. Well, we saved part of one. Or at least we saved the sawdust and discarded grocery bags that would have been used to manufacture the composite decking. Of course, to save the sawdust and bags we imposed burdens at multiple locales in the environment with all the driving and planing and sawing and sealing we did. Still, if we ever do submit 19th Street House for a rating from the givers of green awards, we will get points for re-use. The applause will be pleasant. It will compensate me for that huge splinter I drove under my thumbnail handling that damnable old lumber. Memory of

it will comfort me as I recoat that deck every other year for the rest of my life.

Consider the second prescription of the mantra. House builders of all stripes are becoming adept at *recycling*. Tract builders grind up concrete, lumber scrap, and drywall remnants and put it all right to work in their projects as components of drainage systems or as soil amendments. Home manufacturers, namely builders who assemble houses in factories rather than building them right on site, claim to recycle virtually all scrap, and house factories are often, therefore, touted as a greener way of building.

My experience suggests that equal possibilities for recycling exist for individual, site-built homes. All that is needed, just as at a tract or in a factory, is economic motivation, a system that simplifies the recycling, and personnel trained to use the system. Years ago when I first set up the simple system of bins visible in the photo below, I did not label the bins emphatically enough. I ended up with soda bottles mingled with copper wiring, fast food containers and cardboard gooped together with banana peels and the remnants of peanut butter sandwiches and tacos. Now I have added big labels to the bins. My co-workers and I get the recyclables into the right bins, where they are easily scooped into cans or bags for curbside pickup. At 19th Street I intended to apply tract builder practices of cycling bulk items (like the soil from the foundation drill holes that would be used for landscaping) right into the project, and use my bins for smaller items. I aimed to reduce waste from the eight tons reported as typical for new houses by 95 percent, and carry no more than a pickup truck load to the dump.

But even if I did succeed in achieving 95 percent recycling, would the effort significantly lower the load our project would place on the environment? Recycling, like re-use, requires a sequence of energy and material inputs parallel to those engendered by new-use. The primary difference is that extraction is replaced by separation. Does separation impose less environmental burden than extraction? Answers must be worked out on a case-by-case basis. For one material maybe yes, for another perhaps no. In one circumstance maybe, in another probably not. Moreover, the answers change as techniques and technologies evolve. But at a minimum, separation is difficult.

As mayor of San Francisco, Gavin Newsom became so frustrated with the difficulty of separation in San Francisco's recycling efforts that he proposed having garbage collectors do double duty as cops and issue citations to citizens who failed to properly separate out recyclables from other throwaways. Of course, as they penned the tickets, the garbage collectors' huge trucks would be idling at curbside. Would the damage done by the additional diesel particulate they were spewing into the air have been offset by any additional separation that the citations encouraged? And even if they did succeed in encouraging separation, would impacts be lowered? Not necessarily. Recycling is worthwhile only if there is a factory to which the recycled material can be hauled at reasonable dollar and environmental cost, as well as a market for the products the factory will make. Often there is not. And when there is not, the recycled material will likely go to the dump. With diligent effort and plentiful investment in recycling plants, San Franciscans have achieved a nearly 75 percent recycling rate. They are world leaders at recycling. But because there is often not sufficient demand for their recycled materials, sometimes half of it ends up in the dump. Along with the materials, of course, all the efforts of the citizenry to recycle and all the energy and material used to construct and operate the recycling plants are also getting dumped.

So now consider *reduction*. It is possible at three levels: First, *not building at all*. Second, if building cannot be avoided, *building small*, as compactly as practicable. Third, building with systems that will consume the *feasible minimum* of material and energy for construction and operation across their useful life. Our pier and grade beam was the first of such systems implemented at 19th Street. Others will be put in place as we stand the house up on its foundation. Each of the systems is straightforward enough. However, integrating them in a single house while meeting all the other expectations we have for houses, now that was the hard work.

Beyond my project at 19th Street, on the larger scale in American society, there are serious obstacles to achieving reduction. They include difficulties in speeding the development and deployment of efficient technologies, from energy-sipping refrigerators to methods for effectively insulating and sealing older buildings. The greatest obstacles to reduction, however, may be cultural. We Americans seem impelled toward ever-increasing consumption. How often do we choose less, even when less is enough, if more is available? Sometimes bigger is even required by law. A client of mine wanted to build a one-bedroom retirement home on land he owns in the mountains. We agreed on a plan for an 800 square foot cottage. The building department would not allow it. "Too small," they said, and required that the square footage be nearly doubled.

When not encoded in law, upsizing is embedded in our habits. They can be hard to shake. The architect Sarah Susanka won fame and fortune with her *Not So Big House* series of books. At first her books featured quite compact places. But within a few years Susanka was promoting a "showhouse" at a builder's convention that, all told, incorporates nearly 4,000 square feet of living area. Supersizing, it seems, is as difficult to resist in building as it is in fast food. During my lifetime, the size of new American homes has grown by roughly 250 percent. I regularly find myself being urged to supersize. When we get together for our annual preparation of my tax returns, my accountant sometimes cajoles my wife and me to increase our consumption. "You can't take it with you," she tells me.

I don't doubt she's right. However, it's also the case that you can leave something behind for other living creatures. And, it is my personal sense that freedom comes with restraining one's consumption. The debt, clutter, and burdens of maintenance resulting from compulsive consumption feel imprisoning to me. But even for readers who do not share my less-is-more sensibility, who don't much care for the idea of reducing by not building, who are put off by compact structures, even for you there are rewards in reducing. Implementing more efficient systems for construction (or renovation) and operation saves money, a great deal of it over the long haul, along with sparing the air, water, animal life, plant habitat, and therefore us. And in contrast to re-use and recycling, with reduction the benefits are unambiguous. They are not offset by costs that are often difficult to discern. By not using a beam at all, you really *do* save a tree along with a buck. In fact, compared with the other two prescriptions of the mantra, reduction has such an edge that, at least in the case of building, the mantra should read *reuse—Recycle—REDUCE!*

Single column accounting to life cycle cost assessment

In emphasizing *reducing*, I don't mean to dismiss *reusing* and *recycling*. I simply mean to suggest that we face an accounting challenge. It often takes careful figuring to know whether or not you are committing an environmentally friendly act when you reuse or recycle.

Accounting is simple arithmetic at its heart. In one column you total up your income. In a second column you total your expenses. You subtract the expenses from the income. The remainder is your net earnings, or loss. What is simple is not necessarily easy, however. Accounting, especially for forecasting purposes, is not at all easy in part because of the powerful temptation to overlook the possible unpleasantness in the expense column while tallying the happy news hoped for in the income column. I see it regularly in the building business. A young builder submits a bid of $96,000 and wins his first big job. He's ecstatic. He's sure that he will make a ton of money. He can smell the new pickup truck he will be able to buy at the end of the job. After all, how can you possibly lose money when you are taking in that much? When the job is over, he knows the answer: spend $104,000 to build the project while collecting only $90,000 because the owner decided to stiff you, and your lawyer said it would cost more in legal expenses than you'd ever realize from a lawsuit to recover the final $6,000.

The environment considerate building movement has been plagued with such single column optimism, the tendency to exult over future benefits and gloss over costs. The roof garden installer described earlier, bent on feeding his sense of self, balks at cost/benefit analyses of his projects. He hides from the fact that he is exploiting natural habitat to create little patches of artificial habitat. I succumb to single column accounting with my decision to recycle the Julia Morgan deck material. So proud am I to be putting old lumber to new use that I neglect to carefully account for the environmental *costs* as well as *benefits* of re-use, and fail to realize that the costs may outweigh the benefits.

Similarly, as you may have noticed, the advocates of fly ash concrete, to whom I gave voice in the first chapter, wax so enthusiastic over its benefits they neglect to raise even the possibility of costs. Fly ash makes strong concrete, they say, and the toxic substances it contains are best entombed in concrete rather than left loose in the larger environment where they will eventually make their way into streams and lakes. Eventually, however, the structures in which fly ash is incorporated will live out their useful lives and be demolished. What will happen to the toxics then? As fly ash concrete gains wider acceptance, are we simply guaranteeing the widespread dispersal of the toxics it contains? Fly ash advocates skip past the question. Their cost/benefit accounting, in fact, includes no costs at all, only benefits.

Such examples of single column accounting abound. I will not belabor them further. If you are of a mind to, you will readily spot the tendency to celebrate benefits while ignoring costs in one green building initiative after another, even the best intentioned.

Partly because of the temptation and hazards of single column accounting, building scientists have developed a new accounting method. Known as life cycle cost assessment (LCA), it is an attempt to measure the environmental costs of making and using a product from "cradle to cradle," from the initial harvesting of raw material through recycling of the used-up product. In theory, a well-developed database of LCAs would allow you to compare the environmental impacts of the alternate products you were considering for a project, for example, bamboo flooring from China versus oak flooring produced according to Forest Stewardship Council standards and grown and milled locally. Life cycle cost assessment is now well established, at least as a concept. In the more sophisticated sectors of the environment considerate building community, it has surpassed reduce—reuse—recycle as the dominant mantra. Various institutions are performing life cycle cost assessment and collecting their data into life cycle inventories (LSIs).

But just as we can too readily assume we are being environment considerate simply because we are recycling or reusing, we can be seduced by the quantitative character of life cycle assessments into giving them more credibility than they are due. Scot Horst, chair of the steering committee of Leadership in Energy and Environmental Design (LEED), the most prominent of the agencies that evaluate construction projects for their "greenness," summarizes both the attractions and the hazards of LCA. He praises it for its holistic character. With LCA he notes we are pushing past the point where we glorify one material as green for an attribute or two, and discard another because it has a bad characteristic. Instead we are attempting to evaluate materials or projects for their overall environmental impact. But Horst, who makes his living providing life cycle assessment tools, admits that "LCA methodology" is "so complex it's easy to get lost" in it. For the moment, he says, what we have is "confusion." Horst thinks we'll get LCA up to speed with more research. We just need to spend the money, to make the investment.

I hope he is right. I have my doubts. My skepticism arises from my experience with construction estimating data. Long ago, when I was just starting out as a builder, a mentor warned me against relying on the costly manuals filled with tables of such data. "They aren't good for much," he told me, "other than bookends." He was right. The rough averages that the manuals report will vary so widely from a particular builder's costs on a specific project that relying on them for estimating the cost to construct that project puts the builder at risk for huge losses.

Compiling estimating cost data appears simple compared with generating useful inventories of life cycle cost data. To create estimating data, the publishers only have to gather and average costs from a sample of builders. For example, they might ask a random selection of builders to report how many person-hours per linear foot it costs to frame eight foot high walls using 2x4 studs, then average the reported costs, and publish the average as a line item in their manual.

By contrast, generating just one LCA involves collecting inputs and outputs that may be registered all across the planet. A full-blown LCI may require doing that for tens or even hundreds of thousands of products. How does one collect numbers for all the necessary inputs of material and energy and outputs of toxic substances and gouged environments to accurately assess the impact of, say, a batch of concrete made with gravel brought in from South America, sand from Canada, portland cement from the East Coast of the United States, fly ash from a coal fired power plant in the Midwest, and a variety of additives from chemical plants in South Africa, Dubai, India, and Texas?

To make the task even more difficult, the technologies used to manufacture the thousands of construction products are in constant flux. A cubic yard of concrete, a bag of insulating material, or a bundle of roofing may require quite different inputs and generate very different life cycle costs this year compared with last year. Next year the inputs and outputs will be different again. And they will vary if the product, or even just one of its components, comes from manufacturer A rather than Z.

Even if the numbers are reasonably reliable, arriving at stable conclusions or making decisions on the basis of an LCA can be a dicey enterprise. An assessment compiled by an English housing agency illustrates the challenge, particularly because it is of limited scope. It attempts to calculate only impacts of global warming, putting aside other environmental costs such as habitat destruction or production of toxics.

The housing agency's assessment was made to resolve arguments between those passionate contestants, building preservationists and developers of new housing. Building preservationists have hitched their wagon to the "green" building train. Ardently they invoke single column accounting to establish the environmental credentials of their cause. Think of the benefits, they urge, of refurbishing older buildings rather than rebuilding from the ground up. Think of the savings of material—Bricks! Mortar! Timber! —and of the energy used to make it when a building structure is reused rather than torn down and carted to the dump. Developers green hitch just as eagerly, also with the aid of single column accounting, promoting demolition of aged structures

to make way for their fresh product. Think of the b
of replacing those old, leaky, energy-hogging boxes w
energy-efficient, new homes.

The English LCA concluded that for a number of y
houses would enjoy an advantage over the new hous
and operation combined would result, over those early years, ... _
emission of greenhouse gases than construction and operation of the
new houses. But gradually the new houses would gain on the refurbished
units. After half a century, remarkably enough, the refurbished and new
homes would, on average, have pulled more or less even in the volume
of emissions they have put into the atmosphere. Buried in the report,
however, is a striking number that undermines the usefulness of its
assessment, even-handed though it is. Sixty-eight percent of the energy
embedded in both the new and old houses (i.e., used for their initial
construction or renovation as opposed to operation and maintenance)
was in their brick facades and walls. Had the new houses been built
with material requiring less energy to produce than brick, they could
have pulled even with the refurbished houses much more quickly and
enjoyed a substantial advantage at the fifty year mark.

One can easily imagine both preservationists and developers seizing
on the study to justify their position. "See," the preservationists would say,
"refurbishment results immediately in less greenhouse gas production. It
helps us move quickly, as we must, to slow global warming."

"Not so fast," the developers will answer. "We will be battling global
warming for a long time, and over the long term our new houses will
help more. We will catch you in a mere half-century at most, and after
that clearly move ahead. What's more, we can build much more efficient
houses than the study gives us credit for, not only by eliminating the
brick facades, but with lots of other measures not included in the houses
in the study. And if we did, our product would surpass your refurbished
houses even more quickly."

"Hold on there," the preservationists will retort. "The lighter materials
you will substitute for brick won't last nearly as long. Maintaining and
replacing those flimsier materials down the road will result in a whole
new series of impacts. Furthermore, while you may be able to build with

ater energy efficiency than you are given credit for, we, too, have made strides. We now know how to refurbish and retrofit houses so that they can be far more energy efficient than those included in the study."

Round and round the argument will go. Life cycle assessment won't definitively settle it. LCA will not help us choose with certainty between renovation and new construction any more than the prescriptive mandates that preceded LCA will enable us to sure-footedly make our way to a green way of building.

Given the limits of both the old and the new mantra, of reduce—reuse—recycle and of life cycle cost assessment, what could I rely on at 19th Street? How could I best fulfill the environment considerate piece of my pyramidal mission statement? I could reuse selectively, attempting to ensure that when I did, re-use was resulting in less and not more environmental impact. I could and would recycle diligently. I would be encouraged by research from Technical University of Denmark indicating that recycling *does* result in lowered environmental impacts roughly 80 percent of the time. I would hope to at least match the 80 percent and hope the benefits would not be canceled by damage done by the other 20 percent of my efforts.

I could, in my pursuit of environment consideration, also look to life cycle assessments for rough guidance in selection of materials. But in the end I would have to make judgment calls compounded of intuition, logic, and ambiguous quantitative analysis. I would have to accept that my results would end up as a porridge of hope and best guesses, nothing more. Finally, most emphatically, I would come back to *reduce*, attempting to lower inputs of resources both for construction and long-term operation—even while staying focused on building a house that people could afford and love. That, it seemed to me, was most likely where the sweet spot lay.

Healthy

Until the later decades of the twentieth century, the construction community—builders, designers, tradespeople, all of us except a few visionaries—were as numb to the health implications as to the environmental consequences of our work. Unwittingly we bombarded our clients and ourselves with dangerous materials. Then came the realizations and the fears. Asbestos in building finishes breaks loose and destroys respiratory systems. Lead in paint impairs brain function in children. Sawdust is carcinogenic. Sawdust from wood saturated with preservatives can be intensely carcinogenic. Mold in damp walls causes chronic illnesses. Indoor air quality in many new houses is far worse than the outside air in the most polluted cities. Carpets are toxic waste sites. With the fear came the outcry of the injured and the lawsuits. And then, rapidly, came an understanding that we had to do better.

The "green" building movement usually bundles health together with general environment consideration. Thinking about the house I wanted to build at 19th Street, I separated the two, placing them at different points of the pyramid. Environment considerate and healthy building do not automatically go hand in hand. Achieving one is no guarantee that you have taken care of the other. A few years ago a new kind of insulating material came onto the market. Made from scraps generated at textile factories, it was appreciated for its recycled content. But it was especially welcomed for its claimed lack of toxicity, which marked it off from the batt insulation, dominant in the market at the time, manufactured of fiberglass strands and a toxic formaldehyde based binder. You can hug a bundle of the cloth stuff without noticeable ill effects. You definitely would not want to hug a bundle of the fiberglass insulation and breathe in the emissions of the volatile formaldehyde.

But the huggable cloth stuff, though apparently healthier, poses problems at the environmental point of our pyramid of building values. Most critically, it does not readily "loft," or puff up sufficiently to fully contact all sides of the framing cavities into which it is placed. And such a deficiency, in ways we will explore later in our story of building 19th Street House, can result in severe loss of energy efficiency. In addition, the cloth insulation is expensive to purchase and can be difficult and costly to put in place. How much greener have you gotten, then, when you fill a wall with batts of the recycled cloth stuff? Yes, you've used a product made of recycled material. Careful life cycle cost accounting might reveal that the recycling resulted in a more resource efficient way of producing insulation than manufacturing from virgin materials. If so, you could claim environmental benefits. But you also endure two costs. Because the material is relatively expensive, you have put out extra dollars that could, perhaps, have been better spent. And, because of the poor lofting qualities of the insulation, you run the risk of losing energy efficiency. The dollar loss hurts immediately; there's never enough money to fully realize all the hopes we have for our building projects. And the energy loss will go on year in and year out over the entire life of the project, gradually adding up to a substantial environmental impact.

While environmental consideration and health issues don't necessarily go hand in hand, they tend also to be concentrated at opposite ends of the construction sequence. Opportunities for lowering environmental impact are concentrated in the earlier phases of a job—in the conceptualizing and drawing up of the project and during the rough work of foundation, framing, cladding, window, and infrastructure installation. That's when you get your big opportunities to reduce initial inputs for construction and to assure minimal inputs for long-term operation and maintenance.

Health protection comes into play relatively little during the rough phases. Yes, you must take care to protect the health and safety of workers at the site. You must avoid incorporating toxic substances in the structural components that might later seep into living spaces. But opportunities to protect the health of the family who will eventually live in the house are concentrated in the finish work. Then it is critical to avoid installing materials with the toxic ingredients that are still too often used in the flooring, cabinets, countertops, and paints the family will come in contact with every day. Because environment consideration and health tend to need attention at opposite ends of the construction sequence, I placed them at separate points of my builder's pyramid.

Form Givers and pattern languages

Along with consideration for the environment and a house healthy for its occupants, I hoped for something else at 19th Street. I hoped for a house people would feel happy to come home to after a day's work, a place that catered to their aesthetic sensibility. But, just as I intended to take on other challenges "with 100 silver B-Bs" rather than a "single silver bullet," I was not aiming for any breakthrough architectural innovation.

In other words, I had no aspirations to follow in the footsteps of what a former head of the American Institute of Architects chapter in Maine has called the "Form Givers," those lionized architects such as Corbusier, Mies van der Rohe, and Frank Lloyd Wright who transformed their contemporaries' idea of how buildings should look. For one thing, I am not an architect (though I sometimes dare to call myself an "architekton," a calling I will tell you more about later). For another, I am a bit put off by the high-falutin' tone of partisans of the Form Giver school. To their way of thinking, the memorable sculptural composition of a building's elements—the unfurling and bending of its surfaces to create poetic interplay of light and shadow—is *all* that *really* matters. Buildings that fall short visually do not, in their belief system, even qualify as "Architecture," with the "A" capitalized to distinguish work that matters from the run-of-the-mill stuff, such as preservation and gradual evolution of traditional building forms.

Among partisans of the Form Giver school, one encounters, when not utter indifference to, at least not much excitement about the functional purposes of building. Philip Johnson, an eminent architect in his own right and a promoter of form-giving from his post at the Museum of Modern Art (MoMA) in New York, said of function, perhaps a bit mischievously but also with seriousness, "It doesn't matter much." Corbusier himself was willing to admit that if a house served practical needs, the builders deserved thanks, like "railway engineers or the telephone service," but their offerings could not express the relationships that moved men's souls as did the work of real Architects.

When Form Giver loyalists turn cool to function, they can collide harshly with clients having more down-to-earth concerns. Earlier in my career, I had once naively set up such a collision. The spectacle had the effect of pushing me toward an alternative school of architectural thought that later contributed to the crafting of 19th Street House.

Not yet quite understanding his breed, I had recommended a local Form Giver loyalist as a possible designer for the remodel project of a new client. When he went to her home to interview for the commission, the architect listened thoughtfully, now and again stroking his neatly trimmed beard, as she talked about her project. However, when he opened his portfolio to show her his work, uneasiness began to develop. My client looked worried. What, she was wondering, did all this architect talk about floating planes and innovative use of materials have to do with her main problem, struggling to feed her kids and guests out of her decrepit and badly laid-out kitchen? When conversation turned from the portfolio back to her project, a tense standoff developed.

The architect was eager to open wide the wall between the kitchen and dining room in my client's traditional home. She did not take to the idea. Why cut a big hole in the wall, which had been there for eighty years nicely doing its job, and now separated the space where she cooked from the one where her family and guests ate and the kids did their homework? Well, the architect explained, a generous opening would provide a visual connection between the two spaces, making each seem larger. The flow of light back and forth through the rooms, now blocked off from one another, would amplify the increased sense of spaciousness. And think, he urged, of the animating play of that natural illumination, varying in effect as the sun passed through the sky each day, entering the rooms from constantly shifting angles. Think of the ever changing tapestry of bright and shadow cast across the interiors.

"Well, no," said my client, her worried look tightening into one of determination. Opening the wall might seem to be a nice idea, but looking at it with practical considerations in mind, she thought not. "Well, yes," said the architect. Back and forth they went, the architect gradually becoming impatient with her inability to sense the opportunities for capital "A" Architecture that lay beyond simply bringing her kitchen up to good operating condition. She must understand, *the opening was essential!* It would provide just that axis of spatial connection the rooms so clearly "wanted."

Now my client was visibly angered. No way! she told the architect. Regardless of what the "space wanted," what *she* wanted was to be comfortable in her kitchen. An opening in the wall would give guests a view of her dirty dishes. And she would not be comfortable with *that.* Around they went, the woman not quite realizing what she was up against, just how deeply rooted was the architect's belief that refined form illuminated in sunlight was what would, in the long run, bring her joy in her new space. She had not read *Home: The History of an Idea,* by Witold Rybczynski, an architect and writer who has pushed back against the Form Givers, and who recalls hearing the word "comfort" used only once in his six years of architectural training. She would have been startled by Philip Johnson's declaration that a chair is *comfortable* if it is *beautiful.* She had not heard the despairing complaint of an acquaintance of mine about the architects with whom he works: "All they care about is what things look like." The acquaintance is a professor of city planning. He holds down a job alongside the architect professors at Harvard, the very university at which the Form Giver loyalist battling with my client over her kitchen had been trained.

But while my client did not understand the architect's loyalties, she did hold strong beliefs of her own. She has an advanced degree from a school as prominent as Harvard. The degree is an MBA in marketing, and she felt that someone running a business, as was the architect, ought to pay close attention to and honor the preferences of his customers. When the architect displayed little inclination to temper his personal priorities with marketing acumen, she dismissed him from her house sans commission. And I, intent on salvaging her project for my company, introduced her to an architect with different inclinations.

The second architect thought of herself as running a service business. At the first meeting with new clients she gave them a detailed questionnaire, and she studied their answers in order to develop a thorough understanding of their needs and concerns. Her work was geared toward "appropriateness," she explained. She wanted the buildings she designed to be comfortable, not only pleasing to look at, but also to move through, operate, and share with family and friends. About one thing she was adamant. Forms should not interfere with functions. She was irritated by a design whose mannerisms and gestures, even if visually compelling, got in the way of the activity a space was intended for.

She did enjoy the work of certain Form Givers (just as many partisans of form-giving can open themselves to the everyday concerns of clients). But her greater interest was in "pattern language," the notion that just as cultures assemble languages of words for making sentences, they develop languages of time-tested patterns for creating their built environment. She had, in fact, studied with Christopher Alexander, lead author of *A Pattern Language* (see Resources), an annotated catalogue of 253 enduring patterns for building that is as admired today as the work of the iconic Form Givers was in earlier decades. It was from among these 253 patterns, as well as from those I had acquired an affection for by building and observing houses for decades, that I hoped to assemble a successful combination of patterns for my considerate house at 19th Street.

Architonic

To express that hope at the fourth point of my pyramid, I decided against using the word "architecture." Though the dictionary definition of "architecture" is broad, in use the meaning has shriveled. The word "architecture" has become too heavily associated with the visually apprehended aspects of buildings. Ask people what they think of when they hear the word. They will tell you it relates to the way buildings *look*. Perhaps that is because of the Form Giver school's influence. Even in a boiled-down version of *A Pattern Language*, written not by Chris Alexander but by his junior co-authors and published twenty-five years later with the title *Patterns of Home*, emphasis is overwhelmingly on what is seen. There is admiration for rhythmically repeated shapes, for the way a building's elements frame views and for views through rooms, for shadow patterns cast by the sun and visual boundaries and varying ceiling forms, for one form seen nestling among others, and for a roof appearing as a dashed line and then dissolving to expose a view. There are sentences about exquisitely delicate structure and others about a march of roof beams. It is as if the sole purpose of design were to give householders something to stand around and look at.

I did want the 19th Street House to be good to look at. But I wanted it also to be attractive in many other ways. I wanted it to be pleasing to touch, easy on the hearing, fresh smelling. About the only sense I did not contemplate it directly pleasing was taste, though I hoped to create an inviting and efficient kitchen where that sense could be happily catered to as well. And, I wanted it to be a place where one could comfortably attend to household duties.

I was aiming for a house that would feel solid when you leaned against its walls or walked across its floors. I hoped that it would feel good under the hand—reassuring when you gripped a stair rail, turned a faucet or a door handle, or pressed your palm against a countertop. I intended that its interior temperature and humidity would hold stable within a comfortable range, feeling pleasant to the skin, our largest sensory organ after all. I hoped that the house would handle sound well, resisting entry of harsh sounds from the outside and appropriately containing desired music or conversation, for a house should offer audio privacy. It is as least as important as visual privacy. I intended that if the house's appliances and other built-in devices made sounds of their own, the sounds should not be distracting. At most the house should produce hushed whispers.

I wanted the house not only to smell fresh, but to quickly ventilate away bad smells. At the prompting of a gardener who suggested that a lemon tree be planted in the front yard so the scent could drift across the porch into the front room, I added the intention that the house admit pleasing smells. I wanted a house that was responsive to kinesthetic needs and abilities (our capacity for movement), that was comfortable to enter, to wander through, and to exit. Doorways in a house should be amply wide. Passageways should not feel congested. They should be useable by people with a range of physical abilities and disabilities, and continue to be useable by long time owners as they age and lose mobility, so that they will be able to remain in their homes if that is what they wish.

In other words, houses should be built for a lifetime, for all kinds of lifetimes. A house should facilitate the physical tasks of operating, maintaining, and living in it. The contraptions built into the house, from cabinets to shades to fixtures, should support graceful and efficient use. The ducts, wires, piping, and equipment that service the house should be accessible enough for ready maintenance and replacement, but not so accessible that they can be damaged or their controls moved inadvertently. Movement of groceries into the house, of furnishings through it, of clothing to the washing machine, and even of walls—so that the house can be readily adjusted for the different families who may live in it over the years—should be made easy.

To express my hope that the house would satisfy in all these many ways and not only visually, I invented the word "architonic" and attached it to the third point of my pyramid.

Dollarwise, too

It was a lot to hope for: environment consideration, healthy construction, and architonic value. But the pyramid was not complete even then. Those first three values had to be realized together with a fourth, respect for dollars, both those of the family who would occupy the house and my own. San Pablo is a town that provides what developers have come to call "workforce housing," homes for nurses, plumbers, office managers, cops, schoolteachers, waitresses, butchers, carpenters, clerks, and cooks. Houses in San Pablo sell toward the lower end of the cost ladder for the metropolitan Bay Area. Building a house in range of the people attracted to San Pablo would require strict budgetary discipline.

It would be stricter yet because the house also needed to give the builder, namely me, a decent return on investment of time and money. Otherwise it would not be real. It might be an interesting experiment in meeting the new environmental and health demands that confront builders. It might be architonically pleasing; visitors might be quite taken with it. Building it might be an entertaining way for me to pass the time and a way of working out the notions I had been mulling over and wanted to express in a book. But it would fail to be real, because a house subsidized by some financially fortunate person as a way of expressing his values and pet preferences (and there are a lot of such houses featured in various building magazines) would not be of much actual value to society. What we do require as a society are ideas for building houses that are healthier, more environment considerate, and architonic, and *at the same time economically feasible* both for a broad spectrum of purchasers and for the people who make their living creating the houses. Otherwise the houses won't get built.

As a term for expressing my financial hopes for 19th Street House in the pyramid, the familiar "affordable" came first to mind. But "affordable" did not quite get it. "Affordable" is too much of a moving target, pushed sharply up and down by market forces so that at one moment a large number of buyers can afford a particular house and at another very few. "Affordable" is also associated with "cheap," and cheap quickly gets expensive and unaffordable as the building fails early in its life and repairs mount.

For 19th Street House what I had in mind was something else: allocating the limited dollars available with great care in order to substantially achieve consideration for the environment, health, and architonic value expressed in the pyramid, and ending up with a house that would prove a sound investment for myself and for succeeding owners over the long term. To describe that hope I settled on "dollarwise," and attached it to the fourth point of the pyramid.

I did not expect to score 100 percent as I set out in pursuit of my pyramid of hopes. I have never crafted a project that did not end with my realizing that it could have been better conceived and better built. I have stood outside completed projects with their architects and heard them lament missed opportunity. At 19th Street, before even sketching a promising form for the house, I would make several false starts, foundering on my misapprehensions of the neighborhood, potholes in my knowledge, or hurdles thrown up by government.

HOUSES NOT BUILT AND WHY

The 19th Street House was not my first project in San Pablo. A couple of years before installing its foundation, I had renovated the existing house next door. "Lake Street House" I call it because it sits on the corner where 19th Street intersects Lake. During the several months I worked on Lake Street House, I became friendly with many of the neighbors as they stopped by to check out the new window trim, paint colors, and roof shingles transforming the house they had been living alongside for years. Several of the neighbors invited me to their places. I was struck by how well each of the houses functioned as a family home even though, like Lake Street House, they were only a quarter to a third the size of the McMansions that were being thrown up in suburbs across the country at the time.

Lessons from the Lake Street House

Lake Street House, along with the neighboring homes, demonstrated to me the viability of a modest-sized home. The house comprises (measuring to the exterior of the walls) only 1,050 square feet of habitable space, plus an oversized single-car garage. But within that compact area is a three-bedroom, two-bath house with a kitchen, dining room, living room, laundry, shop, and large storage area. How was so much functionality achieved? With a simple but well-organized floor plan which, crucially, devotes only a tiny percentage of the total square footage to areas that serve for circulation only.

In his excellent book, *Building an Affordable House* (see Resources), Fernando Pagés Ruiz recommends that areas used for circulation only—foyers, hallways, and stairways—be held to 6 percent or less of total square footage. That's a challenging goal. Houses often go the other way, squandering square footage on the areas that people merely pass through on the way to the places in the house where they actually sleep, work and attend to chores, prepare food and eat, or gather with friends. In fact, it is not unusual to see houses devoting a third of their space to circulation. At Lake Street House, the hallways and other circulation-only areas consume merely 4 percent of the total interior square footage. Movement through the house is largely along the edges of the living room and dining area or through the kitchen.

While Lake Street's builder did create an efficient floor plan, he also made serious mistakes. Two of them provided additional useful lessons for 19th Street House. First, the builder crafted his front porch poorly. Lake Street House is surrounded by homes with useable front porches

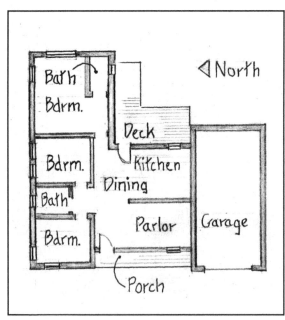

where teenagers gather after school, a mother spends her afternoons watching her young children play, and a disabled woman sits, exchanges gossip with passersby, and chats with the carpenters working across the street. The builder of Lake Street House, however, created a porch only three feet wide. With steps at one end and the front door at the other, the porch is too narrow to be of use other than as a path to the entry. Had he built it two feet wider, it would have, like the neighbors' porches, functioned as a pleasant outdoor room, a place to visit with friends on a hot summer afternoon.

Even more unfortunate, the builder placed the garage on the southern side of the house—on the *sunny* side. As a result, the garage blocked sunlight from coming into the house, except for morning light entering the rear bedroom and a bit of evening light making its way under the porch overhang into the living room. The wonderful all-day southern sunshine with its power to warm, to cheer, and to reduce energy use for heating and lighting was blocked off from the interior of the house by the mass of the garage.

While Lake Street House taught much about architonic matters by both its deficiencies and its efficient use of space, it also modeled—simply by successfully being small—a strategy for fulfilling the environment considerate requirement of the builder's pyramid. Houses impact the environment in five ways: Initial construction. Use of energy for operation. Consumption of material and energy for maintenance. Deconstruction and construction for remodeling and renovation. Tear-down and recycling or dumping at the end of useful life. Somewhat surprisingly, of the five, the second and third are by far the most impactful. It is variously estimated that, on average, operation and maintenance of American homes over their lifetimes registers from half a dozen to several dozen times the impact of initial construction.

Building a house small not only lowers the energy and material inputs for initial construction; it saves a great number of inputs thereafter. A small house consumes less energy for heating each chilly morning. It will need only a fraction of the glass when its windowpanes must be replaced. Compared with a 3,500 square foot house, a 1,200 square foot house will save roughly two-thirds of the floor covering, paint, cabinets, countertops, fixtures, and many smaller items that will be replaced, discarded, and replaced again as the house is repeatedly improved and renovated over the decades.

The lowered impacts of a smaller house might seem so obvious you may wonder why I bother to point them out. Here's why. While the issue of size gets more attention than it did earlier in the green building movement (and especially since the financial panic of '07 rocked our world), it remains underemphasized. Bloated houses, 4,000 square feet and larger, are heralded as steps toward a more environmentally friendly way of life because they are decked out with a variety of dubiously "green" gestures—like bamboo flooring hauled across the ocean from China, tankless water heaters, to be discussed (or lampooned) later in our story, and rooftop gardens. It was as if the act of building a huge house with all its magnified immediate and long-term impacts somehow transformed into an act of environmental responsibility because the house was fitted with "green" goodies, all of which would, of course, impose their own repeated impacts for maintenance over time, sometimes even more than the construction they supplanted.

Beyond the architonic and environmental lessons, Lake Street taught me something else. By building a small house, I would be exercising dollar wisdom with respect to my own pocketbook. There would be a market for this house. A small, pleasing, well-built, functionally efficient house would attract customers. After our realtor listed the carefully renovated, 1,050 square foot Lake Street house, he soon became desperate to close a deal. He was so deluged with calls, they were keeping him from his other work.

Real money

Even as constructing a small house made financial sense for me as a developer, it would be a dollarwise purchase for its eventual owners. It would reduce their burden of mortgage payments, insurance, and taxes. And over the long run, it would consume far less of their income for energy and maintenance than a larger house, freeing them to save and invest for the financial security of themselves and their families.

Anyone who has owned one knows how voraciously houses consume money for energy, water, maintenance, repair, and renovation. Not without reason are they satirized as "money pits" in Hollywood comedies. Not without reason are first-time buyers—who are focused only on the mortgage, tax, and insurance costs of owning a home—often shocked when the full costs settle down upon them.

Yet people often think that pouring money into a bigger or more luxurious house is a smart investment. "We feel that putting money in our house is the best investment we can make," one friend told me during a recent ballooning of housing prices as he pumped $100,000 of his savings into a remodel. "My house is my retirement program," said another who steadily spends her discretionary income for improvements of her home. "We haven't done very well in the stock market lately," a neighbor told me, "and so we will try putting our money in our house." All seem to believe that by buying a house and making improvements, they are creating an asset that will, over the long term, gain in *real* dollar value (that is, in dollars adjusted for inflation) like a portfolio of stocks in companies that are increasing their free cash flows.

In actuality a *house*—as crucially distinct from an entire residential property including the lot, house, and improvements—is rarely an appreciating asset, though there are exceptions to the rule such as highly regarded historical structures. A house is a depreciating asset, one that declines in value rather than gaining value. It is more like a car or any other big-ticket consumer item than it is like shares of businesses that increase earnings over time and therefore gain value. As it gets older, its parts—roofing, windows, cabinets and flooring, heating and plumbing and electrical systems, even frame and foundation—all wear out. They depreciate; they lose value. And if you fix the house up to push its value back up, the improvements themselves depreciate.

The investment made in a house can lose value the instant you put it into use, just as a new car does the moment you drive it off the lot. That was made clear by a bizarrely misleading ad that appeared some years ago in a home and garden magazine. Remodel your kitchen, the article urged, promising a "96 percent return" on the investment. Now, if the claim were true, that would be wonderful news for a builder like me. I would be able to tell clients that for every $100 they paid me to remodel their kitchen, they would instantaneously add $196 to the value of their home. If I could deliver that kind of return, Warren Buffett, the prominent investor from Nebraska, would be on bended knee at my doorstep, begging me to load up my pickup truck and come on out to Omaha to remodel his place. Alas, a closer look at the ad revealed that it meant something different (and sneaky) by its use of the word "return." It meant that for every $100 invested, you would get back ninety-six dollars in value added to your house. The other four bucks would evaporate immediately. That is, of course, a 4 percent loss rather than a gain or return, much less a 96 percent gain.

When people enjoy large *real* gains on the original investment in their *property*, it is typically because the *lot*, not the *house*, went up in value. And most likely, the lot appreciated because it is in an area where there was high demand for homes and a scarcity of buildable land. That is why you see builders buying lots with old houses on them in high-demand neighborhoods, then demolishing the houses and building new ones. The lots have become valuable even as the houses have lost value. That is why a craftsman bungalow fixer-upper in Wichita, Kansas, where there is much buildable land available cheaply, could be had for $10,000 a few years ago when much the same place in Berkeley, California, where there are virtually no empty lots, cost half a million and up. In both locales, the houses are worn out and have little value. But while demand for the lot under the house in Wichita is limited, there's a great deal of demand for the lot under the house in Berkeley. In fact, a neighbor of mine, living on the Berkeley border, was told by a realtor that he would be able to increase the sales price of his home if he removed his dilapidated house and offered buyers a pristine parcel for which they could envision the house of their dreams.

Home owners mistakenly come to think of their houses and the improvements they make to them as good investments that gain real dollar value because they are not separately tracking the values of the house, the improvements, and the lot—and are not paying attention to the effect of inflation. If they did, they would realize they have made (or lost) money on their homes over the long run because they have had good (or bad) luck as land speculators, not because of "investments" they have made in their houses. They would understand what people who purchase manufactured houses and lease space for them in mobile home parks already realize. They know their houses decline in value. They see that used houses in their parks drop in price relative to new ones just as a used Ford or Honda sells for less than a new one. They know they are not making money on an investment, but slowly wearing out a consumer good. It's the park owner who makes money leasing the house owners parking places for their houses, and, if he has luck as a land speculator, enjoys a rise in the value of his property as well.

Architekton

With Lake Street renovated and sold, I felt I had the beginnings of a sound program for a project that would accomplish the compact mission diagramed in my pyramid. As a small house, it would be more considerate of the environment and would make dollar sense for me and for the eventual owners, especially if I built a house that was both durable and energy efficient. I even had a few of the fundamental architonic features in mind. With an ample front porch, the house would connect nicely to the outdoors and the neighborhood. With plentiful windows on the sunny southern exposure, it would not only enjoy a head start toward energy efficiency, but would offer rooms bright with the Bay Area's abundant sunlight. Now it was time to envision answers to such questions as:

- What sort of family might eventually come to live in the house, and what would they need it to do for them?

- What limitations would the building codes place on the size and shape of the house? How much of the lot could it cover? How close to property lines could it be built? How tall could it be?

- What geometric form and volume would best meet the needs of the family while also staying within the limitations imposed by the code?

- Should the form, and also the exterior finish, be similar to what was already present in the neighborhood, or could something new be introduced?

- How should the form and volume of the house relate to those of its immediate neighbors? In what ways must it be considerate of their needs?

- What kinds of rooms, and how many of them, should be included inside the volume? How should they be arranged, and how should space be allocated among them?

- What shapes should the rooms themselves take? How should they flow together (or not); how should they open to the outside?

- How could I finish the exterior of the house and the interior of its rooms with materials that are beautiful, considerate of neighbors and the larger environment, yet within my tight budget?

Of course, all these questions had to be answered in ways consistent with the requirements of the pyramid. The questions did not constitute a checklist. I would keep coming back to each of them. Answers to one would continuously shape the answers to others until the project reached its final functionality, form, and finish.

To begin working out answers to the questions, I had to draw the house and work out the specifications for its construction. In the world of home building these days, we have architects and other designers who draw and write specifications. And we have building contractors and craftspeople who construct. From both sides of the design/build division we hear complaints. "Builders don't bother to read drawings." "Architects draw stuff that is not buildable." "Contractors are crooks, and clients need to be protected from them (by architects)." "Designers draw structural elements and detail that is ridiculously expensive to build, and their clients need protection (by builders who know their stuff)." Many anecdotes, quite a few of them true enough, can be marshaled to support each of the accusations.

Out of frustration with one another, or to increase their control over a project, or to increase earning power, or for the sheer joy and satisfaction of crafting a building from first imagining through the finish details, both designers and builders have taken up so-called "design-build." Christopher Alexander, architect and author of *A Pattern Language*, has advocated design-build and tried his hand at it. In another of his books, *The Production of Homes*, Alexander chronicles his experience building a cluster of houses in a Mexican village and calls upon other architects to follow his lead. He urges them to take on fewer projects, and for those projects to provide hands-on leadership all the way through. Extrapolating from his own experience in Mexico, he promises a profound encounter: "It was not merely that we were responsible for both [design and construction]. It was something much more, a physical love for the buildings and the building materials . . . a feeling that we were actually *making* these buildings, not merely designing them, and that we were therefore responsible for every detail in a way that had to be understood through hands and fingers—thoroughly understood, the way a painter understands his paint or a good cook understands the soup by tasting it."

During the years I ran my construction company, I attempted to bridge the designer/builder divide by developing a collaborative method for working with designers from the first conceptual stages of a project through completion of construction. I wrote about my collaborative approach in my books on running construction companies and have heard from many builders who have adapted my approach to their own operations. But by the time of 19th Street, I was reaching back to an earlier way of being a builder. I was reaching back to the way of the ancient Greeks. The Greeks had a word "architekton." Though it is the root of "architect," it actually meant "chief carpenter," suggesting that the divorce between designers and builders had not yet taken place, and that architecting and building were understood as a unified process.

The chief carpenter tradition thrived deep into the Middle Ages when a chief, just as likely a chief mason as a carpenter, took charge of crafting a manor house or a castle or a cathedral from the drawing through the hewing and placement of stone blocks and timber roof beams. The tradition lives on today, practiced by men and women, some trained in architecture schools, some having come up through trade apprenticeships, some entirely self-taught, who crave the full experience of building. In fact, the ancient way of the architekton may be also the way of the future. Design-build is an increasingly prevalent practice, while membership in the American Institute of Architects (AIA), the professional association of architects, has declined steeply in recent years.

For 19th Street House, I appointed myself architekton—to the dismay of one architect friend who insists one should not design buildings without first undergoing years of academic training, but with the approval of another who describes his architectural schooling as mostly "jumping though hoops." It fell to me, as architekton, to craft the drawings. For the work, I chose a humble technology with roots reaching as far back as the chief carpenter tradition itself, paper and pencil.

Computer assisted design (CAD) software, so widely in use today, does have its advantages. The software rapidly produces repetitive details, such as exposed rafter tails. You draw one, and with a few clicks of the mouse you will have the computer filling in all the rest. The computer will take you on a virtual walk through a three-dimensional blowup of your design, allowing you to take in the volumes, proportions, and flow of the rooms somewhat as an occupant might actually experience them. If you make a change on one page of your drawings, CAD can even extend the changes to related details on other pages. Computers have also allowed designers such as Frank Gehry to draw and order up the construction of undulating forms that would otherwise not have been possible to build. But CAD has its downsides, too. CAD software is costly, and the costs keep coming. Another architekton I know likes to say, "Three things are inescapable: death, taxes, and computer upgrades." To my eye, computer drawings have a lifeless quality. They look machine-made. I have wondered if that contributes to a degree of sterility in buildings constructed from them.

The greatest disadvantage of CAD derives from the computer's very strength at filling in the drawings for you. If the computer does it, you don't, and you know your building that much less intimately. While that might not matter to an architectural office, which will have precious little if any role to play in construction of their building, for a chief carpenter it is a loss. Every bit of knowledge you gain crafting your drawings will strengthen your hand as you extend into the crafting of the building itself.

For a personal reason, as well, I favor pencil and paper. I enjoy shaping the views of the building with a pencil, just as I enjoy shaping material with my carpentry tools. I feel myself traveling down the same path that Chris Alexander celebrates, but from the opposite direction. Just as he discovered the visceral joy in shaping and placing the actual material of the structures he had conceived, when I draw with a pencil I feel deeply connected to the house, as if I am making it hands-on. That precious sense of connection is diminished when I design with a computer, clicking with a mouse or issuing commands through a keyboard and watching lines fly into place on the screen. I have an environmental reason for using a pencil: Computers consume much electrical power; good mechanical pencils only a few skinny sticks of graphite. I wrote, printed rather than scrawled, the first draft of this book with a pencil on the backsides of once-used sheets of paper. I am pretty sure the first draft was stronger for it. Instead of words spewing onto a screen as I pounded a keyboard, infatuated with some line of thought I was developing, each word was being put down with effort that inspired economy.

Two cubes

The starting point for drawing a building is often a vision of a form. The sprawling home of the owner of Real Goods, a Northern California vendor of "green" goods, was inspired by a hawk in full flight, and that of the athletic facility at the University of California's Santa Cruz campus by the shape of traditional barns. One of my favorite houses was first envisioned as a broad roof that would shelter as yet unseen clusters of rooms below from the storms and powerful sun of its Caribbean location.

The form I began to envision and draw for 19th Street House was more modest. I first saw the house as a cube (or something close to a cube) with a roof. The cube has strong architonic possibilities. Among the most comfortable and handsome houses I have ever experienced, certain homes of the Georgian style in Scotland and in North Carolina, are essentially two-story cubes with a roof. The cube can help achieve environment consideration and dollar wisdom as well. It gives you maximum environmental and financial bang for your input of resources and your buck. Of all the geometric forms used in house construction (with the possible exception of the rarely employed octagon), it will give you the greatest volume and square footage for the material, energy, and labor invested.

I sketched not only one but two possible cubes with roofs for the 19th Street lot. With two cubes, I thought that I could most effectively utilize the lot and serve the family who might come to live in the spaces I would build, while still taking into account the needs of the neighborhood. I thought I could also meet building code requirements by capitalizing, as I had years earlier for another project, on a certain California housing law, which was intended to promote construction of small second units on lots previously restricted to a single-family house. The law makes good dollar and environmental sense. The second units can piggyback on the utilities—sewer, gas, and electrical—already in place for the main house. They respond to the desire of single people of modest means, whether renters or tenants-in-common, to have a detached home rather than being limited to a choice of units in an apartment building. And as "infill construction," new housing within already existing towns or cities, they help reduce sprawl of the metropolis into the countryside with all the associated environmental impacts that it imposes: maintaining highways and other infrastructure, paving over farmland and wildlife habitat, and long-distance commuting.

In San Pablo, second units have an additional attraction. Many of the town's residents, carrying on the traditions of their home countries, live as multigenerational families. The eventual owners of 19th Street House could rent out the second cube if they liked. But it could also be the grandparents' house while the parents and their children had bedrooms on the upper level of the main house, and all three generations of the family gathered for meals on its lower level.

Together, the two cubes with roofs that I was imagining—a house of about 1,200 square feet and a second unit of about 600 square feet—would cover only one-quarter of the lot, leaving 3,000 square feet for a variety of outdoor spaces. They would have been particularly appropriate to the beginning of the new century during which they would be built. The phony-money real estate boom, which had spawned a sprawl of huge houses in the late twentieth century and first years of the twenty-first, would be collapsing. Observers of the housing industry were predicting that as the world moved deeper into an era of costly energy and material, many of the far-flung, bloated new suburban homes would so burden their owners with costs for operation, upkeep, and commuting, they would be put on the block at fire-sale prices, or even abandoned altogether. One real estate economist forecast darkly that 25 million of the houses would be degraded to surplus and left to decay in their tracts, taken over by homeless people and gangs, or carved up into apartments by slum landlords. As the behemoths rotted, he predicted, housing that was closer to urban cores and centers of employment, that was compact and efficient—precisely the characteristics of the two cubes I hoped to build—would come increasingly into demand.

At 19th Street, I never got the chance to develop the pair of cubes. I was tripped up by a provision of the very second-unit law that I had counted on. Anticipating that if the legislation left them any wiggle room at all, many cities and towns would block development of second units (Great idea! But not in my town!), the state required that local governments create ordinances with *reasonable* requirements for the units, and that projects meeting the requirements be approved promptly while projects that fell short be turned down. To reduce blackballing of reasonable proposals to a minimum, no appeals or hearings or variances were allowed. It was either up or down.

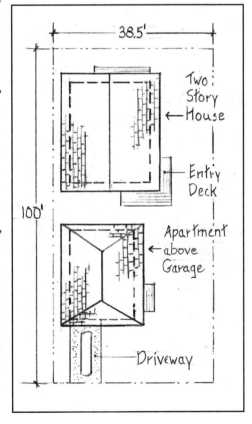

The ordinance that San Pablo enacted to comply with the state law allowed second units only on lots fifty feet or more in width. Quite reasonably, the town did not want its many neighborhoods with very narrow lots and an already congested feel to become yet more crowded. I felt, however, that the concern did not apply at my 19th Street parcel, for while it was only thirty-eight and a half feet wide, it was surrounded by homes on large lots. I argued for my second unit in a letter to the city planner. But he insisted that the law left him no leeway.

There are times when it is worth fighting City Hall. I have had successes. I rang up the California civil servant charged with monitoring city compliance with the second-unit law. I received from him, in this order: A sympathetic hearing. Assurances that the city planner was misunderstanding the law. Promises of help. No action. And, finally, no response to my follow-up calls. With an uneasy conscience and regret over reduced financial opportunity—for building two units seemed both the most environment considerate and the most profitable development option—but wanting to get on with my project, I decided to go another route. The drawings for the two cubes with roofs went in the drawer.

Lessons from two bad ideas

Where to next, I wondered. Feeling depleted from my setback, I first sketched a single-story house. "Boy, this will be easy to build," I was thinking. No hauling lumber up to a roof ridge twenty-five feet above the ground. No laboring up and down a scaffolding to install windows at second-story walls. No carrying 300-pound bathtubs up a flight of stairs to the bathrooms.

At first, the single-story concept showed promise. By building a basically rectangular box and pushing it at front, back, and sides right to the legally required setbacks, I was able to capture enough square footage for a three-bedroom, two-bath house. Two small decks, one facing south and one west, connected the interior spaces to the outdoors. With different exposures to sun and wind, they would be inviting in different weather and seasons, and at different times of day. Together with a garage popped out at the front, the decks articulated the simple box into an interesting form.

A shed roof, rising north to south, sheltered the entire house, and under its high southern eave provided ample room for windows to let light deep into the house. With the eave well proportioned and detailed, and with siding, doors, and windows thoughtfully placed and trimmed out, the house could look good from the street. But the one-story concept had problems as well. The structure crowded out open space on the lot, covering half again as much of the lot as the now banished two-cubes-with-roofs while providing considerably less habitable space. The roof sloped exactly the wrong direction to carry solar panels to produce hot water and electricity (a possibility I did not intend to exploit immediately but wanted to preserve), for solar panels require southern exposure.

On the other hand, if the roof slope were reversed to accommodate solar devices, it would not allow nearly as much southern sunshine to make its way into the house. In technical language, I would be sacrificing passive solar for active solar, a really dumb move, sort of like digging a 300 foot deep well when good water can be dipped right from a spring.

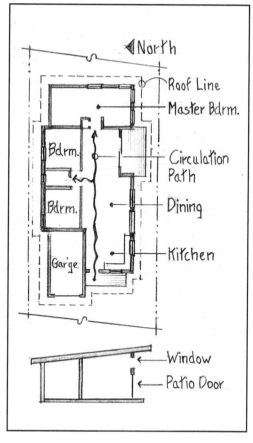

Though different roof forms did partially solve the problems, they introduced others. And whatever roof was used, the interior of the house did not work. The narrowness of the lot coupled with San Pablo's setback requirements forced the creation of awkward, compromised spaces. The smaller bedrooms ended up with a window on one exposure only, not two as is necessary for balanced natural lighting. That window would take in only the relatively dull northern light. And while the front area along the southern side did accommodate a comfortable sitting and TV room, the leftover space allowed only a cramped kitchen and a dining table that ended up stranded in the middle of pathways through the house.

All variations of the one-story plan I was able to imagine had similar problems or created others. Too much of the lot was covered with building, wiping out space for gardening and play. Bedrooms became too "carrot shaped," too narrow to handle furniture well or to permit comfortable movement. Circulation took up too much space or required dark hallways or pathways so long they gave the house a shotgun quality. Rooms with plumbing—kitchen, baths, laundry, hot water closet—ended up scattered about the house, thereby needing the long pipe runs from the hot water heater that would impose higher initial construction costs and, as we will see in Chapter Six, "Infrastructure," startlingly higher operating costs over the life of the building.

Any one-story structure would, in addition, use more material and labor than a cube of equivalent square footage. It would move 19th Street House away from the goals of environmental consideration and dollar wisdom. In the end, I was unable to come up with a satisfactory one-story plan that made both architonic and financial sense in the San Pablo market. And so the one-story concept, too, slid into the drawer.

Moving on, I began making sketches for a single cube, somewhat bigger than the main house in my initial two-cube concept. At first, from sheer love of their big-shouldered forms, I drew a flat-roofed house with an exterior in the Santa Fe style. But soon I realized that I needed to modify the form. Sitting and drawing at my home office in my own neighborhood, where the occasional Santa Fe house fits in well, I had lost touch with the 19th Street neighborhood. Its greatest architectural strength lies in the rhythmic repetition of simple gable-end cottage roofs marching up the streets toward the green hills. A flat-roofed Santa Fe style building would disrupt that rhythm. It would feel like an alien import to the street. And, I feared it would be inconsiderate of its one-story neighbors, a bulky block of a building looming heavily above them.

The Santa Fe drawings, too, had to go in the drawer—a third house to be not built. But as is often the case with early drafts for any sort of creative effort, the sketching had not been in vain. The Santa Fe design, in particular, had pushed me in a promising direction—toward a somewhat enlarged cube that could house a multigenerational family while still covering less than a quarter of the lot, leaving sizeable side- and backyard space for trees, a vegetable garden, play areas, and a deck. With a south-facing wall, it would let sunshine into both downstairs family spaces and upstairs bedrooms. With a moderately pitched gable roof and porch, it could sit comfortably alongside its neighbors and complement the visual rhythm of the street.

Its interior space would accommodate all the functionality needed in a modern home. In fact, I was at the beginning of amazement (that eventually would be expressed also by visitors to the completed 19th Street House) at the amount of family and private space that could be provided by a home of only 1,400 square feet, around half the size of average houses being built in the United States at the time. Now I had a concept for the house. It was time to craft working drawings that would define rooms and their connections, call out all the myriad structural, exterior, and interior details of the house-to-be, and guide me and my crew as we built it.

CRAFTING THE DRAWINGS

It's a rare builder, at least in my part of the world, who would think of starting construction of a house before it had been drawn in detail. He would no more hit the job site without plans than a National Basketball Association coach would start the season without a playbook. Every project of any size I have ever been involved with has been constructed in accordance with a thick roll of documents. Dictating virtually every detail and produced at costs running as high as a fifth of the cost of the actual construction, they were constantly furled and unfurled, checked and rechecked as the project progressed. Drawing first, constructing second, that's been a given; and it continues to be so even as digital documents supplant paper plans at building sites.

I had never even considered that it might be otherwise—not until I read Christopher Alexander's *The Production of Houses*, his account of building a cluster of small homes in Mexico. Working together with the families who would occupy them, Alexander and his team used stakes and lines to mark out the positions of the homes and their rooms directly on the soil of the empty lots. Then, dispensing with drawing altogether, they commenced construction right from the markers. Spurred by Alexander's account, I wondered, would it be possible here in the United States? Could an architekton, a chief carpenter in the old sense, a person capable in both design and construction, simply imagine a house and then build straightaway without drawing? Could he or she lay out the perimeters of the spaces on the ground; walk through and around them imagining functions, volume, detail, and building systems; then order materials, commence construction, and end up with a house up to snuff in all the ways my pyramid requires? Could you—oh tempting thought—actually get around the expense of drawing and compiling specifications and put the savings into upping construction quality instead? You know, I think it might just be possible—if you could get away with it, that is.

There may be locales in the United States where you could get away with it. Nineteenth Street in San Pablo, California, is not one of them. If you tried, the vigorous building department, backed by the efficient police department, would shut down your site and order you to get permits. For those permits you would be required to present detailed drawings showing your intention to build in compliance with the ever-denser demands of planning and building codes. Only after your documentation had been approved and your permit payments delivered (in the case of 19th Street House, four payments totaling $25,000 for four separate permits) would you be allowed to build.

Why draw?

Though it might be possible to dispense with it, drawing before constructing is worthwhile for reasons beyond obtaining the blessing of the building department. We have come to ask a great deal of our homes, and in consequence a modern house is bogglingly complex, required to address many, many concerns. Here is a very small sampling:

- Will the structural components and connections keep the house upright under normal stress and strain over many decades? Will they handle the extraordinary stress of an earthquake or cyclonic windstorm, which might come only once in many decades?

- Will it be possible to weave through the structure all the ducts, pipes, and wires for the many devices, from washing machines to computers to electric toothbrushes, we expect our houses to support?

- Will the openings in the structure do all that we hope for in providing light, warmth, insulation against cold, good views, fresh air, access to the outside, and visual effect?

- Are rooms big enough to serve their intended purposes? Will it be possible to get the necessary furniture into and out of them?

- Are doorways wide enough? Will doors conflict with one another or impede the efficient and comfortable use of interior space?

- Will there be sufficient room to the sides and in front of the toilets? Space to get into and out of the shower and to dry off? To work comfortably back and forth between sink, stove, and refrigerator in the kitchen?

- Is there a place for the cat box and the recycling bins? Have you remembered to include a mailbox?

It might be possible to address all the questions on the run, building upward with just a few stakes and lines on the ground to guide you. But thinking it all through by means of drawing first may prevent many a serious error and oversight. According to one woman, now a successful architect in her own right, who worked with Professor Alexander during her student years on the little houses in the Mexican village, they leaked badly. Without drawings to remind them of the mundane details, Alexander's team apparently got so caught up in constructing the lovely domed roofs they neglected to install an adequate waterproof membrane beneath the earthen material with which the domes were topped.

For architektons who draw and specify as well as lead construction of their projects, drawing offers an additional benefit. When you draw and then build, it is as if you build twice. For all the romantic talk about the joys of "making something with your hands," building is done principally with the mind. It is a matter of imagining a flow of tangible materials from multiple sources into empty space. It is a matter of so concentrating one's attention that the flow is regulated with efficiency. It is a matter of orchestrating the movements of the materials and the many instruments applied to them so that the materials assemble into precisely connected forms. When a job site foreman is frustrated with his carpentry apprentice, he does not slap the lad's hands. He yells, "Pay attention, dammit! Think!" Building well requires enormous mental effort.

Methodically imagining your way through the project on paper is a dress rehearsal for imagining it into place on site. You know your building intimately even before you pick up a hammer. Drawing it thoughtfully and thoroughly may, moreover, stimulate ideas, nuances, and touches (some of which might barely germinate during drawing and flower fully only when you are fastening lumber in place) that might otherwise never surface and that can make the difference between an *ordinary* and a *loved* building.

For clarity, I will have to describe the drawing of 19th Street House as a step-at-a-time process. In reality the process is not necessarily so linear. Yes, for some projects you quickly come upon a governing theme, and the rest of the idea flows logically into place behind it. At other times, crafting of drawings is more like putting together a picture puzzle, except that at the outset you do not quite know what the picture looks like. You don't even know what the pieces look like. You work back and forth, shaping one aspect of your idea, then another, then revising them both to make way for a third. And so, the pieces take shape and change, the picture emerges and evolves. One Bay Area architect says that as she begins her design process she does not even attempt to envision a form or space. Rather she asks herself, "Where do I need a window?" and, "Where do I need a door?" From these modest, gentle beginnings, rich and beautiful designs emerge.

Alternately, you might start with a general program: *The height and square footage of the house,* given the limitations imposed by building ordinances, conditions on the lot, and budget. *The functions that the house needs to serve*—home for a family of one, or six; one generation or two; or home, office, and shop all rolled together. *The form*—long and thin or boxy; peaked roof or flat—that best suits the site and serves the anticipated functions. *The placement of the form on the lot,* again in response to regulations, but also in response to the conditions at the site—prevailing winds, orientation to the sun, location of neighboring houses, slope of the land, direction of the best views, and any unusual topography such as boulders or streams, both above ground and below grade.

Placing the house on the lot

At 19th Street, by drawing the three houses (two cubes, single-story, Santa Fe style) not to be built, I had found my way to parts of my program. Now, how should that *compact cube with porch, exposure to southern sun, and a gable roof* be placed on its lot? Design savants sometimes advise siting a house on the least desirable part of a lot, leaving the choicest natural features undisturbed. Lovely idea. But underlying it can be an assumption that the house will sit on a sizeable acreage—a mythical place with meadows, granite outcroppings or streams wandering through, which you would not want to intrude on, but that happens also to include a barren knoll perfect for a house as it just happens to command a miles-long outlook across a magnificent river valley.

The great majority of our houses are, however, built not on idyllic countryside acreages, but instead on compact suburban parcels, more or less flat, usually rectangular, and hemmed in by other houses. No portion of such a lot is inherently choicer than others. For these typical lots, the guideline needs revision to something like this: site the house so as to preserve open space around it, with as much consideration for the neighbors as you can manage, taking into account sun, wind, and views as you are able.

That is what I set out to do at 19th Street. I moved my cube as far toward the street and toward the Lake Street House, i.e., toward the northern and western edge of the lot, as the codes would allow. That positioning placed the house alongside Lake Street's garage so that it would not be visible from the windows of Lake Street's living spaces, and would cast a shadow across only a small corner of Lake Street's rear yard. At the same time, the northwest positioning placed the house as far back as possible from the neighbors to the south, who would see it from windows of their living spaces. Thus, my 19th Street House was removed from the shadow of the southern neighbor's home, maximizing the exposure of 19ᵗʰ Street House to sunlight.

The northwest positioning also created a dollar and environmental benefit. Paths for utility and service connections (sewer, water, gas, electrical, phone, cable) were kept as short as possible, saving material and energy at both initial installation and for the inevitable eventual maintenance

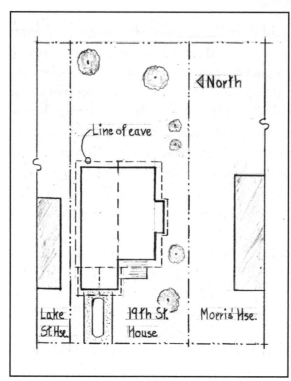

and replacements. The positioning created three areas of open yard: a compact front area already hosting several mature shrubs and a plum tree; a southern strip wide enough for new trees that would soften the house for the southern neighbors and shade lower level rooms against summer sun; and at the back, a yard big enough for an oak I hoped to plant, a vegetable garden, and leisure and play areas.

Bubble clusters

With form and placement on the lot worked out, another question arose. What could and should be built inside of the intended cubic volume of the house? Seeking the answer with a traditional method, I drew bubbles, each representing a space, and sorted the bubbles into four groups. Had I been building for clients, they would have been in large part responsible for naming the bubbles, for they would have known what sort of spaces they desired for their home. In the case of 19ᵗʰ Street House, however, I was building for an unknown client. I did not know who would come to occupy the house, but I had made a decision to build a home that would serve a family with children, or even a multigenerational family. The interior of the cube could just as readily have been carved into a hip work/live loft or a posh, one-bedroom pad with office spaces. But a house for a larger family seemed to me what was most needed in San Pablo.

The first group of bubbles represented family spaces that would likely be clustered together in the house, though just how would have to be puzzled out later. The second group represented a minimum of private spaces, three bedrooms, and a bath, also likely to be clustered. In the third group, I placed bubbles representing spaces that, while necessary, did not have to be clustered, but could be allowed to find their various appropriate places alongside the family and private clusters.

In that third group, I included a bubble representing a garage. I did so with regret, only because I was forced to. In the Bay Area's climate, garaging cars is not a must. Generally, people do not put their cars in their garages. As I have seen over and over when building for clients, garages instead end up as costly storage space for stuff people do not use, don't need, don't remember they have, and would not be able to find in the garage if they did need it and were able to remember they already owned it. The stuff is typically worth far less than the garage itself, but the owners nevertheless keep it piled there for decades on end thinking they just might have use for it someday, then finally, with a sigh of relief, recycle it all when I come along and explain that my crew and I will need the garage as a staging area if we are to work efficiently. There are ways to provide for questionable storage that are far less costly in both dollars and environmental impact than building a garage with a concrete foundation and heavy-duty walls and roof. But the City of San Pablo, adhering to the fiction that its people put their cars in their garages rather than cluttering up the streets with them, required that I build one.

Along with the garage, the third bubble group called for a laundry space. Compact, moderate-cost houses sometimes have the washer and dryer in a niche or a closet off the hallway. For 19th Street House, because I imagined it might someday serve as home for a sizeable extended family with grandpa and grandma, mom and dad, and three kids moving through it, I felt something more was needed. The house needed a laundry space big enough to step into, where washing and drying and ironing could be done out of the way of daily household traffic, so that laundry would not end up spilling into and congesting circulation areas.

In the third group, I included a bubble representing a "service core," a centrally located area for the space and water heaters, the primary plumbing pipes, and the electrical panel. In houses with no service core, these items tend to end up in whatever leftover area can be found, often remote from the functions they support. Runs of duct and pipe and wire are greatly lengthened, resulting in waste for installation and operation. Lengthier runs of all three eat up more material and labor during construction. And the long runs of furnace ducting and hot water lines can, as mentioned earlier and as we will see in startling detail later, dissipate astonishing amounts of heat in delivering it to points of use.

The fourth and final group of bubbles expressed not necessities but hopes, three of them. Would it be somehow possible within the small cube and its restrained square footage to fit in a second full bath to service the private spaces and even a half bath to service the family spaces? Would it be possible, also, to fit in a fourth bedroom, a good-sized one—a potential grandparents' place—along with a spacious-enough parents' bedroom and two bedrooms for children?

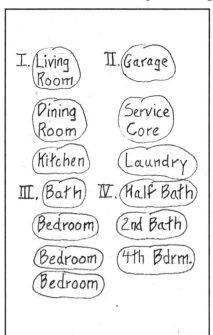

Altogether, the four bubble clusters of necessities and hopes added up to one big question. Could a roughly cubic form about twenty-six feet wide, high, and tall, with a total floor area of 1,352 square feet, contain a comfortable four-bedroom, two-and-a-half-bath home with a laundry as well as a service core? If so, it would provide all the functionality (though a good deal less gratuitous circulation area and less space per room) of the new American home typical of its day, but with about half the square footage.

Honoring the intimacy gradient

Moving from bubble clusters toward actual working drawings, I had to answer two major questions. The first was, where should the garage go? Ironically, yes, the placement of that dubious space would shape and influence every design decision that would follow. Two options for the garage were quickly scotched. It could have gone in the far southern corner of the lot; the city would have allowed that. But putting it there would have required paving over the entire southern edge of the yard for a driveway, wiping out existing plants in the front yard, and eliminating the possibility of planting trees in the side yard. Placing the entire garage out to the front of the house would push the house too far back, squeezing its rear yard down to a narrow strip, and imposing its bulk over the northern neighbor's rear yard. The solution I settled on—placing the garage largely within the cube but popping it out at the front—had promise. It took away much less of the yard. It created an "L" formed by the sidewall of the garage and the front wall of the house that would nicely enclose the front porch I'd long had in mind, making it a more sheltering outdoor room.

Popping the garage out at the front also added potential for a more interesting "face," as one architect calls the front of his houses—for more "curb appeal," as realtors say. Exactly how the potential might be realized would emerge only further down the line. I would be chasing after it and refining it all the way through the drawing of the floor plans and of the front and side views of the house, the "exterior elevations" as they are called in building parlance. But I sensed there was a chance for something pretty nice.

Along with answering the garage question, I needed to determine whether I should, just maybe, build the house upside down, placing family spaces on an upper floor and bedrooms at the entry level. In my own neighborhood, a builder had recently done just that to capture views of the San Francisco Bay from upstairs living and dining rooms. But I have noticed that entering that house amidst the bedrooms at the lower level unsettles visitors. They feel they are invading private territory. The upside-down arrangement seems to violate a deeply held expectation, reinforced by the way we have built for centuries, that homes will be organized according to an "intimacy gradient," as it is called in pattern language. When the intimacy gradient is honored, the rooms where a family might host someone they don't know very well—like a door-to-door fund-raiser they have allowed inside—are placed closest to the entry. Spaces into which they would invite friends to share meals or a cup of coffee are further into the house. Deeper in still are the family's private bedrooms and bathrooms.

Like the upside-down house built near my home, the 19th Street House would enjoy good views—though of coastal mountains and hills rather than the San Francisco Bay—from its upper level. It would have been nice

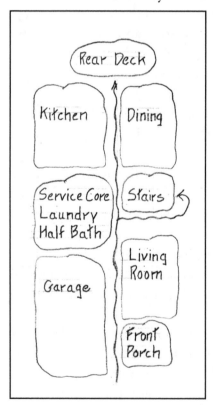

to enjoy those views during daylight hours from upstairs family spaces. I decided, however, to stay with the usual arrangement, to honor the expectation of the intimacy gradient with family spaces placed on the lower floor and private spaces above. Further along in its development, in the choice of heating systems and finish flooring, for example, the house would be pushing the boundaries of convention quite enough. I did not want to push it so far it would feel too weird to too many people and be difficult to sell or rent. Any lingering inclination I had toward upside down was squelched by my wife. "No one," she said firmly, "wants to carry groceries upstairs to a kitchen. I wouldn't."

With a garage located and the interior spaces arranged right side up, I began organizing bubbles into rough versions of a potential first-floor plan. It included family spaces organized in a traditional pattern. It serviced those spaces with a half bath and served the entire house with a heating/plumbing/electrical core at a central location. It even suggested comfortable circulation that used little floor area. A straight path extended from a front entry along the edge of the living room to the rear of the house, and at its midpoint branched off to the stairway.

Four bedrooms and an inspiration

As I drew a bubble sketch of the second floor, I included a fourth bedroom, one large enough to serve an older couple as both a sleeping area and a daytime retreat. The fourth bedroom represented a remnant of that grandparents' place, the second unit I had wanted to include in the two cube plan rejected by the city on the grounds that my lot was too narrow. I still felt it was important to build the 19th Street House so that it could accommodate a multigenerational family in some comfort. While renovating Lake Street, I had become acquainted with several such San Pablo families trying to cram themselves into homes with too few bedrooms. I had seen families jury-rigging garages to function as sleeping space. I had seen what a difference would have been made by an extra bedroom or two, even if compact, allowing parents and grandparents and the oldest child to have spaces of their own.

The second-floor bubble plan also carried forward the intention that 19th Street House be environment considerate in its use of resources for both construction and living. The upstairs bathrooms were backed up against one another and stood directly over the first-floor half bath and service core so that water supply and waste lines could be both shared and short. The distance from the water heater to each of the bathrooms, where most hot water would be consumed, was just a few feet. All rooms on the second floor (as was also the case for the first floor) had an edge along the center line of the house where a heat register could be located only a short duct run from the space heater. Thus the opportunity for heat loss from water and air en route to point of use would be minimized.

Similarly, working together with the simple T-circulation pattern on the lower level, a central foyer serving the second story minimized the square footage needed for circulation, and thereby minimized the material and energy needed both for its construction and for its long-term maintenance.

While the initial bubble sketches held possibilities for a good house, they also made visible some of the problems still to be solved. The laundry space had yet to find its place. It was still hovering off to the side. And, the sketches warned, the stairway and upstairs foyer, located as they were in the middle of the house, could evolve into cramped, dark places. I knew of the danger from my own home. There the entry foyer and stairwell are largely shut off from natural light by the rooms they lead to. Even the quarter sawn oak flooring and the mahogany mirror, ten square feet in size, made in my great-grandfather's furniture factory in Germany during the nineteenth century and now hanging at the stair landing, do not save the space from feeling dim.

I also knew of the danger—as well as the possibility of turning the liability into an asset—from rebuilding the large home of my beloved clients Don and Carol Aird some years earlier. The stairway in the Airds' original house had been a dark, three-story, vertical tunnel closed off from natural light by surrounding rooms. But with the Airds and their architect in the lead, and the structural engineer, cabinetmaker, carpentry crew, and me all contributing ideas, the stairway was transformed. When reconstruction of the house was completed, it had become a sunlit four-story library extending all the way up to a retractable skylight, which gave access to a roof deck. It is a pleasure to use that stairway, sliding your hand along the smooth steel banister, pausing to pull a book from the shelves, leaning back on the padded bench below the skylight. I could not hope to match the Aird stairway on my 19th Street House budget. But eventually during drawing and construction I would be inspired by it.

Making it work

From hopeful bubble sketches to useful working drawings is a long journey. Smaller houses demand especially intense focus lest you draw something that can't be built—or worse, will not work after it is built.

Every increment of horizontal and vertical dimension counts. Let a wall slip over a fraction of an inch, and your tub will not fit into its allotted space during construction. Let it slip a couple of inches in the other direction, and you have squeezed out space for comfortable entry into a bedroom or made a closet so small a coat hanger will not fit into it. Place a beam too high in a floor frame, and you block heating ducts from reaching a corner bedroom. Move a window a few inches too far away from the corner of a room, and there will not be enough wall space for a bureau to stand without blocking the view and ventilation.

To achieve all that is necessary and all that you hope for in the limited square footage that is available, you arrange and rearrange. You shift windows and doors. You adjust stairway step heights and tread depths by a thirty-second of an inch. You scrimp for smidgens of space, turning studs sideways to allow pantry shelves deep enough for five cans of soup, not four and four-tenths. You get a little desperate at times: how am I possibly going to fit in a decent-sized closet and a homework table here in the smallest child's bedroom, yet free up enough space so that the kid can move around the bed to make it up in the morning? At other times, you smile and think, this is happening. It is going to work. I am puzzling the picture together. It's looking good.

You roll out your drawings for friends, some of them building or design professionals and others not, but all of them people who have aptitude around architonic issues, a feeling for the qualities that make a house a pleasure to move through, tend to and operate, rest in, touch, and look at and out of. They see possibilities that had escaped you. Rooms switch places and then switch again. A door moves from one wall to an adjacent one. Your house gets a little longer and a touch taller. Here and there, a bay pops out of a wall to house a landing or a display niche.

All this and much more happened as the 19th Street House bubble sketches evolved into working drawings. A fellow architekton, who had just finished crafting a small home and thought his place a bit tight, urged me to stretch the house to thirty-two feet in length (not including the garage pop out). I accepted his idea, rationalizing away my unease about the environment and dollar impacts of building bigger. If some future owners felt compelled to tear the house apart to gain a little extra space, the impact would be far greater than if I made the house big enough to begin with. Moreover, a small lengthening of the house would have only moderate impact at initial construction compared with the impact of a later addition.

Another friend spotted efficiencies in locating the laundry space on the first floor, clustering it with the half bath and the service core rather than placing it upstairs. A fellow builder pointed out, however, that the downstairs location had a drawback. Most laundry, he pointed out, is generated in baths and bedrooms, and carting laundry downstairs and back up is inconvenient. He was right. But putting the laundry space upstairs would have required elimination of the fourth bedroom or making the house yet bigger by extending it into and shrinking the backyard. So downstairs the laundry went, close by the service core, where it would require only the shortest of pipe and electrical runs.

Likewise a doorway connecting the garage and the interior

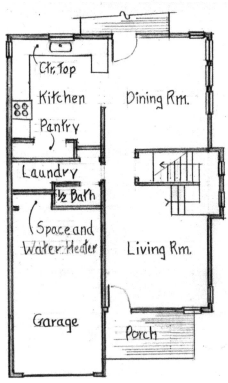

space was removed from the drawings. Healthy house experts emphasize that garages are often storehouses of toxics—including combustion fumes when they are actually used to park cars. Interior doors to garages get left open or even propped open. The toxics and fumes seep into the house. Houses built tightly for efficient heating and cooling, as houses are increasingly required to be these days, and as 19th Street House would certainly be, hold the toxics in. Children especially are sickened, though maybe so gradually that parents are not aware of the damage being done or of its source. For that reason, garages are best not connected directly to living spaces.

After looking over the first-floor layout, an architect friend, avid for open plan designs, proposed that I change the stairway orientation. He pointed out that by rising south to north, i.e., rising from the right or south side of the house toward the left or north side, as I had anticipated in the bubble sketches and included in the working drawings, the stairway would divide the family space into two major areas, an entry parlor at the front and an area for cooking and dining at the rear. I should swing my stairway against the southern wall, into a west-to-east orientation, he urged. By doing that, I would open the lower floor areas to one another and create wonderful, long interior views. And if I wished, he added, the family spaces could be artfully differentiated by changes in level, with cabinetry and built-ins, or with ceiling constructions such as soffits.

I knew what he meant. Open plans can be visually dramatic. Some are virtual sculpture galleries, featuring imaginative yet functional formations conjured by their designers—a skillfully crafted niche for an antique clock, sensuously curving soffits housing indirect lighting, even indoor trellises. But open plans have a steep downside. When all the different members of a household are in that big space with each doing his or her own thing, you get cacophony. Not long before drawing 19th Street House, I went to a party at the home of another architect. He greatly regretted the open plan he had designed for his house. Too noisy! No privacy! He declared that if he had the chance to build himself another home, he would not make that mistake again. Ironically, the open plan, intended to make his house seem spacious, had actually made it feel smaller by putting the family members right up against one another.

Taking the second architect's emphatic cue, I decided that at 19th Street House, the stairway should remain oriented south to north, separating the front and rear areas of the downstairs family space. The kitchen and dining spaces were, however, left open to one another, divided only by a cabinet peninsula and a beam supporting the floor above. Some household cooks would not like that. They would prefer a wall, or at least ceiling-hung cabinets above the peninsula, to create a more complete barrier between their workspace and the dining area. However, I decided to leave the areas for food preparation and eating as shared, communal space. Thinking ahead to the dining area windows, I wanted the southern light they would admit to be able to flow freely all the way to the far side of the kitchen. Southern sun can effectively illuminate space up to twenty-five feet deep. That is exactly the distance from the dining room windows to the far side of the kitchen at 19th Street House.

Sunlight and a little specialness

Not all climates encourage opening the southern wall to let sunlight flow in. I have seen hunkered-down desert homes with their backs, thick windowless walls, turned to the south, barring the savage sun from direct entry. In the South, older homes from the era before air conditioning, as well as thoughtfully designed newer houses for an era when energy conservation looms large, have broad porches positioned on their southern exposures to prevent the penetration of sunlight into indoor spaces on sultry summer days. But in San Pablo, which enjoys the easy, mild climate of the San Francisco Bay Area, southern sun is to be welcomed. Entering through windows, it provides natural lighting all year around, saving electricity. And it promotes mental health. People who live in the Bay Area celebrate their sunlight as much as the English complain about their incessant rain. Sunlight is widely acknowledged to stimulate happiness and diminish depression. Additionally, it provides low-cost heating—not *no*-cost, not by any means, for windows are not free. Good windows are among the most expensive components of a house. Cheap windows, which will fail earlier and need replacement, may be even more costly in the long run.

To take in the sun, 19th Street House's windows are concentrated on the southern side. Fully half its windows face directly south. In the upstairs bedrooms and downstairs family spaces, additional windows face east and west, providing those rooms with light from two directions—an antidote to glare. If you have ever stayed in a hotel room with a window on one side only and noticed the light conditions, you will understand the concern. The rooms can feel like caves with the brightly lit window wall and the shadowed interior walls contrasting harshly.

At the north wall, the cold side of the house, windows were minimized for the sake of holding down heat loss and maximizing energy efficiency. Rooms that could do without windows were placed on the north side of the house. The garage suffered little if any for lack of windows. Natural lighting in the laundry would have been pleasant but was not essential. The two upstairs bathrooms were also placed to the north and drawn without windows—though not without a tussle with an architect friend who critiqued my design decisions.

"How could you do that?" he demanded in the half playful yet quite serious way we usually debated architectural issues. How could I, he asked, patting at his purple bowtie in a gesture of mock bewilderment, possibly deprive the family of the lovely view of the hills to the north, which would be visible through bathroom windows? I laid out my reasons: energy efficiency, environment consideration, and dollar wisdom. I asked whether he thought I should contribute a little more to the destruction of the planet's environment so people could enjoy a peek at it while they were showering.

He dismissed my thinking, insisting that two small windows would allow only trivial amounts of heat energy to escape. The loss might be very little on any given day, I told him, but it would be substantial over the long term, and would come on top of considerable energy expended to create and install windows in the first place "Why, it might be just enough," I suggested, "that the associated global warming would push one more polar bear over the edge into extinction. And if not, it would assuredly impinge on some animal habitat somewhere."

He said he thought I was probably exaggerating. All I was willing to concede was that while my estimate of impact due to energy loss through the windows was not much more than a wild guess, one thing was sure: windows built into shower walls leak. When they leak, they cause rot in their walls. The rotted walls have to be repaired. And over the decades, all the repair work occasioned by designers who felt their showers just had to have a window in them has certainly added up to great environmental impact, not to mention financial burden on owners.

The architect was incredulous and told me I should just waterproof the window. "I've got him; he's on my turf now," I thought to myself. Patiently—well, maybe with a touch of triumph—I explained to him that no waterproofing is perfect, that all waterproofing fails over the years as surely as the leaves of the maple turn yellow and tumble to the ground each fall.

"Oh, come now, we specify this sort of thing all the time. We never have a problem."

"That," I told him, "is because when there is a problem, the clients do not call you. When their building fails, they don't call the *architect*. They call the *builder*—and the builder does not tell you about the problem because he does not want to lose your confidence."

"David," he said with finality, falling back on the papal mode of the Form Givers handing down one of their *fatwas* with that certain confidence of infallibility. "It was a mistake." There's no arguing with true believers, I thought, but decided to indulge in one more shot. During what percentage of their showers, I asked my friend, did he figure the family members would pause to take in the view?

"Why, every shower, of course," he said. I chuckled. But as things turned out, he would enjoy the last smile. Focusing intently on the reasons to keep costly, heat-losing windows out of the bathroom, I failed to see another and much more dollar- and environment-friendly way of bringing sunlight into them. That oversight would only be discovered far deeper into our story, a year and a half after the family moved into the house. Just adjacent to the bathrooms, however, another problem surfaced immediately, and out of it an architonic and an environmental opportunity emerged hand in hand. The problem was that the stairs would not fit in the space I had at first allotted.

To conform to the building code and feel familiar, a stairway must meet several requirements. The steps, or "risers," must all be the same height and the treads the same width to within a small fraction of an inch. In order that they not feel uncomfortably steep, the steps should not much exceed seven and a half inches in height, and the height of the step plus the depth of the tread (the "rise and run," in carpenter lingo) should be close to eighteen inches. For example, a seven and a half inch rise plus a ten and a half inch run will give you a comfortable stairway. But 19ᵗʰ Street House, at its originally intended width and layout of rooms, could not accommodate a comfortable and safe stairway. With an acceptable step height and tread depth, the stairway would have extended almost all the way to the bathroom walls, leaving a ridiculously narrow upstairs landing. On the other hand, to leave adequate landing space in front of the bathroom walls, the stairway would have had to be excessively steep, with high risers and shallow treads.

For the stairway to work, it would have to begin beyond the intended exterior south wall of the house. But, of course, the stairway could not just poke out through that south wall and be left hanging in midair. It needed to be enclosed in a bay jutting out of the southern wall. A bay would be costly. Any time you incorporate changes in direction in a building, you add substantial material and labor for both rough and finish work. A bay incorporates multiple changes in direction: two inside corners, two outside corners, and a roof jutting out from a wall.

All told, the bay came close to doubling the cost of framing, cladding, and interior finish at the southern wall. But the investment seemed dollarwise. It was essential to preserving the intended first-floor plan. It would add variety and interest to the highly visible southern wall.

And, that architectural interest would arise out of necessary function, not merely for the sake of decoration in the manner of the shallow fake pop outs lathered across much recent production housing. It would be a form following function even if, alas, falling a little short of the "perfect spiritual union of form and function" that Frank Lloyd Wright

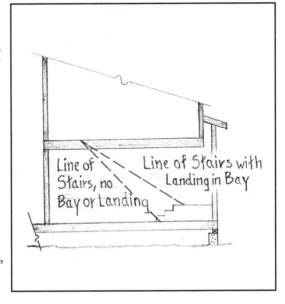

advocated when he came to feel that the "form follows function" dictum was being misinterpreted.

At the interior, the bay added an alcove, an inviting little getaway beyond the expected family and private spaces. I imagined pillows on the landing, propped against the bay's sidewalls, and children playing there or teenagers talking. The bay added visual depth to the entry parlor, giving that constrained space a greater volume. The two tall windows centered in its south-facing wall would add to the mix of light in the entry room, contribute to the warming of the house in the winter, and powerfully illuminate the stairwell—moving it away from the dismal tunnel I had feared. It was moving the stairway design in the direction I had been inspired to go by the Airds' sunlit vertical library.

The stairway and its landings would continue to evolve, even deep into construction. But as it took its place in the drawings, I was beginning to feel that the house was acquiring a bit of specialness. The garage pop out and bay were moving the house beyond the boxy configurations typical of moderate-cost housing. Downstairs, the six windows in the kitchen and dining area would flood that space with welcoming, warming sunlight.

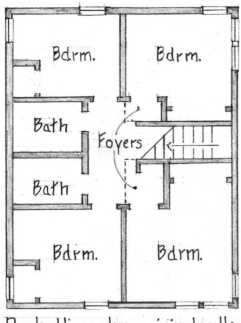

Dashed lines show original walls.

On the upper level, with so little square footage gobbled up for circulation, there was, it turned out, room for those four bedrooms. One child's bedroom would be snug, only a third larger than the legal minimum of seventy square feet. But the other would be big enough for two young children. And the two larger bedrooms would each be comfortable for adult couples. Every bedroom would have a sizeable closet. None would be your basic rectangle. In each, a wall would turn a corner to form a niche or alcove. In the children's bedrooms, I imagined building a desk into the alcove, providing a place softly lit by indirect northern sunlight to do homework.

The two adult bedrooms each acquired an additional distinctive feature thanks to a fellow architekton who spotted an idea that had escaped me. With a few strokes of his pencil he proposed slightly rearranging the walls and entry doors to the adult bedrooms. Now when you entered the rooms, instead of looking at the end of a closet, you looked across the rooms and out through a window. Now, each of the bedrooms had acquired a foyer of its own, a place for bookshelves or art that signaled a transition to private adult spaces, distinguishing them from the child's bedrooms whose doors opened directly onto the main landing. For all the benefit they provided, the foyers added nothing in material and only an hour or so of carpentry labor for each bedroom.

The third dimension, restraint, and X-ray vision

"Don't forget the third dimension," I was once advised. There is more to an interior space than the two horizontal dimensions of the floor plan. The horizontal dimensions largely define function and flow, determining what we will do in a building, where we will do it, and how we will get from space to space. The vertical dimensions most contribute to the personality and presence of a room as we encounter it. They surround

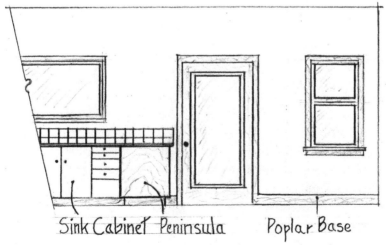

Sink Cabinet Peninsula   Poplar Base

us. They stare us in the face. One architect I have worked with attaches so much importance to the vertical compositions that if his clients' budgets allowed he would draw a straight-on view, an "elevation," of every single interior wall, and not at the usual scale with a quarter inch representing one foot, but four times that size.

For 19th Street House I settled on drawing three categories of elevations: Walls that were typical of several others. Walls that supported a great deal of function. And walls that were unique. For example, I drew a wall with typical windows, casings, and baseboards, trusting that if they worked at one wall they would work at others. I drew views of the kitchen cabinet walls and of the bathroom plumbing wall, for they were loaded with function, and I needed to make sure that it all fitted into the allotted space. I drew the stairway wall, for that was what family members would confront when they stepped in from the front porch. If both wall and porch were well conceived and constructed, they would evoke the feeling, "I have come home to a good place."

The person who urged me to remember the third dimension might well have added, "And don't forget to look up." Rooms have ceilings, too. They can be enhanced for relatively little cost. A coffered ceiling can be created with a small amount of lumber and drywall. A simple molding just below the junction of the ceiling and the walls adds a distinctive cap to a room, especially if the area above the molding is painted a different color than the walls below. Light-colored or painted wood can contribute warmth and texture. However, a badly chosen species, such as redwood, which will darken greatly over time, can end up creating a gloomy feeling. The need to consider what a building will become, not only what it will be at the moment of completion, is sometimes not sufficiently considered.

I did sketch possibilities for the adult bedroom ceilings, but rather than incorporating one of the treatments into the working drawings, I set them aside for reconsideration during construction. I suspected that the ceilings would remain unadorned, that the rooms would have character enough with their niches, alcoves, natural pine window trim, and prominent baseboards. There are houses where the designer has laid his hands on too heavily, applying his signature to every surface, nook, and cranny. Looking at a well-known picture book of such places, my mother, a weaver of subdued, elegant linen fabrics in her youth, said, "None of these places are restful."

It's hard to make a home inside an overly design-intensive house. It is as if the designer never leaves but is always insisting to you, "Look how creative I am." The designer's presence overpowers the owner's touches, furnishings, and arrangements. Some people seem to like living inside someone else's noisy artwork. I have had a few clients who happily inhabit densely detailed interiors created by their prestigious designer. I enjoyed building those interiors, but would not want to live in them. One thing I greatly appreciate about my own home is that while it is well conceived and constructed, it stays in the background in a way that allows my wife and me to create the personalities of our rooms.

Even if ceilings are left unadorned, you must look up during drawing. At the very least there will be electrical lights up there, and they need to be positioned carefully in relation to what lies below. For 19th Street House, I took the standard shortcut to create a view of the ceiling lights and their relationship to floors and walls. I simply copied the floor plans, leaving out measurements and notes, and drew in the lights. The "reflected ceiling plan," as it is called, also served as a place to note all the other wiring terminations such as outlets, phone jacks, and cable connections, along with the lights.

It is necessary during drawing to look not only down at floors, up at ceilings, and at walls. You need to look *inside* walls. That's work often skipped over during house design. Too often the complex of ducts, pipes, metal boxes, and wires—along with the components of the thermal barrier—that will be hidden from view behind finish surfaces are given no consideration during drawing. It is left to the tradespeople to get them into place. The frame goes up, and then the heating, ventilation, and air conditioning (HVAC) installers and the plumbers hack their way through it—in the worst cases angrily battling for space, weakening the structure, and disrupting finish surfaces. For example, for lack of forethought, in a recent Bay Area remodel, a heat register ended up off-center above a double door and crammed awkwardly against a curved wall-to-ceiling transition so that big gaps showed between its flanges and the plaster. In another, because ductwork was not planned out in advance, it ended up exposed to the inside of the wall frame. It had to be concealed by a chase, a box of framing lumber and drywall, from floor to ceiling. The chase bulges out awkwardly in one corner of the master bedroom, forever visible from the bed, sure to dampen romance many a night as the husband flags, distracted by thoughts of the architect and builder he paid so much for such thoughtless work.

Inevitably, during construction you have to refine the layout of the larger pipes and ducts. But if you make sure to allocate sufficient separate space for your heating, plumbing, electrical, and media systems during drawing, you will have a much easier time during construction. Anticipating what is inside your structural frame, what I am going to be calling "infrastructure" in a coming chapter, is especially important in the small house with the compact service core. Again, every fraction of an inch counts. You are intending to fit a lot of function into restricted volumes. For 19th Street House, I drew both a plan and section view of my service core and looked the drawings over with my subcontractors to make sure each would have the space needed.

Keeping the house up

Even now, drawing is not done. There is this small matter: the building must stand up, hopefully for a long time, against the most violent batterings of nature as well as its imperceptibly gradual erosions. Most of the structural work that keeps a typical frame house erect is hidden from view, but it must be envisioned and specified in the working drawings.

For 19th Street House, the structural portion of the drawings (and accompanying specifications) ran to eleven pages, nearly as many as the floor plans, elevations, reflected ceiling views, and related detail combined. I crafted the structural drawings, and my engineer reviewed my work. He added a couple of straps, a few rows of nails, and several clips. Then he saved me construction costs nearly equal to his $1,500 fee by suggesting bigger foundation piers but fewer of them. After I had altered my drawings in keeping with his recommendations, he stamped them with his official seal.

I could have gotten my building permit without the seal. But it made the building department happy. In earthquake country, building departments want as much assurance as they can get. Environment consideration demands strong structure as well. If a building goes down in The Big One, every bit of consideration that went into it will be wasted.

Structural drawings indicate the size of all structural components. Equally important, they show how the components are connected together. In *Why Buildings Fall Down*, Matthys Levy and Mario Salvadori tell a story that makes vivid the importance of connections. One morning in 1968, Ms. Ivy Hodge, not realizing that her apartment in a twenty-two-story tower east of London, England, had filled with gas leaking from her stove, began preparing breakfast, and struck a match to light a burner. The gas exploded. Ms. Hodge was knocked to the floor. She suffered second-degree burns on her face and arms. Otherwise, she was not injured. Her eardrums were not even damaged.

The tower in which Ms. Hodge lived, however, did not get off so easily. The explosion knocked an exterior wall of her living room completely off the floor that supported the wall. Now, the floor above, which Ms. Hodge's wall had held up, was left without support from below. As a result, that floor collapsed, leaving the wall *it* held up with no support as well. Domino style—wall, then floor, then wall, then the next floor—the sequence of collapse continued until an entire corner of Ms. Hodge's apartment tower lay in rubble on the ground below. Ms. Hodge, sprawled in front of her stove, found herself staring into empty space that seconds earlier had been her living room.

The reason for the collapse? The wall and floor of Ms. Hodge's apartment, both made of premanufactured concrete slabs, had been joined together only by a thin bed of mortar, as if they were mere bricks in a garden wall. Steel connectors of the kind installed to tie together the walls and floors in similar apartment towers had been omitted. For lack of such connection, a relatively mild explosion—one not strong enough to severely injure, much less kill, a person right next to it—was enough to take down an entire corner of a mid-rise building.

Sizing of structural members and connections relies on experience, mathematical calculation, and computer simulation. It relies as well on information from experiments conducted by building scientists. In labs in California, builders and engineers erect full-size houses atop giant shaking tables that simulate a seismic event, and then examine the house for failures and deformations to determine how future buildings might be strengthened against earthquakes. But for all the figuring and study that goes into crafting structure, the goal is simple. A building must stand up against "the loads," as engineers say, imposed upon it. The loads generate forces, and the forces boil down to just two types: compression and tension. Buildings get pushed (compressed), and they get pulled (tensed). We must build them so they can withstand the greatest pushing and pulling they are liable to experience. We do not want to build our apartment towers so that a little mishap during the preparation of a tenant's breakfast will generate a push sufficient to tumble a good portion of the tower to the ground.

Though all loads generate compression and/or tension, the loads can be divided into several types. Houses, such as the one I was planning to build at 19th Street, experience *dead loads*, namely their own weight. Remodeling older homes, I have seen floors sagging into gentle arcs, pushed downward by the weight of walls inadequately supported from below by the floor frame. The homes are slowly being defeated by their own dead weight.

Houses experience *live loads*, the stress imposed by the family who lives in the house, their possessions, and their guests. Live loads may normally be light. But they can become concentrated, as when fifteen friends crowd into the entry parlor to watch the Super Bowl. Houses also sustain *dynamic loads*, those that strike it suddenly and with amplified force. You can observe dynamic load by getting on and off your bathroom scale. Step on, and the scale registers, say, 172 pounds. Hop on, and for an instant the scale registers over 300 pounds. If the Super Bowl guests were to leap up joyfully and come back down in unison as their team completed a long pass to set up the go-ahead field goal, they would inflict a dynamic load.

For a fascinating tour through further nuances of load, read *Why Buildings Fall Down* and the companion volume, *Why Buildings Stand Up*. With a series of vivid case studies, the authors will take you deep into the ways that builders and engineers have tried, failed, and succeeded in creating structures that hold together against the force of storms, earthquakes, and human use and abuse. You will learn about: The *varying* loads imposed by wind as it gradually increases and decreases pressure on a building. The way compression can create tension in a beam. And, most startling of all, the way tension and compression combine to create a stress on buildings called "shear," analogous to the force of shears cutting through sheet metal.

For this story of 19th Street House, it will be enough to mention two principles of structural design especially important in house building. First, components should be *redundant*. Second, connections should be *continuous*. Both principles can be seen at work in my structural section. Reduced to simple terms, redundancy calls for putting in structural members in excess of what the building will need in ordinary circumstances. Then if a member fails, there will be backup in place to pick up the load.

In other words, redundancy parallels principles we rely on to maintain margin of safety in other aspects of life, such as "save something for a rainy day."

The structural drawings for 19th Street House imposed redundancy by, to cite one instance, calling for roof trusses every two feet. The trusses could have been spaced further apart and might have functioned just fine, at least initially. I have remodeled houses with rafters much less frequently placed and much weaker than the 19th Street House trusses, and those rafters have held up

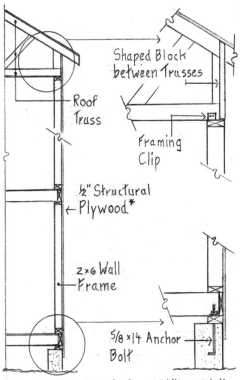

Shaped Block between Trusses

Roof Truss

Framing Clip

½" Structural Plywood*

2×6 Wall Frame

5/8 ×14 Anchor Bolt

* See nailing schedule for addit'l requir'm'ts.

their roofs for decades. Of course, it remains to be seen whether they will survive the dynamic load to be imposed on that "rainy day" when a violent to very violent earthquake rumbles through. With their greater strength and redundancy, the trusses at 19th Street House should have a better chance.

From the foundation all the way to the roof trusses at 19th Street House, the connections are continuous. Follow the path up in the structural section. The mudsill is bolted to the foundation. The joists and rim are nailed to the mudsill. The subfloor and the wall plate are spiked to both joists and rim, while the studs are connected to the plate. The heavily nailed wall sheathing ties together everything from the mudsill through the second-story wall frame, and so on, until finally the trusses are attached to the second story wall with metal brackets fastened with substantial screws.

If any in the series of connections were left out, a potentially deadly weakness such as existed at Ms. Hodge's tower would result. Under an extraordinary load, the house could come apart right at the point of discontinuity. In hurricanes, roof assemblies do rip off the walls below because the rafters or trusses were barely nailed in place. In earthquakes, older homes continuously tied together by wall and roof sheathing sometimes stay largely intact from the mudsill up to the roof ridge but hop right off their foundations for lack of attachment of mudsill to concrete.

Softened craftsman

In some of the most beloved of our edifices—the Eiffel Tower, Gothic cathedrals, the Golden Gate Bridge—structural elements and form are unified. You cannot imagine the one without the other. Even in house construction, though the structural components are generally invisible, they are interdependent. Structural drawing follows architectural drawing, with the hope that structure can be developed that will support the intended form for an acceptable cost. If not, the form must be modified. In contrast to the close relationship of structure and form, the interior and exterior shape and look of a house can be, to a surprising degree, independent of one another. It's quite possible to build a minimalist, open-plan, twenty-first-century loft inside a nineteenth-century brownstone, or, for that matter, inside an eighty-year-old Masonic Temple, with little necessary alteration of its exterior, as was done a mile down the road from my own home.

Interior and exterior can be quite independent of one another even in the matter of fenestration, namely the arrangement of windows and doors—certain obvious practical matters aside. Clients of mine once hired a designer who neglected to coordinate exterior and interior placement of a window. He located it so that it appeared to fit gracefully into a wall as seen from the street, but on the interior—had we actually installed the window as drawn—it would have been split by the floor line, with a lower portion jutting down into a study on the first floor and the upper portion sticking up into the new master bedroom above.

But otherwise, fenestration is mostly a matter of preference. One well-known California architect simply placed his windows where they best provided natural light and view on the interior and let them fall where they might, sometimes quite erratically, across the exterior of his buildings. Other designers skillfully give emphasis to exterior appearance, using windows to provide decorative bands, dramatic corners, exclamation, and emphasis.

At 19th Street House I wanted it all. I wanted everything that windows have to give. View from within. Natural light from without. Warmth on cool days. Ventilation on warm days. A contribution to the exterior articulation and fabric of the house and a contribution to interior visual appeal. Windows, it seems to me, are arguably the single most important component of a house. They govern our sense of connection (or lack thereof) of inside to outside. The mix of natural light they provide, or not, sets the tone of interior space. They can be decorative or very ugly. Change the windows, the way they are built into the walls of a house and their edges trimmed out (or not), and you alter the visual impact of the house, transforming it from blank and dull to pleasing, from crisp and clean to cluttered, from inviting to off-putting, or the other way around. The type, size, and placement of windows determine to a significant extent the energy efficiency of a house and, thus, its long-term environmental impact. If there is any room in a house construction budget for a splurge, the money should probably go first to windows. They are far more important than other features such as certain slick finishes that real estate ads gush over or the various contraptions and new materials hyped by salespeople of so-called "green" building components. They are a dollarwise investment to be sure.

I had first placed and sized the windows for 19th Street House in the floor plan and interior elevations with an eye toward the way they would light the interior and serve the anticipated uses of the rooms. As I began drawing the exteriors, I reviewed their placement for alignment and balance and for proportion to the surrounding exterior surfaces, making small adjustments. When it came to the actual choice of windows, I decided on insulated fiberglass frames with a clear pine finish on the interior. While far above the quality of the inexpensive vinyl windows in such wide use now, and also three times their cost, they nevertheless fit (barely) within my tight budget. The manufacturer claimed energy efficiency, durability, and ease of maintenance for his frames. We shall see; we have in the past been offered windows made with advanced materials that were touted as good for a century but deteriorated within a few years. I am hopeful about the 19th Street House windows. The manufacturer had been making similar product for fifteen years by the time I purchased mine. If they perform as promised, the windows will offer visual pleasure and register an environmental plus, contributing to lowered consumption of fuel for heating and lowered investment of material and energy for maintenance over a very long term.

With the windows placed, I had a free hand with the exterior. I stayed with the gabled form that was both in tune with the neighborhood and considerate of the immediate neighbors. Selecting finishes, I drew on the wealth of details used in the craftsman style homes in the Bay Area. For variety and richness of texture, I specified three materials for the wall cladding: At the lower level, stucco for a visually strong base. At the upper level, lapped planks. At the gables and for the garage pop out, plywood and 1x6 applied in a board-and-batten pattern. After studying similar bays on other recently built homes, I realized that as an entity distinct from the main mass of the 19th Street House, its bay should be clad in one material. So I drew it with its stucco finish extending all the way to its roof line.

At the pitched roof, the upper 2x6s of the trusses (their top chords) were extended out past the walls—like the rafters of a traditional craftsman design—to support a broad, sheltering eave. Pitched roofs with broad eaves, certain observers of house design have concluded, provide a powerful sense of shelter absent from homes with roofs clipped off at or close to the wall line. Certain scholars, probing the primal symbolism projected by the pitched roof with broad eaves, have suggested it may even respond to some need deep within our psyche. In support of the notion, *Pattern Language* cites a survey of children who lived in eaveless apartment towers. When asked to draw pictures of homes, they typically made a drawing of a cottage

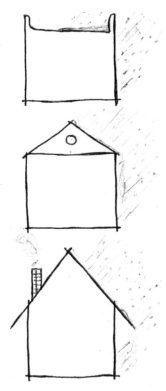

with, yes, a pitched gable roof with a sheltering eave. Perhaps there is something primal at work here. But it may also be that such a roof says "shelter" simply because it actually, obviously does provide more shelter against wind and rain than a flat or even a pitched but eaveless roof—and kids just get that.

While the traditional gabled, broadly eaved craftsman houses are handsome places, they can also be a bit severe. Their stucco walls are often flat, with only a slightly pebbly or grainy texture. Window and door trim is installed with sharp mitered joints executing militarily perfect ninety degree angles. And rafter tails are cut to sharp points, marching along the underside of the eave like a row of spikes set to defend the house against invaders. At 19th Street House, I sought to gentle the presence of the house, even as I applied the traditional craftsman vernacular. I specified stucco with a mildly rolling, not a flat finish. Window trim was butt jointed with the headpiece thicker than the vertical pieces so as to cast a softening shadow line. Edges of the trim were eased with a slight roundover rather than being left with sharp corners. And the rafters, along with the barge boards at the front and back of the house, as well as the beams and rafters of the porch, were terminated with a strong curve, or "deep radius" as carpenters say.

Despite feeling uneasy about using a good part of a tree merely for aesthetic effect, I drew two 6x6 posts supporting the roof at the front porch. A single 4x4 or even a skinny steel pipe would have done the job. A pair of stout porch posts, however, adds to the face of a house a reassuring presence that a single, more slender even if structurally

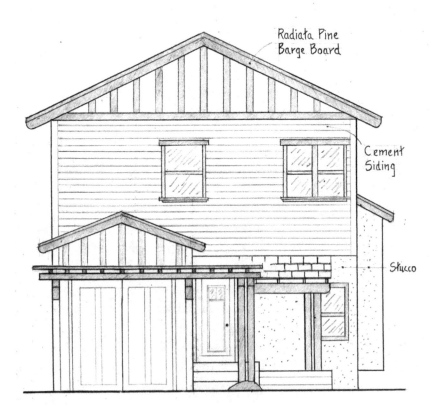

Radiata Pine
Barge Board

Cement
Siding

Stucco

adequate post just can't convey. By comparison, it feels skimpy and looks stark.

Detailing of the exterior was not done for visual effect only. The health point of my pyramid also came into play—here in the form of concern for physical safety. An architect friend urged making the roof steeper, increasing its pitch to six or seven in twelve, i.e., to six or seven inches of vertical rise for each twelve inches of horizontal run. The steeper roof he was advocating would have given the house a more distinctive presence. I was greatly tempted to build it. But the roof pitch stayed at five in twelve. Roofs pitched more steeply than that are dangerous for the people who have to climb onto them to do maintenance. Two builder friends of mine have been badly injured sliding off steep, albeit dramatic looking, roofs. At 19th Street House, various architonic, environment, dollar, and health values usually could be served simultaneously. But not in the matter of the porch posts and not in the matter of the steepened roof. In the one, architonic trumped environment, and in the other, health and safety trumped visual concerns.

Durability and a dollop of ambiguity

The cladding of the exterior walls was chosen with an eye to pattern, texture, and cost—with emphasis not on immediate cost but on durability and life cycle cost. Green building experts advocate for durability as key to environment consideration. Build for the long run rather than using vulnerable materials that will need replacement far earlier, they urge. You may increase first costs, but you will enjoy dollar payback over time even while benefiting the environment. In his book, *Your Green House,* Alex Wilson, a leader in the green construction movement, promotes the building of durable structures as a basic principle of environment considerate building.

At a glance the principle seems incontrovertible, and at 19th Street House I responded to the principle by electing to use stucco—which I have seen hold up for a century and more in the Bay Area climate—for the lower level, where the walls are most exposed to impact. For the second story, I settled on a plank siding made of cement and fibers and touted for its durability. At the garage and gable peaks, I specified high-quality, engineered lumber products, i.e., products manufactured with combinations of wood and resins, namely five-ply, resawn Douglas fir plywood and finger-jointed Radiata 1x6 battens. The plywood is less durable than the cementatious planking and stucco. But it would be sheltered from destructive sun and rain by the deep eaves. And it would do double duty. Even while serving as the finish surface, it would provide the required structural strength that, at the areas of the house finished with stucco or planking, would have to be provided by an underlying sheet of plywood.

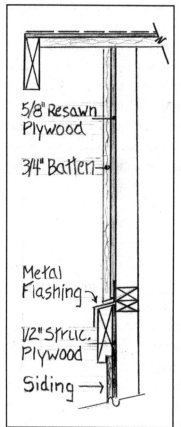

Wall claddings that would have been much cheaper, such as those manufactured of plastics or pressed board, are available. Some might look good right after installation. But after twenty-five years, by my rough estimate, they would be in failure and require removal and replacement. The stucco, cementatious planking, and engineered products would, in contrast, need only repainting—probably their first repainting—at the quarter century mark. The choice of the durable cladding for 19th Street House went right to the difference, I felt sure, between "affordability" and "dollar wisdom." Yes, the cheaper material would have shaved half a percent off the cost of the house and knocked ten dollars off a monthly mortgage held by future owners. But would that have been money well saved? Or, would the misery of having to replace the siding twenty-five years down the road make "affordable" then look like just a cheap, bad choice made by a forgotten builder?

For me, the instinctive answer to these questions was an emphatic "no" and a confident "yes." I was not, for the sake of a few bucks, about to inflict on some future owners the job of recladding their entire house. As a builder, I want to construct houses that will hold up. I hope for them to be standing tall, doing their job, a hundred years after I have driven the last nail. At 19th Street House, I went with my instinct and desire. I welcomed the advocacy of Alex Wilson as support for my own inclinations.

But as I wrote these paragraphs equating durable with environment friendly, it dawned on me I had fallen into a way of thinking that I had criticized in certain other partisans of the green building movement. I was hitching my passion for durable work to the green train without any data to justify the hookup, just as they were attaching their own pet causes. I was behaving like the green roof builder described earlier. You remember him. The biologist who was so excited about creating habitat for birds and bees that he was unwilling to look at accounting that might suggest his work resulted in net environmental damage, not improvement.

A parallel observation could be made about my decisions to go durable, for I do not actually know their long-term, net environmental impact. The old bugaboo, the sheer difficulty of doing life cycle cost assessment with precision, raises its head. As odd and counterintuitive as it might seem, some of the decisions to build durable might not be at all environment considerate in the long run. My choices of stucco and cementatious siding for the exterior of 19th Street House are a case in point. All I know for sure is they are more expensive initially than flimsier material; the cement they contain is produced at great environmental cost; and building with the durable product makes me feel good (nourishes my "sense of self," as the biologist said of his work). But I do not know whether the manufacture, installation, and maintenance of the materials I chose will have more or less environmental impact over the course of fifty years or a hundred years than would making, installing, maintaining, and replacing flimsier material over those periods of time.

It is quite possible that technological innovation already under way will soon result in a new cladding that contains no toxic substances, requires little energy to manufacture or recycle, needs no maintenance, does double duty as high-value insulation, and is embedded with cells that can generate more electrical power from sunlight than the house will use. If so, the flimsier siding could be replaced with the advanced product in a few decades. And once the numbers have been crunched, my choice of durable construction could well turn out to have been a wrong turn environmentally and financially, serving no other purpose than to bolster my psyche.

Fortunately, not quite so much ambiguity pervades every aspect of the attempt to craft a house that is at once environment considerate, dollarwise, architonic, and healthy. There are things one can do—with as much certainty as one can know anything about the future—that are steps in the right direction. At 19th Street House, one such measure was building a foundation that used far less material and energy than the conventional choice. Another was drawing up a small house. Still another was staying close to a roughly cubic form to get a great deal of function within a modest square footage. As my crew and I began crafting floors and wall frames atop the foundation installed by the concrete maestro Dave Kendall, we aimed to capitalize on other opportunities.

CRAFTING THE SHELL

The 2x6 Hem-Fir boards we had used to form the foundation lay in neat stacks at the rear of the site, awaiting construction into wall frames. As I looked over the lumber and strapped on my carpenter bags, a pleasurable anticipation settled on me. I do love framing. Framers are dismissed as mere "rough carpenters." In the public perception, they have skills much inferior to those of the finish carpenters who install doors, baseboards, cabinets, crown moldings, and paneling. In fact, in recent years the relationship of rough to finish skills has been turned upside down by the invention of new tools: Precise, powerful, sliding saws that quickly adjust to any angle or combination of angles needed to fit one board to another. Carbide tipped blades that cut wood mirror smooth. Orbital jigsaws with a blade action so steady and precise they'll slice a shaving off a board thin enough that light will pass through. And all manner of jigs and devices that automate the once demanding tasks of laying out and joining finish materials. Finish carpentry has been simplified enough so that an able apprentice can, in a few months, become proficient at the basics—the exception being stair building. But stairs as often as not are now precut in factories and delivered to jobsites ready for assembly.

Meanwhile, engineering advances and environmental demands have made framing far more complicated.

Framers must know exactly where and how to place a complex assortment of lumber types from old-fashioned 2x4s to new, engineered materials composed of wood strands, synthetic fibers, and resins. They must know how to tie the varieties of lumber together with a thick catalogue's worth of fasteners and connectors. Even as the requirements for finish remain relatively static, framers must steadily adjust their practices as new materials come on line and designs evolve to increase structural strength and support more energy-efficient construction.

At the same time, framers are under tremendous economic pressure to produce rapidly—for the frame may represent a sixth of the cost of a house, and as it grows more expensive, the budget for the other, more visible items that draw customers is squeezed. Good framers are graceful and powerful athletes as much as they are craftspeople. They move with no waste of motion, making decisions as they move, hefting and placing boards, beams, and heavy hardware with rapid precision. The work of a really good framer is tight and in every respect true. It is dead level, plumb, and square, so that floors and walls are

seen to plane evenly when you sight them end to end. When you see a good frame, you sense a sculptural beauty in its crisp orderliness and in the way it foreshadows the quality of the well-built house it will support.

A top-notch carpenter, walking onto the site of a well-crafted frame, will say to the crew that has put it up, "Clean work, guys. Real clean." He will see the trueness of line, the nails set flat and snug, evenly spaced, none missing their target and poking out of a board, waiting to rip open the skin of an unsuspecting carpenter passing by. Any that went awry when the frame was nailed together have been pulled and tossed on the scrap metal heap.

New kinds of sticks

I was hoping to build a very clean frame for 19th Street House. It might be my last, I was thinking. I'd done my first framing forty years earlier. My joints sometimes felt a bit stiff in the morning, and I realized I was fortunate to still be able to handle the physical rigors of carpentry at a construction site. Looking at the stacks of 2x6s, and alongside them the floor and roof framing materials my lumber company had trucked to the empty lot, I realized something else, too. The stacks represented an evolution in materials technology as relentless, if much less proclaimed, as the media evolution that has filled our lives with computers and mobile communication devices. There was hardly an item in the stacks that had even existed in the early 1970s when I began working as a framer. Had a fellow framer from those years gone to sleep á la Rip van Winkle, awakened four decades later, and shown up for work at 19th Street House, he would look at our lumber with puzzlement. He would not know what to do with it.

Gone were the punishingly heavy solid lumber joists—twelve inches wide, two inches thick, and up to twenty feet long—used to support floors in his day. In their place were stacks of truss joists, or TJIs as they are called, using the initials of one manufacturer. The new joists, designed by engineers and concocted of thin strips and flakes of wood bonded with adhesives, were made in plants rather than sawn in mills. They are so light I can hold a twenty-footer in one hand like an elongated briefcase. Gone were the beams—used to span windows, entries, and passageways—that had been sawn whole from large trees. In their place was a new kind of beam, designed not in a forest by nature but in a test laboratory by wood scientists, and manufactured of strands of wood fiber extracted from trees much too small for milling into the bygone materials. Missing, too, were the wide, heavy boards for assembling a traditional roof frame of ridge, rafters, and collar ties or ceiling joists. In their place we would be taking delivery of a series of roof trusses—light, lacy webs of 2x4s joined by metal clasps.

Even the stacks of 4x8 panels for wall sheathing puzzle Rip. "What the heck is this stuff?" he asks, running his hand across the wax-coated surface of the top panel of one stack. "OSB—oriented strand board,"

I tell him and explain that it was yet another product made from glue and wood flakes. OSB is rapidly taking the place of the plywood that old Rip was accustomed to. It can be made from much smaller trees, and thereby scores points for greenness. But it does require a protective coating of wax, for unlike plywood, which holds up remarkably well even when repeatedly soaked by rain, if OSB gets soaked a single time it will begin crumbling around the edges into something resembling oatmeal mush. Embarrassed a bit by the look on Rip's face when I admit to using such a pathetic product—though virtually every new house is now built with it—I hasten to emphasize that I use OSB only for walls protected by a broad eave. "I draw the line there," I tell him, and call his attention to the stack of old-fashioned plywood I would use for sheathing the roof and decking the floors, both much more at risk of getting wet than the protected wall surfaces. He grunts; he does not appear much impressed.

As we come to the 2x4s and 2x6s intended for interior and exterior wall frames, Rip feels momentarily in more familiar territory. At a glance, the boards look like the sticks he had built with in the 1970s. But then he notices the differences. They are so light. And each board is stamped with two sets of letters that Rip has not seen before, "KD" and "FSC," the first meaning "kiln dried" to indicate that the lumber had been heated in a chamber so as to bring its moisture content—and incidentally its weight—down gradually without causing distortion or warpage.

For 19th Street House, kiln dried lumber was an option, an upgrade. "Green lumber," lumber that has been dried only in the open air, is often still so wet when it arrives at a jobsite that it releases a spray of water when you slam a nail into it. Green lumber remains widely available at big-box suppliers and old-school lumberyards. But by my calculation, it has become an increasingly poor choice for house framing. These days, green lumber is unstable stuff. Sawn from genetically engineered, rapid growth plantation trees, it has a low proportion of dense and hard winter growth rings to soft, broad summer growth. It cracks as it dries. It cups. It twists and winds. It oozes gobs of sap, which gum up carpenters' hands and tools. It soaks up water easily and sprouts dark patches of mold.

True, green lumber is cheaper. At the time we ordered material for 19th Street House, it was running about 20 percent less than KD. But by the time you have culled out the bad boards, invested labor in straightening others, and scrubbed off the sap, the savings is eaten up by wasted material and labor. Further along in the construction of your house, you will still be battling the bad lumber. You will see studs spiraling like licorice sticks and bowing badly out of line with the intended plane of your walls. You will fight the distortions all the way through finish work. Green lumber was not material for the clean frame I planned to build. Thinking it would prove dollarwise, I paid the premium charge for KD.

As for Rip, he has now grown disgusted: "What kind of craziness has framing come to? You guys have to wax your sheathing? You have to cook your wood in some kind of oven to get straight stock? Seems like to me you've cooked the guts out of it, feels like a stack of feathers to me. You use wood flakes stuck together with glue to stiffen up your walls? I'm outta here. Going back to sleep. Hopefully when I wake up again, wood butchers will be back to working with honest sticks. Good-bye to you so-called framers and your phony lumber." Rip does not even give me a chance to explain "FSC," nor the concepts of environment consideration underlying the letters. In his day, green was a concept still far over the horizon for all but a tiny number of construction guys. Too bad he took off so abruptly; the FSC thing, he might have liked it.

Forestry stewardship

While building 19th Street House, I would find that environment consideration paid off repeatedly, not only by reducing long-term maintenance cost but immediately, in dollar savings. I came to think the assumption "green costs more" resulted from the association of green with complex and expensive adding on of gadgetry as opposed to straightforward reducing of material and energy for construction and operation. I concluded that if you are spending more rather than saving dollars, it's a warning signal that you are likely going *against* environment consideration, not gaining green but getting into the red.

There are, however, exceptions to my contrarian principle. One exception is the next step I took toward environment consideration by opting for the "FSC" stamped lumber. The letters certify that the lumber comes from forests managed in accordance with the high standards of environment protection encouraged by the Forest Stewardship Council. This green gesture cost me rather than reducing expenses. It added about three cents (roughly 6 percent) to my costs per foot of lumber for walls and roof frames. I spent my extra money, not with an eye to financial outcomes, but instead as an investment in the sort of world I want to live in. I had seen forests mined for lumber without heed to the kinds of standards set by the Council. Those once beautiful and vibrant forests are a dismaying sight: Huge stretches of hills and valleys reduced to a patchwork of stump land. Crisscrossing access roads rutted and eroding, streams below choked with silt, riparian life suffocated. And homes downstream flooded with muddy water from too-rapid runoff because the denuded hillsides cannot retain rainfall.

The FSC stamp is offered as a guarantee that the lumber on which it appears has been taken from forests in a far more considerate fashion. The Forest Stewardship Council was initiated in 1990, and not by tree huggers alone. The first meetings that led to the formal founding of the FSC were attended by environmental activists, by representatives of people who managed the production and use of timber, by advocates for the rights of aboriginal peoples living in forests, and by men and women who work for wages harvesting and processing forest products. The FSC summarized its aims with a crisp slogan and three succinctly stated goals: "Because Forests Matter" they should be managed in a way that is environmentally appropriate, socially beneficial, and economically viable.

The three goals are, in turn, detailed in ten principles spelled out in a document you can enjoy for yourself at the FSC Web site. A sampling: Forest managers are required to respect the ownership rights of indigenous peoples. They are required to meet or exceed the health and safety standards of the nation in which they are operating and to honor the rights of workers to organize. Forest managers must minimize waste, protect watersheds, and—here is a big one—not harvest at rates that can't be *permanently* sustained. Forest managers must avoid the use of toxic chemicals and protect threatened species. To ensure that a forestry operation's embrace of the principles is not merely a marketing ploy, it is required to produce an action plan and demonstrate adherence by submitting the forest to monitoring by an FSC accredited inspector.

Good and hopeful stuff to my way of thinking, though I had concerns, too. Who were the monitors? Did they have the know-how to range across a forest and actually determine that it was being harvested sustainably, that waterways and stands of ancient trees and species diversity were being protected, that safety practices were up to snuff, that the entire complex of principles was being met to a reasonable degree (not perfectly, for the FSC wisely required good but not flawless performance).

And how susceptible was the monitoring system to corruption? After all, inspection agencies are always vulnerable to the greasing of the palm, especially when their income is provided by the businesses they inspect. The Forest Stewardship Council is sustained by fees from the very operations that produce and sell the products carrying its seal of approval.

Strapping on my carpenter's belt out at 19th Street, I did not know the answer to these questions, only that an FSC stamp brought applause in the green building movement. I plunked my money down, hoped for the best, and got unexpectedly good value. To my delight, the particular batch of FSC stamped and kiln dried boards delivered to 19th Street was the best framing lumber I'd seen in years. I did not have to cull out a single stick, not one. Every 2x6 and 2x4 was free of cracks, with all knots tight, true, and straight. It was gorgeous lumber. I think after he got over his initial shock old Rip would have loved standing up walls with the stuff.

Contenders

Joe Lstiburek probably would not have been so impressed with my lumber stack as I was. Joe is among the best-known building scientists in the United States. A broad shouldered, big bellied, sometimes bellicose man, he travels the continent educating and evangelizing construction professionals about optimal insulation installation, efficient heating and cooling, waterproofing, and other nuts and bolts of resource conserving, durable construction. He's a man with a gift for the pithy phrase and enjoys dropping on his audiences such proclamations as this one: "If wood were invented today, we would not allow it to be used as a building material." He has a point. (Just about everything Joe has to say about construction is on target. His manuals of principles and details for building in a variety of climates are highly recommended in the Resources section.) Wood rots. It is eroded by sunlight and rain. It is food for mold, and, if it remains wet, becomes covered with black slime. A variety of insects eat it. Others make their nests in wood. It splinters, cracks, and can twist and wind to the point of uselessness. As it ages, it grows so hard you cannot drive a nail into it without predrilling. The dust it throws off when you saw it is carcinogenic. And, the rapidly grown plantation lumber with its low proportion of dense winter rings is so vulnerable to decay it must be shot full of toxic chemicals if it is to have any chance of surviving direct contact with earth or concrete.

All in all, wood would seem an easy target, ripe for replacement by other materials. "Stick built" houses—the carpenters' name for buildings such as we were about to construct from our stack of newfangled lumber at 19th Street—has seen many challengers. They have been coming (and for the most part going) since long before I began building. First came the hay bale house, a house whose walls were made with bales of hay stacked one upon another, pegged together with steel rods or bamboo pins, and plastered over inside and out. Enthusiasts promote hay bale construction avidly: Anyone can build one for himself or herself, for anyone can manage to stack bales of hay in place. Hay bale houses are durable; if protected from water they will (and some have) lasted a century and more. With their thick walls and deep windowsills they can be handsome homes, and with the thick bales superinsulating the interiors, they require little energy for heating or cooling. Moreover, argue the enthusiasts, they can be made from the straw left behind after a harvest—thus sparing forests by replacing framing lumber with material that would otherwise go to waste.

After hay bales came metal. During periods when lumber prices soared, house builders became interested in substituting hollow metal studs for 2x4s and 2x6s of wood—or "tin cans" for "sticks" in carpenter lingo. Tin cans, like hay bales, were extolled by their promoters. They did not rot. They did not burn. They were far lighter than green, sappy, wet wood studs and far easier on carpenters' backs, allowing old-timers to extend their careers by switching from stick to tin can framing. They spared forests; metal studs could be made from waste—old cars, the shells of discarded appliances, empty sardine tins.

More recently another product, the Structural Insulated Panel or SIP, has been heralded as the contender sure to knock off stick framing. To envision an SIP, imagine a giant ice cream sandwich, but one made of a thick block of foam in place of the ice cream and with full-sized sheets of plywood rather than cookie dough adhered to either side. An SIP house is built of such giant foam and plywood sandwiches connected together by bands of lumber (i.e., top and bottom plates) with holes punched through the sandwiches for doors and windows. SIPs are lauded for saving forests. They are admired for their high insulating and air sealing values. And, because they arrive at jobsites precut and ready to connect together, they are heralded as a way of shortening the time needed to get a house built.

Factory constructors and counterpunchers

Hay bales. Tin cans. Foam sandwiches. And the contenders keep coming. We have heard from advocates for earthen houses, with walls constructed of soil rammed into place between two-sided forms or mixed with cement and sprayed against one-sided forms. Ads and articles in the builders' magazines promote houses constructed of poured concrete or of blocks manufactured from a combination of concrete and foam that stack together to form walls. Yet another challenger has come to the front as the one sure to replace the familiar site-built stick house. "It's the future for sure," certain builders proclaim. This contender is different not so much for how it is built (it can be assembled of wood sticks or SIPs, or either combined with steel frames), as for where it is built, namely in a factory.

A few decades back, factory builders manufactured only simple and cheap trailerlike homes. Now factories are producing homes of good quality in styles ranging from craftsman bungalows to sleek modernist boxes. In Austria, where factory construction is advanced, the floor, wall, and roof components of whole condominium complexes—with plumbing, electrical, and heating systems all in place—have been factory built, trucked across the European continent and under the English Channel to be assembled atop foundations in Ireland. The best of the factory builders are hailed not only for producing quality homes but also for virtually eliminating waste by recycling nearly every scrap of material produced in their plants.

Yet, for all the challengers, stick built houses framed on site by carpenters have held their ground. Ninety-five out of 100 homes constructed in the United States are stick built on site. It turns out that the challengers' promoters, while celebrating benefits, have neglected costs and, therefore, overestimated the success their products were likely to enjoy. And costs there surely are. Hay bale houses, a close look reveals, would be more accurately described as houses with bales used for a portion of the walls. They require substantial amounts of lumber to frame window and door openings and for structural connection and continuity. As a result, the bales displace only the insulation and a portion of the material used in the walls—never mind foundations, floors, roofs, infrastructure, and finish—and constitute, all told, only five to ten percent of the material (measured in dollars) that goes into a new house. Contrary to the enthusiasm of bale house advocates, the bales are not necessarily free, nor even necessarily waste. (Nothing is waste until you waste it, right?) Left in the fields after the harvest, the straw from which the bales are made provides way stations for migratory birds that have lost much of their natural habitat to human settlement and industry. The birds return the hospitality by generously fertilizing the fields for the coming season's crop. Moreover, when they are used for wall construction, hay bales occupy a lot of space. Had I specified bales for constructing the exterior walls of 19th Street House, I would have lost roughly a fifth of my floor area, and the rooms would have become unpleasantly narrow.

Tin can construction imposes costs as well. The tin cans may not rot, but they do rust. Their thin walls offer little grip for the screws attaching drywall or cladding on the inside or outside. They quickly transfer to the outdoors the energy used to heat or cool a house; for, of course, metal is a splendid conductor of heat and cold—about fifty times as good a conductor as wood. As for Structural Insulated Panels, the returns are just beginning to come in. But some troubling reports have surfaced. If not built just right, SIP houses squeak. As an old-time stick builder, I wonder about the wisdom of building with foam sandwiches as the prime structural component. What if the foam and plywood begin to separate; does the house become dangerous to inhabit? It may be merely an anomaly, but in the case of one house, the answer was yes. Its SIPs weakened so much that the house was condemned a year after being constructed. It is difficult to imagine such a rapid and complete structural failure with a stick built home.

Perhaps factory built houses will be the contender that finally prevails. Over the course of the twentieth century, factory built housing, appearing first in one form and then another—from an all-steel assemblage to a kit of wooden parts sold by Sears and Roebuck among others—has repeatedly been heralded as "the future." But to date factory built housing has not made much headway, remaining always an "idea whose time never quite comes," as one observer puts it. Perhaps, its time has finally come now. *Builder* magazine reported that during the first housing construction cycle of the twenty-first century, factory building gained market share during both boom times and slow times.

It is too early, however, to know if factory builders will hold onto their gains, much less acquire a substantial share of the housing market over the longer term. For while their promoters claim that building houses in factories offers a great cost advantage, it is also true that factories impose heavy cost burdens of their own—financing, depreciation, maintenance, and operation of a huge building and large machines—mostly absent from on-site house production. A factory's costs keep running whether it is in use or not; we will see how many factory builders survive the severe downturn in the housing market that began in 2006. As of this writing, in 2009 a number of them have already gone bankrupt.

Other benefits claimed by factory boosters do not come automatically. The promoters of manufactured housing proclaim its quality as if it were somehow inherent in the factory process. It ain't necessarily so. (I am thinking of my name brand refrigerator that lasted only six years, the high-end washer that failed after a week, and computer after computer that goes down in a blaze of lost data.) It is conscientious, appropriately organized humans skillfully selecting and employing technology, not technology itself, that creates quality.

Some house factories produce well-crafted products. Others do not, just as some site builders do and some do not—though the site builders all enjoy one indisputable advantage over factory builders: their products are not subjected to the pounding that factory houses experience as they are transported by truck over potholed highways. Similarly, though factory builders claim their houses are less costly along with being better built, the alleged savings can turn out to be illusory. A friend of mine in need of a new house decided to purchase a home produced by a much publicized architect-turned-factory-builder. He was attracted enough by the modernist design and very much by the $200 per square foot price tag advertised on the Web, for it was half of what he would have had to pay for a new house built by a reliable general contractor. But by the time he walked out of the factory builder's sales office, having learned about and totaled up additional costs for supplementary design fees, utility tie-ins, foundation, and finish work not included in the $200, the price of his hoped-for factory built home had *tripled*. It would have cost him 50 percent more than the site built house he had in mind, and would not have suited his lot and neighborhood nearly as well.

All in all, it seems, enthusiasts for the various challengers to stick built have been seduced by the siren call of single column accounting, so dazzled by the possibilities of new materials and methods that they don't see the costs. Meanwhile, as the challengers come and recede, stick builders have not been standing still. Manufacturers, tradespeople, managers, engineers, and designers have moved ahead in concert to create processes of stick building on site that are increasingly competitive in the *very arenas where the challengers claim an edge: environment consideration and dollar wisdom.* There has been no revolutionary breakthrough. Rather, small increments of change are steadily achieved so that, in total, we've come a long distance. The changes may be seen as falling into three categories: The *materials we build with*, such as the fly ash concrete and engineered lumber used at 19th Street House. Our *process for assembling* materials. The *efficiency with which we utilize* materials, as in frugal framing (which will shortly make its appearance in our story).

Stick builders, whether they are local firms selling two dozen homes a year or national companies marketing thousands, have evolved their jobsites into outdoor factories-in-reverse. The homes do not move along an assembly line staffed by workers, as in a factory. Instead, the workers move in teams along the line, from house to house. Each team executes its specialty, then gives way to the following team and moves up the line to the next house. In their turn, excavators, foundation crews, framers, heating and air conditioning mechanics, plumbers, electricians, drywallers, finish carpenters, and painters add to the house until fifteen or more specialized teams have made their contribution. Even in the building of a single custom home, such as 19th Street House, a rationalized factory-like process occurs as one specialized subcontractor after another arrives at the site, does their work, and makes way for the next.

The efficiency and speed of construction achieved at the outdoor factories can be staggering. In specially organized events, teams of precisely choreographed tradespeople have built large wood framed homes in less than a day (this is not a misprint). Habitat for Humanity® claims the world record for speedy house construction, having stood up and completed one of its modest homes in less than three hours (this is not a misprint either; in fact, you can watch the Habitat team go to town yourself on YouTube). At normal forty hour a week jobsites with disciplined scheduling and organization, builders have been able to reduce start-to-completion time for a large house to a couple of months, on par with what it takes to prepare a site for a factory made house, take delivery of the house, install it atop a foundation, tie it into utilities, and detail it out.

At the same time, the best of the stick builders have intensified quality control. Making sure to insulate the inspectors from the craftspeople whose work they inspect so that cozy relationships do not compromise strictness of evaluation, these builders send inspectors through their houses behind each team of craftspeople. Using detailed checklists, the inspectors catch and see to the correction of even the smallest before the house is sold. Builders who deploy quality inspectors claim they deliver houses that are virtually fault free. Nineteenth Street House verifies that defect-free construction is as possible on site as in a factory. During the first two years after completion of the house, only a single construction error, a loose connection in the exhaust line of the central vacuum, cropped up. With two minutes' labor, the defect was corrected.

Frugal framing

Even as builders have been refining the overall organization of their outdoor factory process, tradespeople have been adopting efficiencies in putting materials together. Each taken alone may seem insignificantly small, shaving just minutes off the time needed to build a house. Lead carpenters mark the positions for studs along a wall plate with a dash, saving half the labor of marking with an "X." Apprentices learn to pull a handful of nails at a time from their pouches, quickly sift the nails so that all heads face up, and roll a nail into ready position on their fingertips as they drive the previous one. Altogether, thousands of the small efficiencies have been invented and have seeped through the trades as they are shared at jobsites or in the Tips and Tricks columns of construction magazines and Web sites. The small improvements add up. We reach the point where a pair of skilled carpenters can nail together and stand the entire wall frame of a three-bedroom house in a single day.

Among the most powerful reductions of cost and of environmental impact achieved by site builders is the reduction resulting from step-by-step rethinking of the way lumber is arranged in the frames of stick built houses. Old-school carpenters instinctively resist the new and far more efficient use of lumber. More lumber in a wall *must* make for a better and stronger wall, they instinctively insist. How could it be otherwise? How could less be just as good or better? Trying for strength, or just out of habit, they pile lumber into a wall at every opportunity. Look at the framing, typical of old-school work, shown in the drawing. A total of seven studs have been jammed into a ten and one-half inch space, between the two window openings. Four are superfluous, holding up nothing but themselves. Two can be replaced with metal clips. And, even one of the full-length studs between the windows could be replaced if the headers, the horizontal framing members over the tops of the windows, shared the remaining one.

The new way of framing with less lumber goes by several names. Engineers term it Optimal Value Engineered (OVE) framing to indicate that it provides necessary structural support with the optimal, i.e., least, investment of material and labor. It will give you all the bang you need for as few bucks as possible. A second name, Highly Efficient Framing, is used by a respected thermal boundary expert—a man with deep knowledge of the much undervalued craft of insulating and sealing buildings against loss of the energy used to heat and cool them. He uses his term to stress that the less lumber in a house frame the lower is its embedded energy and its tendency to waste operating energy, for wood, he emphasizes, is a very poor insulator and a surprisingly good conductor of heat and cold. A wood stud transmits heat four times as fast as the insulated space next to

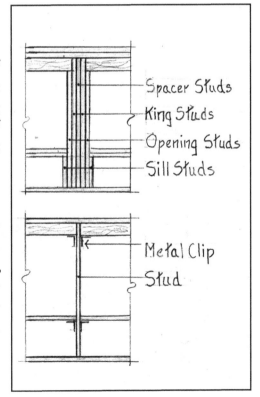

Spacer Studs

King Studs

Opening Studs

Sill Studs

Metal Clip Stud

it. The less of it you have in a wall, the less the thermal boundary is compromised.

I call the new framing simply frugal framing, meaning "not wasteful" (Webster's). The move to frugal framing from old-school, overstuffed framing began with the realization that the traditional spacing of wall studs sixteen inches apart is rooted in a practice that began three and one half centuries ago, but that became unnecessary three-quarters of a century ago. Sixteen inches was the spacing required to support the slender wooden sticks of lathing long ago fastened to studs as a grid to support troweled-on plaster. Wooden lath was disappearing from use before World War II and with it the need to space the studs at sixteen inches, for the drywall and plywood that replaced the wood lath can span two feet.

With the studs spread to two feet, as a second step in the evolution of frugal framing, the joists and roof trusses are likewise spread so that the three components, studs, joists, and trusses, are aligned vertically, and the loads they carry pass straight down to the foundation. At 19th Street House (which already required only about half the lumber of an average new American home because of its compactness), framing at two feet saved some 800 linear feet of lumber—a stack of studs approximately twelve feet tall for the walls alone. If frugal wall framing were extended to all the homes (houses plus apartments) built in the United States in a boom year, the stack of saved lumber would grow to a conservatively estimated height of 6,000 miles.

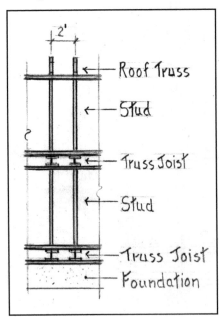

But frugal framing only begins with spreading of studs, joists, and trusses to two feet on center. Next comes elimination of superfluous studs where walls intersect. Then comes reduction of waste at window and door openings. Next comes elimination of the top plate, replacing it with metal clips to tie together intersecting walls. Together, all these measures can produce a reduction of 50 percent or even more in the lumber consumed by a wall.

There are, of course, costs accompanying the benefits (no free lunch here either, no single column accounting allowed). Frugal framing requires the use of 2x6 studs on the first story of two-story houses, because 2x4s will not have sufficient strength to carry the loads. And, it requires use of five-eighths drywall; the cheaper half-inch stuff will not span the two foot centers without sagging. Carpentry crews new to frugal framing will have to retool their thinking and adjust their moves. They may lose some efficiency the first time they execute it. But the costs are trivial compared with the benefits, for the reduced amount of lumber in a frugal frame not only reduces dollar outlay for material, it also saves much labor. Fewer sticks to measure, cut, and nail equates to less labor consumed.

For 19th Street House, we added a final frugality to our framing. Two problems became one another's solutions with a jobsite invention I stumbled on and celebrated by naming it the "Gerstel corner." Problem number one: my drywaller balked at using the metal clips, generally called for in frugal framing,

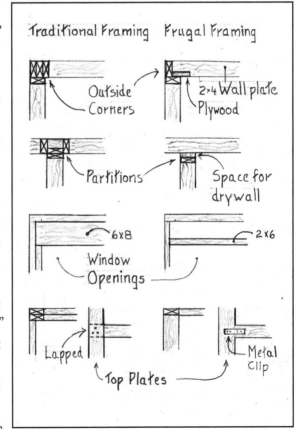

to provide support for his drywall panels at the inside corners of walls and at wall and ceiling junctures. He did not think the clips would provide enough support. Problem two: as typical for a new house under construction, large scraps of plywood and Oriented Strand Board (OSB), destined for the dump, were piling up alongside our recycling bins.

The solution: at the cost of a couple of hours' labor and wear and tear on the table saw, my apprentice ripped the scraps into six inch strips. Then he nailed the rippings, in place of the metal clips, to the backs of studs and top plates. The savings: Ordering and purchasing the clips. The labor and fuel used for taking the plywood and OSB to the dump. And the dump fees, high in our metropolitan area. Extended across a boom year's worth of home building, Gerstel corners could save something like 1 billion corner clips. They would divert from our landfills a stack of plywood and OSB roughly four feet square at the base and 3,000 miles high. My conscientious drywall specialist liked the corners. "Yeah," he said, "they're good."

The hardest working guy and the prodigy

When I began framing, a veteran carpenter warned me, "It's the hardest work in the world except mining coal with a pick and shovel; studies have proved it." The new framing—with lightweight, kiln dried studs and engineered products replacing the waterlogged, green lumber and massive beams and planks that carpenters once had to manhandle—has made the framer's work easier. Even so, it's still demanding. That is one reason I was interested in interviewing Grant Reading for a job at 19th Street House. "He's the hardest working guy I ever met," my former lead carpenter, Fred Blodgett, now an outstanding builder with his own company, told me when he urged me to hire Grant. "It's difficult to get the guy to stop for lunch, much less take a morning break."

A sturdily built man with thick blond hair, Grant greeted me with a smile, a direct look, and the granite handshake of someone who has been driving nails for a living. Like me and many of the men and women I have worked with in construction, Grant had been a serious jock as a kid. Tennis had been his game. He had been drawn to construction by the athleticism of the work, by the challenge of solving problems on the run while rapidly and precisely joining materials together.

As we assembled our pile of sticks into a frame, Grant worked with a fierce, focused impatience to get the job done and get it done well. Down went the first-floor frame of TJIs and parallel strand beams. Up went the first-floor walls of kiln dried and FSC lumber. Down went the upper-level floor and up the walls. As the last of the walls were being braced in place, a flatbed truck carrying a load of roof trusses pulled to the curb. Deftly the driver unfurled its boom and outriggers to convert it into a massive crane. Moments later, he had placed the trusses atop the second-floor walls. And by the late afternoon, they were spaced out, nailed down, and braced plumb to form the roof frame. A couple of days later, the roof was sheathed in plywood, the walls of the house clad in OSB. We now had in place a tawny yellow, rough, crude, and merely schematic but full-size version of the house envisioned in the drawings—a stretched-out cube with bumpouts for the garage and stairway bay.

"Buildings never look or feel like they do in photos," an architect friend once said to me. "You have to go see them and experience them." They never look or feel just like they do in drawings either. When a house rises to its full size during framing, you or a friend or client see a possibility that escaped you during drawing when a couple of inches of pencil line represented eight feet of actual construction. Now, another strength of stick framing shows itself. A stick frame is remarkably easy to reconfigure. With a few measurements, snapping of chalk lines, saw cuts, and a bit of renailing, the planes of a building can be moved, removed, opened, shortened, or extended.

At 19th Street House, Grant discovered a problem as he framed the hatchway to the attic. Politely he pointed it out to me. All the full-height walls we had framed in the upper circulation area turned it into a warren of small spaces. "Cut the walls enclosing the upper stretch of the stairway down to about head height," Grant suggested. Likewise, a visiting friend stood in the framed opening of the front door and stared at the wall separating the entry parlor from the lower portion of the stairway. "Lower that wall, replace it with an open banister, and you will get an increased sense of spaciousness in the front room well worth the labor of making the change," she urged. With a couple of hours' carpentry, the frame had been adjusted upstairs and down. The upper circulation area was transformed into a visually continuous single space. The stairway and entry parlor had merged into a pleasing larger volume.

Now, other requirements became apparent at the upper circulation area. It needed natural daylighting to balance the light coming up the stairs from the two tall windows in the bay. Also, a focal point, something to invite you up the stairs, something more than a blank wall, was called for on the far side of the landing. At the head of the stairs, Grant installed a solar tube, a skylight with a highly reflective pipe reaching through the attic and terminating at a lens in the ceiling. Below it, I framed into the wall a niche echoing the gable form of the house. On

clear days, the skylight lit up the niche wall with startling brightness. Pointing to the sun-washed niche we told visitors we had named it "The Church." Mostly they smiled or nodded in agreement, as if to say, "What else?" One subcontractor, raised in the Confucian tradition, looked puzzled for a moment, then nodded solemnly, "Oh yes, the people who come to live in the house, they will put that lady there, what is her name, oh yes, Miss Virgin Mary."

Looking for other missed opportunities, I walked through the framed form of the house. Mostly, it felt right. Sunlight flowed into interior spaces from several directions. Nooks gave interesting shape to rooms and provided little getaway spaces. An archway gracefully connected the living room to the dining room. The floor felt solid underfoot. Movement through the house felt easy. Even as we pushed to minimize environmental impact and exercise dollar wisdom, were we achieving a house with architonic value? I was thinking, yes we are on our way. Then, as I looked at the exterior of the house from the south, my confidence faltered. The pop out that housed the stair landing, it did not seem right. Was it too high? Too low? Had I gone wrong on the proportion of the pop out to the wall from which it sprang?

Proportion matters, so much so that design savants have devoted themselves to creating mathematical formulas, axioms, and rules of thumb intended to regulate the geometric relationships of a building's components. For example, the authors of *Patterns of Home* advise that the side and end walls of rooms not be markedly different in length. The aim, they say, is to create "potato shaped" rooms rather than "carrot shaped" ones, i.e., long, skinny spaces. Another architect reports, however, that while he was required to learn rules of proportion in school, he never consciously invokes them when he draws, and somehow things come

out right. He has come to believe that people have an innate aptitude for proportion that strengthens through use.

For the 19th Street House, I had relied on instinct, not formulas, when it came to its relationship with the rest of the building. The bay pop out had been drawn in two versions, the first with the upper edge of its roof aligning with the ridge of the garage at the other side of the house, the second a foot higher. I had built the second option, feeling it more gracefully proportioned to the immediately surrounding mass of my building. In the end, I would stay with my decision, anticipating that my second-guessing would evaporate when the finish skin of the house was applied. But meanwhile I experienced the anxiety every builder knows, the abrupt three A.M. awakening, the sudden conviction that you have done something abysmally ignorant, far dumber than any error committed by any other builder, ever.

Soon enough the anxiety subsided. It always does now for me after decades of these "Oh my, what have I done" moments. Eventually, you learn things do work out, that after a good night's sleep you will get up in the morning, go out to the job, and see how to fix matters. This time, along with the relaxing, came a small surge of pride, a feeling that an idea for adjusting the height of the pop out roof, which had come into my head, was really quite ingenious. Yes, it does suggest a certain mastery of the craft, I bragged to myself. I decided to pose the problem of adjusting the roof height to Grant and our younger apprentice, Ryan, at lunch the next day. It would be a good carpentry lesson, I thought, and I looked forward to their expressions of respect when I explained the solution I had figured out.

Grant took the problem in, grunted "hmmmm," and looked thoughtful. Ryan gave me one of his ever-friendly smiles and took a swallow of his energy drink. I'd had doubts about Ryan when he first came to work. Ryan had learned his carpentry first from TV and then in classes. As a high school student, he had holed up in his room with his dog and gobbled up shows on house construction and renovation the way some kids dive into video games. When he entered college, he enrolled in carpentry classes along with the usual academic courses. He'd risen to the head of the class and had fallen in love with building.

But 19th Street House was Ryan's first construction job with economic as well as educational consequences. Ryan had not experienced the time-crazed reality of construction, where labor is so costly and profit margins so tenuous that every minute must be used optimally. On the TV, he'd watched structures fly together between commercials, no one ever making a mistake, work never having to be ripped out and done over with the foreman cursing in frustration as he watched time and dollars evaporate. On television builders never grew terrified of losing their entire life savings on an underbid project. They never anxiously drove their crews to work faster and faster.

Ryan had not yet experienced a stressed foreman snapping at him for not knowing how to do and not getting done what no one had ever yet taught him. He had no experience with barbed Douglas fir splinters driven beneath a fingernail, shoulders bruised by loads of studs, a throat sore from dust, dust masks more irritating than a sore throat, sliced fingertips and gouged forearms, hammer-smashed thumbs—all part of a week's work at a construction site. He was big and strong, but not construction strong. After he spent several hours digging and hauling lumber one searing hot day early in the job, I found him on his hands and knees at the gutter along the street. He looked up at me, wiped his mouth, grinned, and said, "I told you I would work till I vomited."

Ryan quickly gained stamina and responded to the economic realities. "Consolidate your motions," I told him. "Don't measure, then cut, and then nail up a board. Make all your measurements, all cuts, then nail all the sticks in place." I had to tell him only once. Soon he was inventing efficiencies of his own.

I came to feel that in Ryan I had found a young man with exceptional mental gifts for building. Often friends with office-bound careers tell me "working with your hands" must be very satisfying. It is. But carpentry is first and foremost done with the mind. Carpenters envision, analyze, organize, and sequence, then move. Their hands are simply instruments of their minds, and just as there are exceptional legal, scientific, and literary minds, there are minds exceptional at seeing—even on the move with tools in hand—the way material should come together for the sake of both efficiency and beauty. Ryan smiled as I explained the problem at the bay roof and leaned back, expecting to give my young carpenters a moment to grasp the gravity of the situation at the bay, and then to enjoy their applause as I laid out my brilliant solution. When I was done talking, Ryan took another swallow of his energy drink, smiled once more, and offered the exact idea I had labored to find during a restless night. "Well, that might work," I allowed. "Awright. Lunchtime is up. Let's hit it."

Building skin

For all his talent, Ryan was low man at 19th Street House, and assigned to the simple repetitive tasks that new apprentices can do speedily enough to justify their employment. Handing Ryan a new hammer with a titanium head, I told him to nail off the 100 sheets of OSB sheathing that we had earlier hung on the wall frame with only a few nails each. Titanium hammers do not make the pleasing ring of steel hammers. That ring is the sound of vibration. The vibration travels through a carpenter's arm, punishing the joints. Titanium hammers do not vibrate. They cost four times as much as steel hammers, but as a carpenter buddy of mine says, "They're still a damn sight cheaper than elbows." Ryan's determined and attentive work had earned him the bonus of a first-class hammer. He was disappointed, though. He'd looked forward to using our nail gun, powered by an air compressor, to fasten the OSB.

"Not on my job," I told him. Nail guns, more than any other factor, lower framing quality. They are dazzlingly fast. But with a nail gun, you can't feel where the nail has ended up. You don't know whether a nail is embedded in solid lumber or not. And, because density of wood varies while nail guns operate at a fixed setting, nails are often driven too far or not far enough. Strength of attachment is lost. Frequently there is no attachment at all—especially of wall and roof sheathing—to the studs or rafters they are supposed to be nailed to. I have often seen buildings with a third and more of the nails fired into wall sheathing completely missing the studs for which they were intended. Not long ago in Savannah, Georgia, exploring the attic of a new home built by a company reputed to be the best in town, I looked up and saw long rows of "shiners," as we carpenters call nails that have missed their mark, poking through the plywood roof sheathing. They marched along in a perfectly straight line, evenly spaced out, clearly set by a carpenter with control of his tools, but a full inch away from the rafters they were intended to fasten the sheathing to. The carpenter probably never knew he had missed his target, that his work lay there loose, waiting for the next big hurricane to snatch it off the roof frame and hurl it into the street.

Strict building inspectors will flunk sloppy nail gun work. Mostly it's let go as heavily booked inspectors hurry from job to job, correcting only the most egregious violations of building health and safety codes, and even missing a lot of those. As a city inspector told me, "When you pass a building inspection, all that means is that you got a 'D–'" In other words, it does not certify you've done 'A+' or even 'C+' work. You may have. But passing your inspection is not proof one way or the other.

When Ryan finished driving 5,000 nails to attach the OSB, every nail was set snug and flush, holding the sheathing tight to the studs, plates, and beams behind. Though the nailing had taken a day longer than would have been required with a gun, I thought, "That is dollar wisdom, a couple of hundred bucks well spent." Not a single shiner showed on the inside of the house. Every nail was fully embedded. Ryan had a new skill. He knew how to swing a framing hammer with a relaxed, powerful motion. Many carpenters reared in the nail gun era never do learn how to swing a hammer. The inspector was happy. "Wish I saw more work like this," he said. We now had a maximally strong, stable base for our building skin, which Grant and I had already begun applying.

You will never see all the thoughtful work incorporated in a properly installed building skin touted in the real estate ads nor in architectural reviews. Yet a good skin is more fundamental to the satisfaction a house provides than all the dazzlements of features, form, feeling, and finish trumpeted to attract us to it. Consider what we ask of a building's skin, namely waterproofing systems we apply against its frame and the windows, doors, claddings, trim materials, and coatings visible at its exterior surfaces.

We require that a building's skin prevent wind from penetrating into the interior and yet allow a breeze to flow through when we wish. That it let sunlight in or keep it out, depending on the season. That it help keep heat in or out, and cold out or coolness in, according to outdoor conditions. That it allow us to pass through easily and comfortably, without disrupting its other functions.

We are now asking, in the most advanced building codes, that a house's skin protect it from immolation; we want it fire resistant. We require that it keep liquid water out, or drain it away if it happens to penetrate the skin; and—here is a complex requirement often befuddling even to builders and designers, never mind homeowners—that it resist or accommodate the passage of water vapor as appropriate to the climate the house experiences. We ask all that while also expecting that a skin will cloak its underlying structural forms in complementary and pleasing ways, supplying attractive texture, color, and pattern. We expect it to be highly durable, requiring little input of material and energy over a long life. And, of course, even as we hope that it will have been produced in an environment considerate way, we want it to be easy on our pocketbooks.

If a building's skin fails in even a small way at any one of its functions, it can cause chronic irritation, inconvenience, or discomfort. If it fails to hold water out, it can cause extended trauma. Such was the case for "Judith," for whom I served as an expert witness in a lawsuit she was forced to bring against her builder and architect. After losing their first home in the firestorm that swept through the eastern hills of the San Francisco Bay Area in 1991, incinerating 3,000 houses, Judith and her husband had decided to replace it with the home of their dreams. At a glance, their new house appeared sound and attractive. White stucco wrapped a well-proportioned Spanish revival exterior. Handsome rooms radiated out from a spacious central hallway. A semicircular stairway rose gracefully to the second floor. Arched mahogany doors opened onto decks and balconies with a view of the Golden Gate Bridge.

Two years after Judith and her husband moved into their new home, he began a losing battle with cancer. The house began to fail also. Its skin was leaking badly. The unpainted, poorly mixed, and weak stucco cladding its exterior walls soaked up water like a sponge. Beneath the stucco, the waterproofing system of flashings and sheets of house wrap were not competently installed. Instead of directing water that made its way through the stucco back toward the outside of the building, the flashings and wraps instead funneled it right into the wood framed walls. Mold thrived inside the wet walls and burst through to the interior face of the drywall, forming huge, black, stinking webs of slime.

Judith called her architect and builder for help but got no response. Both had left the state. During the two years she nursed her husband, she tried to stem the penetration of rain into her house with duct tape and caulk. She did not succeed. Her husband passed away. Even as she grieved, she was forced to retreat into a few back rooms and finally into a cramped attic space above her garage to escape the intensifying mold, and later the repair work that it necessitated. Eventually, she prevailed in her lawsuit, and found a reputable builder to resurrect her house, though the work consumed a good bit of her life savings along with a large settlement paid by her builder's insurance company. A decade after the mold first began feasting on her walls, she was able to relax in her home again.

Judith's story is not unusual. The scope of building skin failure is so great that a whole sub-industry of lawyers, expert witnesses, and repair specialists has sprung up to deal with it. Homeowners are understandably dismayed and outraged by the failures and the costs of correcting the failures. Building water-resistant houses is, however, not a matter of course as people sometimes assume. One veteran builder, particularly skilled and expert at the work, believes it is not possible to achieve 100 percent success. Water, the universal solvent, is simply too difficult to hold out. It tries to get through building skins from every angle. Water can flow down a skin and, if it finds even a tiny hole, right into the frame. Carried by capillary action, it can rise up a frame like kerosene up a wick, sometimes climbing all the way from the foundation to a second story. When held to a horizontal component of the skin by surface tension and driven by wind, water can travel sideways through the skin. Once under way, water keeps going deeper, carried by the sheer force of momentum, as is any other moving object.

Perhaps most bedeviling of all, water can be sucked right through the skin of a building by differences in air pressure. If the air pressure is lower inside the building than outside, it will, in keeping with the laws of physics, tend to equalize. In the process, if liquid water is present on the skin of a building, it will be sucked inward along with air, through joints where windows meet wall cladding, where vents exit, at cracks caused by building movement, or at other openings.

In the 1990s a certain engineer, one of those very fortunate persons who had ridden the technology boom from modest beginnings up into the financial ether, bought a thirty-acre hill overlooking the San Francisco Bay. He had the top scalped off by bulldozers and hired a local architect and contractor to design and build a domed mansion initially costing (in dollars not adjusted for inflation) some $15 million. During the first winter they were ensconced in their new digs, the engineer and his wife discovered rainwater penetrating the immense curving window wall of their gigantic living room. On its hilltop location, the house was frontally exposed to powerful winter storms. Its domed form was parting the wind in such a way that negative pressures were created at its backside, depressurizing the house. With the wind pushing, and the depressurization sucking, the window wall could not hold the rain out. Each rainy season, the wall had to be covered over with gigantic blue tarps, which entirely blocked the grandly impressive view across the bay to the city. The builder gathered together the subcontractors who had a role in construction of the wall and hammered out an agreement to share responsibility. Reconstruction of the wall got under way. Four years and two million dollars later, the repair was accomplished.

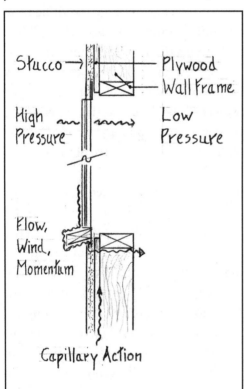

Even modest homes can experience leaks resulting from negative air pressure on the interior. Bath and kitchen fans pump air out. The pressure on the inside of the house turns negative relative to the outside. The pressures try to equalize. In the process, liquid water on the skin is nudged inward, and if it finds an opening, flows right into the frame. From his experience the builder of the domed mansion distilled a lesson that is, therefore, important for all of us who construct houses. *Because it really is impossible to succeed 100*

percent at keeping water out of buildings, you must also provide a means for it to escape. A well-crafted skin provides for escape.

Constructing skin, builders must contend with yet another force bringing water—in this case water vapor—into their structures. That is the so-called "stack effect," the tendency of warm air to rise, carrying water vapor with it, just as hot air carries smoke up a chimney. Warm air rises not only within buildings, from damp basements to first-story and then second-story rooms. It rises through the cavities within a frame. At the same time, vapor can migrate horizontally from the exterior of a house toward its interior, or vice-versa. If the vapor encounters a cold surface on its way through the cavities, say the backside of the drywall of an air-conditioned home, it will condense. Now you have the three necessary conditions for mold growth: Food, the paper backside of the drywall and the wood studs. Air. And water.

Water vapor molecules are particularly tiny. If you are to stop them, you need specialized materials. Proper installation of those materials, not surprisingly called "vapor barriers," varies by climate. In a mild climate, such as that prevailing in San Pablo and at the 19th Street House, it's actually best to forgo the vapor barrier and to allow water vapor to travel freely back and forth from the inside to the outside of the building. But other climates call for sterner measures. (See Resources for books offering guidance.) In hot and humid climates, for example, vapor must be stopped at the exterior of a house lest it condense when it hits the cool, air-conditioned interior surfaces. Other climates require vapor barriers to the interior—or even in the middle of walls.

Houses have always leaked and been permeable to water vapor, though we were not necessarily aware of it in the past. I have pulled apart dozens of older homes and found water damage that never became severe enough to be apparent at the surface. For in those older homes, the framing cavities—the spaces between studs, floor joists, and rafters—were filled with air, which flowed through them as readily as liquid through a sieve. As a result of the airflow, water that made its way into the cavities would, for the most part, dry away harmlessly. Now, in newer and renovated houses, walls are far more airtight. They do not breathe so easily, in some cases not at all. In addition, they have become sponges. Their cavities are filled not with air but with insulation, which retains water (some insulations more, some less). Moreover, the framing materials from the rapidly grown trees out of which we now mill our lumber soak up that water much more readily than the older and denser lumber. Likewise, the paper backside of drywall absorbs moisture more readily than old-fashioned wood lath. All in all, our newer houses absorb and hold water to a much greater extent and are much more susceptible to the decay that water promotes.

A high level of craft is required to install a skin that will protect our vulnerable houses. A single window at 19th Street House, for example, required that a dozen and a half—yes, eighteen—protective components be put in place even before cladding or trim was installed. If any component was installed out of sequence, incorrectly, or sloppily, a pathway for water would have been opened and the structure below put at risk of degradation. By contrast, only half a dozen pieces were needed for the fairly complex wood trim on the interior of each window; and if an item of trim slips, it can be simply reattached and touched up with no further harm done. Skin installation goes unappreciated and underpaid, with finish work drawing the applause. In consequence, especially the unseen components of the skin are often sloppily crafted or outright botched. The dollar and environmental consequences are devastating. It would not surprise me to learn that, on average and over the long term, the energy and material expended in repairing recently built homes due to failures of badly installed building skins will exceed that used to heat and cool them.

Choices

A building skin must not only be skillfully installed; it should be architonic, healthy, environment considerate, and dollarwise. Architonic is not so hard, though involving a nuance or two posed by the guardians of architectural honor, as we will see in a minute. Visual is paramount here. You are concerned with the look of your building's exterior. You can look over samples of materials at the building supply yard; you can look at the way various materials have been used in your neighborhood,

town, or city. Taking into account sunlight, shade, and plantings at
your own project, what you see is pretty much what you will get. You
can even gauge whether your choice will age attractively by looking at
similar earlier installations.

Health is not so hard either. You
can learn, at least to the extent the
manufacturers do not misrepresent or
omit data in the specification sheets the
law requires them to make available, the
degree to which your choices contain toxic
substances. Unfortunately, when it comes
to environment consideration and dollar
wisdom, the task gets harder. You are
confronted with a barrage of claims from
manufacturers and analyses from industry
experts. Only sometimes can you determine
whether their claims and recommendations
are reliable. Often choice comes down to
intuition, guesswork.

At 19th Street House, with window
flashings installed, I had next to choose
the material with which we would entirely
wrap the walls of the house before installing the outermost cladding.
Over the past few decades, a variety of manufacturers have brought
new house wraps to market. There is money to be made. Roughly 400
square miles of wrap is installed in the United States each year when the
housing industry is operating at full throttle. You see buildings cloaked
with the stuff, huge plastic sheets emblazoned with the manufacturer's
name in giant letters. The heavily marketed plastic house wraps have
largely pushed aside an old-fashioned (and far less costly) material. And
that is building felt, the oil-impregnated black paper sold in unassuming
three foot rolls with the manufacturer's name barely visible. You find it
stacked on pallets in back areas of building supply houses.

I have great respect for plain old felt. Often, pulling apart seventy-
five-year-old houses, I have found the felt intact below the siding

or stucco. It had dried out and lost pliability, but it was doing its job, preventing water penetration. The lumber protected by it was in fine condition. The plastic wraps arouse my distrust. I have seen too many plastic building products grow brittle and crack in a short time. How long before a plastic wrap at 19ᵗʰ Street would begin to crack and crumble and leak, I worried. I sought guidance from a detailed article about house wraps in a *Fine Homebuilding* article. Right into the middle of his article, the writer dropped a lengthy sidebar from one of his sources, a university-based building scientist, who commented appreciatively on the new materials. By the way, added the scientist, my own house is wrapped in felt, and if I were building a new house for myself now, I would use felt again. That settled the matter. Felt it was for 19ᵗʰ Street.

For the finish cladding, I had made preliminary choices when crafting the drawings. But as Grant, Ryan, and I framed the house, I reviewed my choices a last time, beginning at the roof and working down. The challenges encountered in choosing illustrate (again) the difficulty of weighing up the pros and cons of competing materials.

Though finding it sterile in appearance, especially for houses, I considered steel roofing. Alex Wilson, that respected cataloguer of green building products, gives steel roofing high ratings for recyclability and durability, passing on manufacturers' claims that it is good for fifty years. When I did my own research, however, I found contradicting information. Web sites out of England projected thirty years as the lifespan. Installers I talked to shrugged and said they'd guess thirty was more likely than fifty. And what about the coatings on the steel roofing, I wondered. Are they highly toxic, as has been the case with durable finishes in the past, liable to erode off the roof into the soil, or poison the air when the roofing is recycled and melted down three to five decades hence?

As an alternative, I considered forty year asphaltic composition shingles. "Yuck," green builders might say. In fact, Alex Wilson disdains the shingles. "Not durable," he says. "Not recyclable." But my experience told me something different. On a house I built a few miles from 19ᵗʰ Street, a so-called "twenty year" asphalt shingle roof has been in service for twenty-five years and is going strong. As for recycling, at the rate we are inventing ways to reuse discarded building materials—turning carpet into wall sheathing—it seemed probable that there'd be a good use for their carcasses when forty year shingles were worn out.

Claims and counterclaims—similar to those made about roofing—popped up around the planking manufactured of cement and fiber that I was considering for the upper level of the house. It is praised for its durability and because its use saves the trees from which the planking would otherwise be made. On the other hand, roof shingles made of the same cementatious material have failed far before they reached the end of their expected life span. And the manufacture of cement, such as is used in the planking, is responsible for a substantial percentage of the emissions thought to cause global warming, which in turn may devastate forests.

Architects raise a different objection to the cementatious planks. One sniffed, "It's fake, I could not use it, I simply could not do fake." He was echoing a line of thought in architecture that calls for "honesty" in use of material. According to *Dwell*, a magazine dedicated to modernist design and to promoting architectural honesty, we must use materials in such a way that they cannot be mistaken for something else. When furniture is made of fiberglass, the fibers must be allowed to show through. No concealing of them allowed. No coating, no painting, no staining, nothing that might lead some unsuspecting observer to mistake the fiberglass for wood or metal or tinted plastic.

But I find the demand for honesty in material an idea with a limited range of convenience. Is glass "dishonest" because you can't see the sand it is made of? And, why is a plank created from fiber and cement more fake than one made from a tree? If cement planks had been invented first, would we be calling the wooden ones "fake" imitations of fiber cement planks? Why, I wondered as I considered my choice of claddings, is the process of mining, heating, mixing, and molding lime (the base ingredient of cement) and fiber into planks more fakery than felling a tree, dragging it from a forest, skinning it, sawing it into boards, and milling the boards to a smooth or rippled surface?

A similar clash of architectural and environmental concerns and counterclaims could be surfaced around my consideration of stucco as well as of a board and batten look for the other exterior wall surfaces. I'll spare you the full tabulation. The point is that with material choice, architectural considerations are highly subjective. And when it comes to environment consideration, there is, as an executive at the University of California charged with greening the institution's maintenance procedures puts it, "a huge information problem." What's true for a university's purchase of paper towels, cleaning chemicals, or a lawn care product holds in spades for building materials. All we know for sure is which materials are cheaper and which we like better.

And so I chose: Old-fashioned felt (at a fraction of the cost of plastic house wraps). Forty year composition shingles at a third the cost of steel roofing—and with an appearance I thought more suited to the softened craftsman look of 19th Street House. Stucco, handsome and good for a century or more. Resawn plywood with battens at the garage and gable. And cementatious planks, so wretchedly dishonest they were molded with a slight ripple similar to that of resawn wood planking.

INFRASTRUCTURE

Perhaps you happened to be renovating an older home at the time Ryan, Grant, and I were constructing our new house at 19th Street. If so, you might have, at roughly the same time, arrived at roughly the same place in your renovation as we did in our new construction. It's just that you would have been working from the opposite direction. While we were *constructing* a foundation, a frame, and a skin, you were *deconstructing*—removing and recycling worn-out parts of your building until you were left with a foundation, a frame, and a skin. From there, our paths might for a time have diverged. While my crew and I made our minor framing adjustments, you might have made bigger changes to enlarge or open up rooms, to improve circulation through your spaces, or to let sunlight in. Quite likely, you would also have had to renovate the skin—including windows. Whatever your tasks, when they were completed, you would, like us, then have what looks very much like a house. But in fact, like us, you would be only about one-third of the way to a completed house. The next third of the way you would be building its infrastructure.

Ever more

As surely as does a city, a house has a hidden infrastructure. If you dig down below the surface of a city or town into the earth, you find an astonishingly dense layering of construction—roadbeds, culverts, pipes, wires, tunnels, conduits, and cables—that supply all the services we are accustomed to enjoying at the surface. Similarly, if you strip away the visible surfaces of a house, especially a recently built one, you will encounter within the frame a maze of ducts, wires large and small, big pipes and little ones, conduits and cables.

The other major components of a house—structure, exterior skin, interior finishes—have been present in buildings for many centuries. Infrastructure has arrived only recently. Outside Charleston, South Carolina, there is a plantation house owned by the National Historic Trust. It was inhabited as recently as a century and a quarter ago, during the lives of the great-grandparents of the baby boomers, but has not been lived in or altered since. In this house, frozen in a moment only 125 years gone, there is not a single fixture or device, not a lamp or heat register or water tap, that hints of an infrastructure beneath the skin; and there is none—not a strand of wire, length of pipe, or run of ductwork. The Charleston house is more or less typical of its time. During the twentieth century, however, infrastructure came on like gangbusters as we ramped up the requirements we make of this invisible portion of our homes.

Each of us now expects that our house will provide us with cold and hot water at the twist of a handle in our kitchen, in two or three bathrooms, in our private laundry, perhaps even at a bar and an outdoor barbecue. We take it for granted that we will have cold water available on demand at two or three locations for car washing, gardening, and children's play. We expect that at the flick of a lever or push of a button the waste we produce inside our home will be carried away. We require that our home provide us instantly with electrical power to operate all manner of devices at every countertop and vanity and at frequent intervals along every wall. If our house is a new one, we expect it to come equipped in almost every room with connections that enable us to communicate with the outside world via voice, print, photo, and video. And, of course, we want the infrastructure of our home to protect us from intruders, sounding an alarm and surreptitiously phoning the police should anyone break in.

We expect artificial light on demand, instantaneously available in every room, closet, and niche, for every task from selecting a tie, to making a sandwich, to paying bills or flossing our teeth. Our demand for light has escalated with particular ferocity. Many of us have come to insist on constant artificial light just as we expect relentless, nonstop sound piped into every inhabited space: living room, car, coffee shop, kitchen, bedroom, mall—or directly into our ears as we walk the streets. Likewise, many of us cannot tolerate dark, apparently can take no enjoyment from shadow or even low light. When I take walks in my neighborhood at night, I see houses in which many rooms with no one in them are brightly lit with multiple lamps. A friend of mine, taken aback by his rising electrical bills, recently counted the bulbs in his house. He found 250 and realized that often he has most of them turned on, even when only he and his wife are home and in their den watching a DVD. "I don't like the dark," he told me.

We require that our house's infrastructure bring us fuel for cooking (increasingly these days at our outdoor barbecues as well as inside), and for conditioning the air in our rooms, no matter whether it's freezing or soggy hot outside, to a temperature within two or three degrees of what we would hope for on a Caribbean isle during a perfect winter vacation day. What's more, we expect our infrastructure and the devices it supports to deliver all that water, power, light, warmth, and coolness quietly, uninterruptedly, and unobtrusively. Of late, we have added a hope that the infrastructure provide for all the requisite services in green fashion, using energy frugally and even gathering the energy on site via geothermal, wind capturing, or solar contraptions. And, of course, we want all the service provided at price points pleasing to our pocketbooks.

Indoor air quality and the healthy house movement

If you are thinking all this is adding up to a very complicated third of a house, you are right. But we are not yet done. The evolution of our houses has given birth to another requirement, namely that they be built with infrastructure for maintaining good quality air within our living spaces. Events have linked up like this: For centuries we built our houses in such a way that they leaked air like a sieve. Much of the time—not always, because on very still days air did not move in and out of them—the leaky houses readily exchanged their air for fresher outdoor air every few hours or even faster. Then in the early 1970s came the first energy crisis as petroleum-rich nations organized to get higher prices for their black gold. As prices rose, so too did our consciousness that as our buildings leaked air, they were also leaking away the dollars spent for heating and cooling the air. To reduce costs we began insulating and plugging leaks in existing houses. And we passed laws mandating that new houses be insulated and sealed against energy and air leakage, that they be constructed with a thermal boundary around the inhabited spaces.

Even though the thermal boundaries were often poorly conceived and badly crafted, and were much less effective than they might have been, our houses became tighter. Some became much tighter. They did not as readily exchange their air for fresher outdoor air, and, in the case of houses with well-crafted thermal boundaries, hardly exchanged it at all. The now entrapped air became polluted from a variety of sources: cooking gas and fumes; shower steam (which contains vaporized chlorine and stimulates mold growth); floor covering, especially carpet, and furnishings saturated with a host of new off-gassing chemicals; cabinets and paint; and, last but not least, people (and pets) who live in the houses. For not only do we drag nasty dust into our homes on our shoes and clothing, but each of us, as the building scientist Joe Lstiburek jokes, is also an "unvented combustion appliance." Just like fake gas logs with no chimney to carry away their deadly exhaust, our bodies are constantly combining air with fuel and releasing the byproducts directly into the interior of our homes.

As houses tightened, warnings sounded. Indoor air quality (IAQ) in some homes was declared to be ten times worse than in downtown Los Angeles on one of its famously smoggy days. Individuals complained. Their houses were making them sick—inducing chronic fatigue, rashes, respiratory problems, and headaches. A new medical term, multiple chemical sensitivity (MCS), emerged to describe the illness of people whose resistance to the pollution in built environments had been broken down. A new literature emerged as well: books and articles joining the words "healthy" and "house" in their titles, and urging changes in construction practice to prevent the health problems caused by poor IAQ.

Naturally, the calls for reform aroused skepticism and resistance. Persons complaining of multiple chemical sensitivity were dismissed as "head cases," hysterics. My own grasp of the reality came only gradually. When I got my first call from a person who told me she needed help because the materials in her beautifully remodeled house were making her so sick she had moved out, I wondered, am I talking to some poor nut case? But then I began to read about healthy house issues. And in preparation for crafting 19th Street House I visited, together with my wife, several model homes I thought might give me useful ideas. From Sandra's reaction, I saw firsthand what bad indoor air can do. When we went into the new homes, Sandra, though she has an unusually high tolerance for physical discomfort, often had to leave immediately. She was beginning to gasp for breath as her respiratory system closed up in response to the indoor pollution.

Build tight! Ventilate right!

Many builders shared my initial skepticism about IAQ issues. Some dug in their heels, angrily resisting the new legislation and the healthy house movement. Construction, they said, was complicated and costly enough without having to turn every house into its own little air quality management district. Politicians should leave building to the folks who knew how to do it. Just as in the old days, they would put up structures that were just leaky enough. Everything would be fine. The healthy house advocates and lawmakers were, however, undeterred. The codes continued to mandate thermal boundaries for energy efficiency. Meanwhile, building scientists fired back at the stressed-out builders. Joe Lstiburek lampooned the idea of maintaining IAQ through leaks as faith based, not reality based. You couldn't count on a house to appropriately ventilate itself, he said. Even leaky houses leaked only erratically. On windy days, they might leak far more than needed to maintain decent IAQ. On still days, they might leak hardly at all;

even opening windows would not get enough air moving through the building to flush out pollutants.

The healthy house advocates and building scientists advanced a slogan to push back against builders' protests: "Build tight! Ventilate right!" In other words, thoroughly insulate and seal for energy efficiency. Ventilate not by leaks and happenstance but with calibrated control, with right-sized mechanical devices—supply fans, exhaust fans, and air exchangers—that would move bad air out and fresher air in.

In his comprehensive and clear book, *The Healthy House* (highly recommended in Resources), John Bower expands the "ventilate" side of the building scientists' mantra to a four-step process: 1) eliminate, 2) separate, 3) ventilate, 4) filtrate. In other words, he instructs, *eliminate* sources of toxicity from your house to the extent reasonably possible. Choose interior finish materials—flooring, paints, cabinets—and also furnishings that do not off-gas pollutants into the air you breathe. If you must, for reasons of budget or availability, use suspect materials in the structure and infrastructure of your building, *separate* them from interior living spaces. For example, if you use insulation held together with hazardous formaldehyde binders, seal the insulation off from interior spaces with airtight drywall. Even if you thoroughly eliminate and separate, *ventilate* as well. Use mechanical devices to flush out dirty air and trade it for cleaner air.

Finally, *filtrate*. Filters ranging from inexpensive paper inserts that will catch only larger particles to high-efficiency particulate accumulators (HEPA) can be integrated into heating (and cooling) systems to clean air before it is pushed out into living areas. There are reasons, however, that filtration is the last of John Bower's four steps. It is the least reliable. Filters must be changed regularly, in some cases monthly. Like other house maintenance tasks, filter change-out gets neglected. The consequences can be severe. My mother began having difficulty breathing after moving into an apartment in a retirement community. The filter for her heating system, it turned out, was difficult to access and had not been changed for a very long time, if ever. It was slick with black mold, dumping contamination into the air stream rather than removing it. When I replaced the filter, my mother's breathing became normal again.

At best, filters clean only the air that actually reaches them; and the mechanical devices that circulate air into and out of our living spaces, pushing it through filters in the process, do not pull in all the air from every corner of a house, never mind suck in all the pollutants residing on surfaces in our homes. Forced air furnaces and air exchangers are not vacuum cleaners. We should not rely on them as if they were, expecting that they will filter away every pollutant in our home. If we don't eliminate, separate, and ventilate, then filtration alone won't protect our air quality.

A house is a system

A few years back, a client of mine returned home just after my crew and I had completed stripping the walls of her kitchen back to the bare studs. With bewilderment, she stared at the exposed tangle of ducts, pipes, and wire. "How in the world do you know how to rearrange all that?" she asked. We explained to her that we relied on an old builder's rule of thumb, "largest first," which helped sort things out. First install the ducts, next the larger plumbing pipes. Then work the smaller pipes around them. Finally wiggle your wires through the space that is left over.

With the infrastructure becoming ever more complex, the old rule of thumb still helps, but more forethought is necessary or you may end up with two components needing to fit into a space where there is room for only one. If you don't plan carefully, you are certain to find a pipe or duct blocked by another from going where it must and forced instead into a zigzagging route. Initial use of material and labor increases, and with it dollar cost and environmental impact. Your poor planning will also—here we come to a terribly important and routinely overlooked consideration—*day by day, relentlessly over the years, lead to increased costs and impacts for operation of the devices serviced by the infrastructure.*

Consider first of all the infrastructure for heating and cooling: Poor duct installation will waste astonishing amounts of energy, far overbalancing the savings achieved by any elaborate and costly high-efficiency furnace or air conditioner attached to it. In an average home, moving up from a standard- to a super-efficiency furnace will lower fuel costs by roughly 12 percent. A poorly crafted duct system will throw away 33 to 50 percent of the heat it transports, increasing fuel costs by equivalent amounts.

In poorly crafted installations, ducts are routed through attics, exterior walls, and crawl spaces. Because they are thinly insulated, if at all, the ducts give up heat to the surrounding relatively cold air or, in the case of air conditioning, absorb heat from the surrounding hot air. The Second Law of Thermodynamics is at work here: temperatures in adjacent spaces—in this case, the inside of a duct and a building cavity—tend to equalize. The cool cavity sucks heat out of the duct.

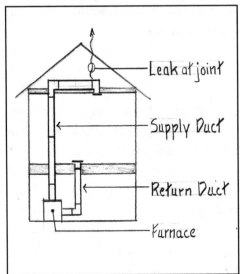

Equally problematic, badly crafted duct systems leak, especially where they are joined together. Before I understood the importance of sealed duct connections, thinking I would be a good green guy and save money at the same time, I had a new and higher-efficiency furnace installed in the crawl space of my home. The following heating season, my fuel consumption and bills went up, not down. Bad workmanship, it turned out, was overwhelming technological advance. At the point where the new furnace was (sloppily) connected to the duct system, hot air was gushing out, nicely warming the crawl space rather than warming the rooms that Sandra, Max the cat, and I inhabit.

My leaky duct system was not unusual. It was typical. It has been estimated that one-quarter of the energy used to heat homes in this country is lost through duct leaks. Just as poorly crafted duct systems waste material and energy, the reverse is true as well. Skilled crafting of ductwork can reduce first costs, and it can radically lower life cycle costs. At 19th Street House, responsibility for crafting the duct system fell to George Nesbitt—sole owner, resident genius, designer, chief installer, and entire full-time crew of Environmental Design/Build of Oakland,

California. George, who perpetually goes about in a broad-brimmed canvas hat pulled down over his brush cut blond hair, is both sybarite and idealist. He loves a big steak, a cozy warm house, and, like all of us builders, a sturdy pickup truck loaded with tools for every possible occasion.

George also believes that we must refurbish our built environment so that it fosters rather than degrades life. We must work, George urges, at resolving the environment/energy crisis from two directions: 1) reducing energy consumption by methods we already possess, and 2) pushing for scientific and technological advances in the production and utilization of energy. George recognizes that the technological advances, such as wind harvesting, solar energy generation, cellulosic fuel production, and all the alternate ways of making energy other than by burning decayed dinosaur carcasses (i.e., petroleum) are the headline grabbers. But, he gently insists, reducing consumption by methods we already possess comes first for a good reason. The less energy we use, the easier it will be for us to produce enough energy by new methods that will inflict less environmental damage, yet still be adequate to maintain our comfortable way of life.

When George arrived in his truck at 19th Street House, it was usually with a covered trailer in tow. Within its extensive system of drawers and shelves, the trailer contained tools for the performance of virtually every trade necessary to house building. George is one of the select group of builders who can perform many of the trades with competence. Because of the diversity of his skills, and his years of studying healthy and environment considerate construction, he understands with acuity the way in which the work of each trade interacts with and influences the functioning of the work performed by other trades. George understands viscerally that, as he likes to say, "A house is a system."

Of course, houses have always been systems: the foundation is connected to the first floor, the floor to the first-story walls, the walls to the second-story floor . . . and so on, all the way up to the roof. The dictum "a house is a system" refers, however, not so much to the classical structural relationships, but to the newer web of interactions that has developed as we load up our houses with ever more infrastructure. One important strand of the web goes like this: Frugal framing uses less lumber, thereby freeing space for more effective insulation. Superior insulation, coupled with sealing of gaps in the frame and skin, reduces loss of heated (or cooled) air. Decreased loss lowers the need to heat or cool air in the first place. The lowered requirements allow use of a smaller furnace. The smaller furnace requires smaller ducts to deliver an adequate supply of air where needed. Smaller ducts are more easily routed to their destination, thus using less labor as well as material, inflicting less cost and environmental impact. And so it goes. Starting with frugal framing, straightforward measures result in the house becoming less costly even as it becomes more environment considerate.

Back during the days when I was completing the drawings for 19th Street House, George, using "house is a system" thinking and specialized software, had calculated that even on the very coldest days that San Pablo would experience, the house would need very little heating beyond that provided by the sun. With its many south-facing windows, tile floors to store heat flowing in through those windows, small number of north-facing windows, and thermal boundary, the house would require only a very small heat source, and along with it only small ducts through which to push heat to a register in each room.

Once construction was under way, George designed and built just such a compact system for 19th Street House. As a last measure, he set out to

eliminate leakage in his system so that virtually all air transported by it would get where it was intended to go. With Ryan and me working as his assistants, George spent hours buttering the joints in the system with a specialized sealant and then connecting the joints snugly. George's intention is to make his ductwork absolutely leak free and thus maximize its long-term efficiency. One day he will succeed. At 19th Street House, as our measurements would later indicate, he limited leakage to about three percent of total air pushed through the ducts.

George included in his system a duct through which fresh air could be pulled from the outside and pushed into the house. That air would slightly pressurize the interior. The pressurization would have the effect of forcing contaminated interior air out. To supplement George's "supply side ventilation," as it is called, Ryan and I provided for exhaust ventilation by installing ducts for exhaust fans in the bathrooms and the kitchen. Along with the ventilation ductwork, we provided piping for an elimination system, namely a central vacuum. Central vacs are large, powerful vacuum cleaners that can be permanently hung in a closet, garage, or basement and connected to interior rooms and to the outside of a building by means of hidden plastic pipes. They are only moderately costly to purchase. Including installation, they run a few hundred bucks more than high-quality, conventional push and pull cleaners. They are delightfully convenient to use, requiring only that you hook up a lightweight hose to a wall outlet. There is some evidence to suggest that people who have central vacs tend to vacuum more often than folks who have to drag around conventional vacuums, and therefore they enjoy cleaner houses and better indoor air quality (IAQ).

At 19th Street House, with a central vac it would be possible to vacuum the entire first floor by attaching the hose to one intake, and the entire second floor by attaching the hose to another. The central vac's powerful motor would pull in dirt through the hose and through the pipes that Ryan and I installed. Then, unlike conventional vacuums—which throw much of the dirt they have just sucked up right back into the interior space, sometimes making the indoor air worse than it was before—our central vac would exhaust it all to the outside.

Our simple ventilation/elimination system—fresh air supply duct, exhaust fans, and central vac—would turn out to work well at 19th Street House. The house would enjoy good quality indoor air with low energy usage. For another house in another climate, however, our system might not be appropriate. In particular, a house of the so-called *Passivhaus* variety, most advanced in Germany but catching on in the United States, requires another technology.

Passive houses feature thermal boundaries with ultra high value insulation and meticulous sealing of all points of potential air leakage. They are the thermos bottles of house construction. They hardly require heating. One construction savant has joked that even in a very, very cold climate you can heat a passive house with a "hot babe," a teenager with a blow dryer in hand.

On the other hand, because they are so tight, passive houses also require exacting attention to the management of indoor air quality, typically provided by a heat-recovery ventilator (HRV). HRVs run continuously using very efficient motors to minimize energy use, expelling air from the dirtiest areas, especially baths and kitchen, while simultaneously drawing in fresh air from the outside and distributing it to bedrooms and the living/dining spaces. Inside the HRV unit, the dirty and fresh air pass by one another through intertwining ducts so that—here is the recovery piece—roughly two-thirds of the heat from the outgoing air is absorbed by the incoming air and carried back inside the house.

Different strokes for different houses and different conditions—in other words, "Green by design, not by ingredient," as one architect nicely describes the challenge of achieving environment considerate construction. Just as a wonderful pickle will not a good clam chowder make, a groovy green product might sour one house while nicely flavoring another. A house is a system.

Water energy

"Green simple," George called 19th Street House. He was contrasting it to the often counterproductive, sometimes merely consumerist efforts to achieve environment consideration by the piling on of impressive, costly technology rather than achieving more with less. "Green simple" was also our approach to crafting our next phase of work, the installation of plumbing pipes. When the house was completed, the plumbing infrastructure would be invisible. But it would make a large contribution to reducing resource consumption in the house—by much more than could have been accomplished via certain showier, so-called green options that we would later decide (adamantly) against.

Reducing water consumption matters because fresh water is a precious and increasingly overtaxed resource. It matters as well because our way of exploiting water resources consumes an enormous amount of energy. All told, in the United States, water use accounts for nearly one-quarter of our stationary energy consumption. (In California, it's closer to a third.)

In a home, every time we flush a toilet, turn on a tap to let cold water flow, take a warm shower, hose down the kids on a hot day, or wash the car, we are consuming energy. The energy is used to lift the water out of the ground, to pump it over mountains and through treatment plants, to filter it and chemicalize it, and to treat and then disburse it after it has been used. Energy is used for the construction of the vast network of dams, pipes, and towers that capture and store the water and carry it to and away from our fixtures and back into the larger environment. When we open a hot water tap, we contribute to all those expenditures of energy and add another for inserting heat into the water. In short, whenever we use water we also use what I call *water energy*.

Efforts to reduce water and water energy use in our houses have focused largely on devices and fixtures. First came improvements in showerheads and faucets that lowered flows from half a dozen gallons per minute to two and a half and then as little as a gallon per minute. Then came thrifty front loading washing machines that cut water and energy use by two-thirds per load. Now we have toilets, "water closets" in plumber's lingo, so intelligently engineered that they use, on average, roughly a gallon of water per flush. That is a reduction of more than 80 percent from the water closets we were installing when I was an apprentice carpenter.

Because of the focus on devices at the surface of our homes, the potential for improvements in the system of pipes largely hidden in the frame—the plumbing infrastructure—has gone mostly unattended. In much the same way as inefficiently routed heating ducts, plumbing infrastructure designed and installed without knowledge of and regard for efficiency wastes dollars and inflicts environmental damage. During construction, far more pipe than necessary is installed to supply fresh water to fixtures and to carry it away, wasting both material and energy used in manufacture and installation. In the case of the hot water lines, the superfluous piping results in heat loss and wastes water energy day by day, decade upon decade. (Exhibit A: the studio apartment I built thirty years ago where I naively placed the water heater as far from the taps as possible.) That pesky Second Law of Thermodynamics, which tells us that temperatures in adjacent spaces or materials tend to equalize,

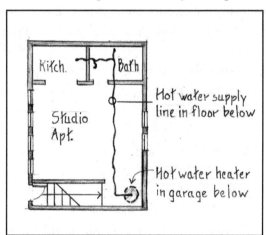

comes into play again as the long lines give up heat (from the water they are carrying) to the surrounding wall cavities, attics, and basements through which they are routed. If the pipes are left uninsulated or if the insulation installation is sloppily done, the rate of loss can double or triple.

In houses with slab foundations, hot water lines are typically routed underground, below the slabs, so that the cool earth—an "infinite heat sink," as engineers say—drains energy and heat away continuously. Hot water lines, especially those made of PEX (cross-linked polyethylene, a plasticlike material that has recently begun to displace copper as the material of choice for water supply lines), are bundled together with cold water lines so that the one is cooled and the other warmed. In extreme cases of such bundling, neither hot water nor cold water ever reaches the taps. Both hot and cold faucets deliver lukewarm water.

Long hot water lines—even when properly separated from cold water supply lines, well insulated, and run within the thermal boundary instead of below grade—waste energy in another and quite startling fashion. To understand, picture yourself at a bathroom sink. You have just finished potting a plant or changing the cat litter. You decide to wash your hands. Going into your second-story bathroom, you turn on the hot water and wait. Then you wait some more. Growing impatient, you decide to duck into the bedroom and grab your car keys while hot water makes its way to the faucet. Just as you leave the bathroom, the hot water begins flowing. It flows for sixty seconds more while you locate your keys, remember what you were doing before you went in search of them and were distracted by the magazine lying on your dresser, and return to the bathroom. When you do, being a good green guy, wanting to minimize your carbon footprint and not waste water and energy, you soap and rinse quickly.

Your good intentions are to no avail. Badly crafted plumbing infrastructure has overwhelmed them. Hot water took so long to arrive at your faucet because the pipe from the water heater, assuming your house is more or less typical, runs eight feet from the top of the heater down to the crawl space, then forty feet through the crawl space, and finally fourteen more feet up to the sink for a total of sixty-two feet. For most of the distance, the pipe is a three-quarter inch line servicing multiple fixtures. For the last few feet, serving only the faucet at the sink, it is half inch.

Each two and one-half feet of your three-quarter line and each five feet of your half inch line holds approximately a cup of water. The sixty-two foot length of pipe from the hot water heater to the tap holds, in total, twenty-four cups or one and a half gallons. That gallon and a half went down the drain while you waited for hot water to arrive. Nearly another two gallons disappeared as you looked for your keys and gazed at the magazine. A quart spilled out while you quickly washed. After you finished washing up, a gallon and a half of hot water was left sitting in the line. If enough time passes before the faucet is used again, that final gallon and a half will have lost all its heat and will, in turn, be dumped at the beginning of the next washing. All told, then, your environmentally aware hand washing consumed enough to fill five one-gallon milk jugs.

Both everyday observation and research by Gary Klein, a leading water energy expert, confirm that brief uses of hot water, like hand washing, constitute a large proportion of our water and water energy consumption. After all, lengthier uses, while consuming much water, are only intermittent. You may shower once a day, do laundry weekly. But sink faucets go on and off frequently. How often is hot water turned on in a kitchen during the preparation of a meal and cleanup afterward? How often is hot water turned on each day in bathrooms for washing up, rinsing, and cleaning? How often is hot water turned on even when cold would do? Each of the uses, if the pipe runs are long, can consume far more water and energy for getting hot water to us than for the actual washing. No low-flow device will save the waste. If the plumbing infrastructure is not optimally efficient, it forces waste. In most houses, I would say based on my experience (and, more significantly, Gary Klein's), it ranges from considerably less than optimal to very, very bad.

We can save enormous amounts of water and energy by building new houses with efficient plumbing infrastructure and, as we renovate existing houses, improving the infrastructure—by installing what Gary Klein calls "structured plumbing®." (Klein's excellent articles on water, water energy, and structured plumbing® are the source of much of the

foregoing narrative and can be accessed over the Web (see Resources.) For a house with hot water production and points of use spread out (as in a 1950s single-story ranch style house), Klein proposes carefully sizing the pipes and using a recirculation pump. For a house like 19th Street, compact and roughly cubic in shape, he suggests an even better option, a "core system." That is exactly the sort of plumbing infrastructure that the house facilitates with its compact form and with its baths, laundry, and hot water heater all tightly clustered together in a central volume. The clustering allows for very short runs of both supply and waste lines, thus minimizing resources used for construction and for getting hot water to the tap.

At 19th Street House, with one exception, hot water lines are twelve feet or less in length, so only three to four cups of water spill from the faucets before hot water arrives from the water heater. Of the seven fixtures drawing hot water, only the kitchen sink is at the end of a lengthier run, and even there, hot water arrives within ten seconds, not a long enough wait to send users wandering off to another task. All the hot water pipe, as well as the last six feet of cold water pipe as it enters the water heater, is insulated.

Our plumbing infrastructure could have been better yet. Once appropriate but now outdated government regulations held us back. Low-flow fixtures and devices such as are now installed in baths, kitchens, and laundries are mandated by law. They do not require nearly as high a volume of water flow as fixtures installed in bygone years. The code for plumbing infrastructure, however, had not, at the time we were building 19th Street House, caught up to the changes in the requirements of low-flow devices. As a result, we had to use a one inch supply line from the meter, three-quarter inch trunk lines, and half inch branches to the fixtures. Had we been allowed to downsize to three-quarters, half, and three-eighths—completely adequate for the low-flow fixtures we would be putting in—we would have saved a great deal of material. And because the smaller pipes hold much less water, at seven of our eight hot water taps we would have come very close to the gold standard that Gary Klein has established for minimizing water and water energy waste: only one cup of water lost before hot water flows from the tap.

Power and light

With plumbing supply and waste lines installed, our electrician, Zichao "Choo" Tang, arrived to install our electrical service and pull wire through the frame for media and phone, security, lighting, and outlets for plug-in devices from appliances to play stations. For Choo's work, as with all that has come before, all four points of our pyramid of values had to be kept in mind. To begin with the health point: around home electrical wiring, the health issues are in part settled matters, in part intensely debated. We are unanimous on one thing: water and electricity don't mix. At areas subject to wetting—baths, kitchens, decks—the codes require installation of ground fault interrupters (GFIs), devices that will interrupt current flow and prevent shock should anyone press a damp finger into an electrically hot outlet.

In addition to imparting shock, electrical currents generate electromagnetic fields. There is intense debate about how much we need to protect ourselves from those fields. Some healthy house advocates urgently sound a warning: keep the service panel as far away from the inhabited areas of your house as possible! Others, including people deeply involved in the healthy house movement, give little credibility to the warnings, thinking that the dangers, if any, are not yet well researched and are far from proven. Even these skeptics may, however, lean toward the precautionary principle: if in doubt, watch out. In crafting 19th Street House, I elected to lean toward precaution. I placed the breaker box—at which high-voltage power from the utility company entered the house—as distant as possible from the inhabited rooms, at the far corner of the garage. Conveniently, that also happens to be a location where the panel is not much visible and does not impair the look of the house.

From the main breaker box at the garage, a single heavy-duty wire was run to a distribution panel at the service core. From that central location, smaller-gauge wire could be pulled with minimal use of material and labor to all the points at which it would be connected to outlets, lights, switches, and other controls. Outlets were placed at frequent intervals along the perimeter of rooms and countertops as the electrical code and the location of appliances dictated. With placement of lights, however, such straightforward guidelines evaporated. Lighting has become a sophisticated craft, involving complex technical and aesthetic choices. The environmental impacts and financial consequences of our collective demands and decisions around lighting are huge. In California, for example, lighting consumes one-quarter of all electrical power used in the state.

In our homes, we have come to expect three kinds of lighting: *Ambient* lighting, i.e., general illumination. *Task* lighting, for cooking, brushing teeth, doing homework, paying bills, illuminating pathways through a house, finding the right pair of pants in a closet. And *accent* lighting, to create interesting patterns of shadow or light on a wall or to illuminate art, a family photo, or collectibles.

But satisfying those demands is not just a matter of sticking a lamp wherever ambient, task, or accent lighting seems called for. What you are lighting and how you will light it also require consideration and decisions—and those decisions must be made before the installation of infrastructure, so that the wiring and boxes support appropriate lighting rather than force you to use fixtures that can't do their job well. To give coherence to the complex task, lighting designers suggest that whether you are choosing ambient, task, or accent lighting, you should bear in mind what they call the "three Ss." Simplifying the concept for use at 19th Street House, I thought of the "three Ss" as follows:

First, the *surface* to be illuminated. When choosing task lighting for kitchen countertops, for example, I kept in mind that they might have a highly reflective surface—as is the case with granite. The wrong lights, or even the right lights wrongly placed, would throw a glare into the eyes of people working over the countertops.

Second, the *system* of lighting. We now have available to us a boggling variety of lighting systems. Among them are recessed cans, surface-mounted fixtures, sconces, pendants, tracks, up lighting, down lighting, combination up and down lighting, and indirect lighting. Along with the light fixtures, we are offered an array of light controls such as dimmers, occupancy sensors, motion sensors, and timers as well as traditional flip switches. And beyond such wall-mounted controls governing one or a few fixtures, we encounter computerized light management systems, which will control lighting for a whole building, adjusting it in response to the degree of natural lighting available and occupancy loads in the building.

Third, the *source* of light. Sources most commonly used in houses now include incandescent bulbs and fluorescents—in the form of both the traditional long tubes and the new compact spiraled tubes generally referred to as CFLs. The ultraefficient and incredibly long-lived light emitting diodes (LEDs) are rapidly making their way into the marketplace. When I began writing this book, LEDs were discouragingly expensive. As I write these lines, you can purchase a strip of undercabinet LEDs, with a claimed life expectancy of fifty thousand hours, for fifty bucks. The evolution of light sources illustrates the financial and environmental benefits of the "reduction first" and "green simple" approach. The initial cost for undercabinet LEDs is about a tenth of a cent per hour of use over their predicted life, while incandescents are approximately three times that much. The LEDs lower operating cost per hour by roughly 95 percent.

It is a challenge to properly outfit a house with ambient, task, and accent lighting, to choose systems and sources appropriate to the surfaces they will illuminate. Thus the rise of the lighting design profession. At 19th Street House, however, the budget could not accommodate a lighting designer other than me. As the designer, I was not only interested in providing the three types of lighting with attention to the "three Ss." I was critically interested in restraining the amount of lighting in order to contain both construction and long-term operating costs. So I boiled my program down to a few steps: Determine where ambient and task light

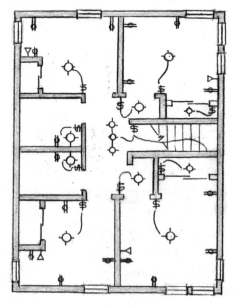

was absolutely necessary. Allow for just a touch of accent lighting if financially feasible. Consider alternative systems and sources with surfaces in mind. Select from promising systems and sources with attention to environment consideration and dollar wisdom.

Because general illumination and the even lighting it throws out over a room is not very interesting or useful, I held infrastructure for ambient light to a minimum. Wiring for a surface-mounted ceiling light was pulled to each bedroom and to the kitchen. But that was all she wrote for ambient lighting. As for task lighting, I assumed that some, particularly for reading at desks, in bed, or in easy chairs, would be provided by plug-in lamps brought by the family who would move into 19th Street House. Wire for task lighting was pulled only to adult bedroom closets, vanities, kitchen countertops, the dining table, and several points along the circulation pathway leading from the front door to the second-floor circulation area.

Just as it had during earlier phases of work, the compact form of the house simultaneously supported dollar wisdom and environment consideration, now by allowing a number of lights to perform double duty. In the small bedrooms, likely to be occupied by children, whose sharp eyes require less light than those of older folks, the wiring for the ceiling light was placed so that it could illuminate the closet as well as provide ambient light for the entire room. Similarly, the lights above the bathroom sink and mirror would provide both task lighting and ambient light to the entire room. The recessed cans that would light the way along the circulation path would likewise do double duty by providing accents, throwing a pleasing pattern of shadow and bright across the walls and nicely illuminating photos, collectibles, or art that might be placed there. At the upper circulation area, wiring was provided for a four-lamp fixture that would be able to light all doorways and also illuminate our "church," the built-in niche we had framed into the wall opposite the stairway. Wiring for light controls was pulled to all the usual places, but with the intention that it would, wherever effective, connect not to standard flip switches or even dimmers but instead to controls that would minimize the waste that comes from leaving lights on when they are not needed.

For all lighting—ambient, task, and accent—Choo, with Ryan and me working as his helpers, pulled wire with the plan that at almost every location the light source we would eventually connect up would be a CFL, a compact fluorescent lamp. Fluorescent light was once cold and unpleasant, but by the time 19th Street House was built, CFLs were available with warmth and capacity for rendering a color tone very close to that of incandescent bulbs. They would generate a soft light that would pleasingly illuminate the surfaces I had in mind for the finishes.

The built-in systems at 19th Street House would include a frugal total of twenty-four fixtures housing a total of thirty bulbs. Total consumption of all built-in ambient, task, and accent lighting, even with every lamp on—a possibility that would be safeguarded against by the controls—would be only some 720 watts. To put it in perspective, that's just 3 percent of the wattage consumed by my earlier-mentioned, darkness-fearing friend with his 240 lamps, all using incandescent bulbs.

Thermal boundary

Experts engage in passionate arguments about the dangers of electromagnetic fields. Knowledgeable builders argue about the best choices for plumbing pipe. Specialists debate the pros and cons of differing approaches to maintaining good-quality indoor air. But these days, it would probably not be possible to find a credible voice arguing against the installation of our last item of infrastructure, a well-crafted thermal boundary. For a relatively modest investment, energy consumption will be slashed. Environmental impact will be profoundly decreased, and bills for heating and cooling will drop sharply or virtually disappear. Simultaneously, comfort will increase as indoor temperatures are stabilized. Even in a mild climate like San Pablo's, payback of the investment will occur in just a few years.

What debate there is about thermal boundaries occurs merely around the margins of the subject, such as the extent to which it is advisable to insulate and seal existing homes. Installing thermal boundaries in existing homes is much tougher than in the open wall frames of new houses or those that have been gutted for a major remodel or renovation. Installers must crawl into cramped attics and basement areas to place insulation and seal gaps. Holes must be drilled in wall surfaces, insulating material pumped in, and walls then plugged and repainted, all without disrupting the water resistance of the building skin. Coming up with procedures and materials that will yield an acceptable return on investment and not damage a house can be difficult. Return on the investment may greatly vary for substantially similar existing houses in different climates. In Montana, a thorough retrofit might yield terrific returns; in San Pablo, the energy savings might never return the dollars spent—and it may be that the dollars would return more environmental bang for the buck if they were invested otherwise.

When it comes to choices of insulating material—foam, blown-in cellulose made of recycled newspapers, fiberglass in either batt or blown-in form, or batts manufactured from recycled fabric—one expert may argue for one, a second for another. There is, also, debate about the optimal quantity of insulation to install. One building scientist argues that because super levels of insulation virtually eliminate the need for heating and cooling, it is the dollarwise and environment considerate thing to do in all cases. Another says, no, that after reaching an insulating value of R-25 (with the R indicating resistance to thermal transference through the structure and skin of a building), piling on more insulation is wasteful; you don't get enough additional performance to make the extra expenditure worthwhile.

But the choices of insulating material and the exact quantity are not the critical things. There are pros and cons to all the materials; the differences in expense for less or more quantity are minor in the context of the overall construction cost for a new or fully renovated building. What is

critical, however, is that the *installation of the insulation and sealants*, of the entire thermal boundary, be both conscientious and skillful. Insulation installation and air sealing involve the attentive filling of all framing cavities and all small gaps so that every channel through which heated or cooled air might flow and escape is closed off. That's easier said than done. Often thermal boundaries are so poorly installed that they lose 50 percent or more

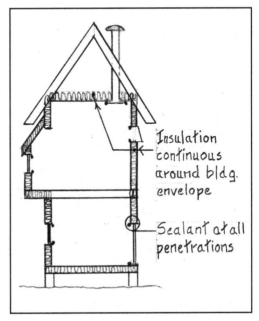

Insulation continuous around bldg. envelope

Sealant at all penetrations

of their potential effectiveness. Rick Chitwood, an insulation and energy efficiency expert headquartered near Mount Shasta, California, tells the story of ineffective work at a large vacation home he was asked to analyze by its very upset owners. Insulation in the house was installed at the R-value required by the code, and the owners assumed their mountain retreat would be reasonably energy efficient. At the end of a holiday, they returned to their primary residence, leaving the heat on at the vacation house so it would not grow moldy in the coming cold months. As winter set in, Rick got a call for help from the owners. They'd just received their latest utility bill. They were horrified. Their costs for keeping their empty house warm were rising toward $16,000 per month.

When Rick drove up to the house, he paused to enjoy the sight of an uncommonly large flock of birds on the roof, and then went inside, intending to perform his usual tests for analyzing air leakage. He was unable to; the leakage was so great his instruments could not fully register it. Puzzled, he began to explore the house, but with all the finishes in place he could not readily detect areas of poor insulation and sealing that might explain the leakage. Then it came to him. The birds! He climbed onto the roof of the house, ascended to the ridge, and placed his hand over the attic vents installed there. He could feel hot air blasting out of them, with nearly the force of a blow dryer. It was that gush of hot air that had attracted the birds to the rooftop.

Rick returned to the interior of the house, noticed that the ceilings on the upper level were wood paneled, and soon diagnosed the problem. Perhaps from bad workmanship, or perhaps because the boards had dried and shrunk, there were small gaps between the individual boards that made up the paneling. Due to normal stack effect, heated air from all levels in the house was rising toward the ceiling, passing through the gaps, and then passing through the insulation above. It was so poorly installed, with so many openings and gaps, it may as well not have been there at all.

Good thermal boundary installers place insulation so that gaps between it and the framing do not exist. They recognize exactly where to place the thermal boundary. They understand which areas of the building should be included within the boundary and which should be placed outside of it—that at 19th Street House the garage could be outside the boundary, but the chases that carried heater ducts along a wall of the garage should be included within the boundary. They know just the right materials—unfaced batts, batts with staple flanges, foam boards, spray foam, caulk, cellulose—to use at different locations as the thermal boundary moves uninterrupted from horizontal to vertical, from crawl space to wall to attic, around windows and doors, soffits and chases, architectural bays and embellishments. They know just how much foam to spray into a gap so that as it expands, it will just fill the gap but not overflow it.

As with installation of window flashings and other work that is terribly important to the performance of buildings but hidden from sight, the crafting of thermal boundaries is greatly undervalued. Did you ever hear your friends extoll their insulating contractor the way they marvel at the work of their cabinetmaker? Probably not, and it is too bad. The insulation installers should not be undervalued. Their work requires the same sort of attentiveness, organization of work flow, and precision required by cabinetmaking. The comfort of our buildings, their energy efficiency, and their impact on our environment depend, in good measure, on the craftspeople with the fiberglass, the foam, and the recycled newspaper. Personally, I'd like to see thermal boundary installers who do their job with excellence get medals, big cash prizes, and a day on *Oprah* every year. They are environmental heroes.

Good thermal boundary installers do not only install the right material with precision in all the right places. Like others who practice their craft day in and day out, like top-notch framers and paperhangers and stair builders, they work with intense focus and with startling grace, speed, and efficiency. The installer at 19th Street House, dispatched by his company when I insisted on first-class work and threatened to send packing anyone who gave me anything less, said hello in the morning, goodbye in the evening. He spoke not another word except to say, in response to a question, that he planned to retire soon, grow vegetables, and raise chickens at the little house he had long owned free and clear. Between utterances, he installed 19th Street's 3,000 square feet of thermal boundary in a day and a morning, near perfectly, working alone.

It was time to install the finishes and fixtures. Our house would then be ready for transformation into a home.

COMPLETION

In most houses, whether they are at the affordable end of the price spectrum or trophy homes costing their owners $500 a square foot to design and build, it is the drywall, or "sheetrock," covering the ceilings and walls that is the most visually dominant element. The four foot by eight foot panels coated with "drywall compound" occupy over half of the visible interior surface of a just-completed house. Yet drywallers who produce excellent work, both the hangers who fit the panels to the ceilings and walls and the finishers who coat and texture them, are rare. I have found only two in my entire career, and not for lack of looking. To find the second one, the man who would do the work at 19th Street House, all I had to do was look up. There he was one afternoon, tall and sturdy with a brilliant white smile on his brown face, leaning against the fence running along the southern boundary of the lot, watching closely as Dave Kendall, Ryan, Grant, and I constructed the foundation forms.

His name is Morris Knight. Morris and his wife and their two sons, just finishing high school and preparing to begin college at the time I was starting to build 19th Street House, live in the house next door. Morris is, in fact, a general building contractor himself, specializing in kitchen and other remodel work. As 19th Street House progressed, he would often come over to study our green simple methods and architonic detail. Morris had not come up an easy path to home ownership, a successful marriage, two boys bound for college, and a growing building business of his own. He had grown up in a public housing project. But his mom did not let him keep bad company. She had a rule: any bad grades, any bad behavior equals no football. She taught Morris to "get with the positive people. You live in the projects, but you don't have to act like you come from the projects. Treat people with respect and expect respect; you will get it." Morris made those words his motto.

After high school, he took up drywall work, finding his way to crews that did the highest quality installation. For years he did the work of a hanger—measuring, cutting, and installing the heavy 4x8 panels. But as he got older, he realized his body would take the physical punishment only for so long. He moved over to becoming a finisher and learned to perform the work of taping, coating, and texturing drywall with exceptional skill. He told me about his premier projects, among them the domed ceiling of a tony new restaurant by the San Francisco Bay. The builder had planned to plaster it. But the plasters could not consistently hold their material to the dome's radius. Morris took over, cutting and fitting his drywall to conform to the domed shape, then taping and coating it to achieve a smooth surface. I have sat underneath the dome. To my critical eye, it appears perfect, a soft blue flowing form with its radius continuous and even at every point. By the time we met at 19th Street, Morris was moving on from drywall and focusing on development of his remodel business. But he was willing to take on the drywall work at 19th Street House. I felt lucky again.

Level five

A drywall job begins with the selection of the wallboard panels—the half inch thick product that is most widely used or fire resistant five-eighths inch thick material. For 19th Street House, I chose five-eighths board. Its measly additional eighth inch of thickness makes a startling difference. For in addition to being thicker, the five-eighths product is also heavier by roughly a third. A wall clad with five-eighths material feels far stouter. By contrast, a wall clad with half inch material feels flimsy. In fact, it is so weak, its use is not even allowed with the two feet on-center frugal framing employed for 19th Street House. Strike five-eighths wallboard with your hand or lean against it and you encounter solid resistance. Don't strike half inch too hard; you will punch right through it. Five-eighths is so sturdy, it even adds to the structural strength of a house. And because of its greater mass and correspondingly greater ability to block sound waves, it quiets a house—particularly important in a compact place like 19th Street House. When the house was completed, a person standing in the living room had to shout to get the attention of someone in an upstairs bedroom, though no special acoustic materials were installed.

For all the benefits it imparts, moving up to five-eighths from half inch wallboard costs only a nickel per square foot of drywall, or roughly thirty bucks per room. At 19th Street House, that translated into a one-tenth of 1 percent increase in total project cost. Or to put it another way, the choice of five-eighths would increase the monthly mortgage for a new owner of 19th Street House by an amount about equal to the cost of a single cup of coffee—and that's regular or decaf at the corner bakery, not one of those creamy confections those candy stores disguised as coffee houses sell you.

With the five-eighths wallboard screwed to the wall and ceiling frames, a drywall job is only a quarter completed, in terms of both time and dollars. Now the wallboard must be finished, the joints taped, the entire surface then coated with compound. The quality of the finish work, accomplished by applying the tape and then the multiple layers of joint compound with large blades shaped something like giant versions of a cook's spatula, or with specialized "bazookas" and "boxes" that speed the work along, can either extend or compromise the quality of the underlying wallboard. Poorly finished, the drywall's expansive surface will degrade the interior of any house. On the other hand, skillfully finished drywall can lend a touch of class to even a moderate-cost home.

At the bottom end of the range of drywall finishes is skip-trowel work, achieved by loading up a long finish blade with drywall compound mixed with sand and skipping it lightly across the surface of the walls and ceilings. Produced by lower-skilled drywall finish crews, skip-trowel looks and feels crude—lumpy, bumpy, and crusty. Better craftspeople can get a better result. But they can also put aside their knives and take a step up, usually at no additional cost, to produce a blown-on texture called "orange peel" for its resemblance to the dimpled surface of an orange. A really skilled drywall finisher with a superbly light touch can achieve an orange peel finish so delicate it is hardly more prominent than the light stipple left by a paint roller.

That is what Morris Knight produced at my request in most of the rooms at 19th Street House. His work is so good it looks virtually smooth from just a few feet away. Yet I have second-guessed my choice ever since making it. For up another notch from a delicate orange peel, we find the highest-grade drywall finish of all. In the trade, we call it "level five" for the five coats of finishing compound that are applied over the entire surface of the walls and ceilings and repeatedly sanded until the walls are silken smooth. Produced by a craftsperson of Morris's capability and painted with equal skill, level five resembles a high-quality plaster job such as one sees in the best houses built during the first half of the

twentieth century. It imparts elegance to an interior space, quietly creating the impression that you are in a house put together by a skilled builder.

All that quality does not come cheap, of course. At 19th Street House, though Morris was charging me neighborly rates ("It's a short commute to the job," he explained), level five throughout the house would have cost roughly $1,500 dollars extra. As I made my final decision about drywall finish, I calculated that those dollars were not in the budget, or that if they were spent for the drywall, I would have to take them away from some other important completion item. But now that the house is built and lived in, I wonder if I should have taken yet fuller advantage of Morris's skills and spent those extra dollars even if it meant going over budget. The walls would have been handsome indeed. The expenditure would have resulted in only a half percent increase in my costs for creating the house, or an eventual additional mortgage payment equivalent to about the cost of a cup of regular coffee with a donut per week.

I have wondered if in holding back from level five, I might have made a mistake that I have often cautioned clients against. At the completion phase of a project, I tell them, one has to guard against impulsively tightening down on a cost here and there. Understandably, you will feel tempted. Construction is stressfully expensive. As you near the end of a project, you may already have encountered some unexpected costs. You may have dug deep into your contingency funds. The cuts you are making may seem attractive in terms of the dollars saved. But for the sake of just a tiny percentage of your investment, you risk sacrificing a really substantial architonic outcome and much of the daily satisfaction you might derive from your home.

Continuity and whimsy

Certain areas of a drywall installation are visually critical, among them the corners where two walls meet. Inside corners must be finished to form a straight line. If they are wobbly, you know you are looking at the work of a finisher not fully competent with the tools. Outside corners likewise must be straight, and their form very much determines the personality of a house. A crisp modernist design will typically call for sharp ninety degree outside corners. For 19th Street House, I asked Morris to install bullnose corners.

The bullnose corners represented a first step in continuing the softened craftsman look I had chosen for the exterior of the house into its interior. To my aesthetic sensibility, continuity is a critical architonic value on the visual side of things. I am not able to appreciate what my wife calls "minestrone gardens," those featuring a variety of plants, all interesting, but planted willy-nilly with no eye toward patterning of their shapes and sizes. I am put off by buildings composed of attractive details that seem, however, to have been crafted by a series of designers totally unaware of or indifferent to what the others are producing, or what exists in the surrounding neighborhood. I do not enjoy neighborhoods in my own town where each house is designed by a different person eager to exercise his or her originality without regard for the neighborhood's character. While much talent is on display, the overall effect, with the lack of connection from one building to the next, is chaos. The neighborhoods feel scrambled and uninviting. At the same time, I admire the architects I have worked with whose designs fit so gracefully into their surrounding traditional neighborhoods, you do not realize that the houses have been entirely transformed. That's why I chose a gable roof for 19th Street House. Even though a hip roof might have been more elegant, the gable roof fell in with the existing rhythm of the street.

Visual continuity, it seems to me, is especially important in a compact place like 19th Street House where one room is likely to be visible from and contribute to the visual experience of another. Supporting continuity, I favor simplicity. I have built and seen houses designed by imaginative but egotistical architects who felt compelled to imprint every surface with evidence that they had, with all the force of their being, *been there*. My clients have seemed happy with their homes, but to my mind, all the powerfully designed form dominates the space to the point they seem like visitors in their own houses.

At 19th Street House, a straightforward place to begin with, strong details are limited to one or two in each interior space. In the bedrooms, it is the clear pine trim of the windows and in the dining room the triple window spanning the south wall. Only at the stairway and landings, a space that I imagined would not come in for much imprinting by future owners, did I allow myself to get more carried away, building in the pair of tall windows, the solar tube, the "church niche," and a prominent rail and balustrade of Douglas fir and copper.

Ryan and I were the carpentry crew now. Grant had taken off for New Zealand. He sent us photos of his bungalow, sitting at the high end of a meadow, looking down to a beach and the Pacific Ocean. But he didn't sound pleased. The Kiwi carpenters he had signed on with put in short weeks, took half-hour tea breaks, and an hour for lunch. Their work ethic did not suit Grant's hard-driving style. I thought he would rather be working with Ryan and me as we turned our attention to the interior finish carpentry, standing up sawhorses in the garage, stacking long lengths of poplar across them, pulling out our routers, inserting roundover bits, and getting to work. Soon the garage slab was covered with tiny white shavings, and the air was filled with the fresh scent of newly milled lumber. Along the edge of each poplar board, we had carved a smaller bullnose to complement the large bullnose of the drywall corners. Moving the poplar into the house, we cut and nailed it in place—1x3 boards for door casings, 1x4 for upper level baseboard, and 1x6 for the first-floor base.

True, poplar does cost more than the skimpy molded trim available in lumberyards or the big-box supply houses, but only about fifty bucks more per room for 19th Street House; or for the whole house, to continue with our coffee cup accounting, about two cups' worth at monthly mortgage payment time. But poplar is solid lumber, tough and dense. It does not off gas as do the cheap moldings made from

particles of wood bonded together with resin. It resists impact much better than soft pine moldings. It paints out beautifully, smoothly. It is a full three-quarter inches or even an inch thick right off the lumberyard rack. In a way that the skimpy trim cannot, its heft visually anchors a wall to a floor and a door to a wall.

Poplar trim was included in even the early drawings for 19th Street House. But not all the details that Ryan and I would construct were so premeditated. When it came time to build the open balustrade at the lower end of the stairs, that as you may recall from Chapter Five, a friend suggested as a way of increasing the sense of spaciousness in the entry parlor, I had as yet made no drawing. I stepped into the backyard. I pulled away the tarp covering all the neatly stacked leftovers from framing and infrastructure construction. There lay a few cutoffs from the clean, straight 2x6s we had used to frame walls, and a 2x4 figured with a rich black and brown burl at one end. There were short lengths of copper pipe remaining from the water supply lines to the kitchens and baths. Somehow, these remnants configured themselves in my imagination into the form of a stair rail, with the wood milled to continue the softened craftsman look. I sketched it on the back of a scrap of drywall, and soon enough the remnants of lumber and pipe became a bit of functional sculpture that caught your eye as you entered the front door. Visitors, I noticed, were drawn to it. And honestly, I was tickled that I could spontaneously craft something so pretty from a pile of leftovers.

Flat-pak cabinetry

As we installed trim, stair rails, and other finish carpentry items, Ryan and I kept an eye on environment consideration and on health along with architonic detail and dollar wisdom. We minimized waste. We recycled scrap or put it to use as pantry shelves or trim inside of bedroom closets. We used poplar for our baseboards and casings, not only for its quality and workability, but also because it is a fast-growing species that can rapidly produce large quantities of lumber and thereby spare forests of slower-growing species like Douglas fir.

Something needs to be said, however, about the extent of environmental benefit we were able to deliver during finish carpentry and, for that matter, the entire completion phase of the house. The benefits were marginal at best. At 19th Street House, as is the case at virtually all houses, opportunities to "green" the project during completion were small potatoes compared with the opportunities that had come during the earlier installation of structure and infrastructure. The reason is simple. The quantity of material used (and, therefore, the energy expended to extract, manufacture, and transport it) during completion is dwarfed by the quantities used earlier. All completion materials for 19th Street House could easily be carried in two or three pickup trucks. Material for the earlier work of building the foundation, frame, skin, and infrastructure, in contrast, required half a dozen large flatbeds and concrete trucks, not to mention the heavy equipment necessary to put it into place. To the extent there are substantial environmental benefits to be contributed during completion, they come not from the construction itself, but from the choice of devices such as low-flow shower heads that will affect later operating impacts.

After trim was nailed in place, I found myself at the next stage of finish work with limited opportunity to exercise environment consideration. Now it was not just the small amount of material involved that limited opportunity. I also faced, for the first time since the choice of Forest Stewardship Council certified (FSC) lumber, a conflict between dollar wisdom and environment consideration. This time it was much sharper. For when it came time to order cabinets, the more environment considerate option proved to be substantially more costly. I had wanted cabinets made with FSC wood products. But they

were available to me only from expensive custom shops or high-end manufacturers. Their charges would have amounted to a tenth or more of my entire budget for the construction of 19th Street House. I couldn't swing it. On the other hand, the cabinet option that would hold down costs while keeping quality up, a so-called "flat-pak" system, was not available to me in FSC material.

Flat-pak cabinet systems arrive at a job site

not assembled into boxes with doors, shelves, and drawers installed, but as a stack of components packed flat on a pallet. Big-box suppliers and a host of storefront countertop and cabinet emporiums offer shabby imported versions of flat-paks. But a number of small manufacturers around the country offer flat-paks of high quality. For a fifth the cost of fully assembled and finished cabinets, a manufacturer two hours' drive from 19ᵗʰ Street delivered top-quality components for every bath and kitchen cabinet in the house.

Modern cabinets have three basic sets of components: The *boxes* (or carcasses as cabinetmakers prettily call them) together with the shelves and drawers they contain. The *doors*. And the *hardware* including drawer slides, shelf slides, and the marvelous Euro-style door hinges capable of opening from ninety to 180 degrees and adjustable in four directions to facilitate door alignment. The hardware delivered with my flat-pak was sturdy; the slides were of the full-extension type so that the drawers and shelves could be pulled out all the way and their contents easily accessed. The carcasses were made with a high grade of three-quarter inch maple plywood, beautifully sealed and clear coated. The doors, a simple frame and panel design with edges eased to complement the softened craftsman detailing used throughout the house, were virtually perfect. And while the components were not FSC, the plywood used for the components was manufactured with relatively benign resins and water

based finishes. While they used part of a tree harvested in an environmentally brutal fashion, they would not damage the respiratory systems of any children exposed to them.

Unlike other materials (such as certain types of advanced particle board used even in costly cabinetry), the plywood would release little in the way of formaldehyde or other deadly volatile organic compounds (VOCs) that would have compromised the air quality in the kitchen and dining space. That was critical. Opportunity for environment consideration may be limited during the completion phase of house building. But completion is also the time when health protection comes to the fore. By eliminating toxic materials from the interior finish surfaces, a builder exercises his or her best opportunity to protect the health of the people who will come to live in the house.

Flooring matters

With cabinets in place, the next of three major opportunities to eliminate toxics from the interior finish came with flooring selection and installation. Materials for flooring should be free of toxic substances embedded during manufacture. Simultaneously, flooring poses an architonic challenge. Different areas of a house require different flooring. But if the appearance of the floorings is not coordinated, the house can acquire a jarringly patchy look. Variety is necessary, and can be pleasing if managed properly. Continuity is essential (at least to my sensibility).

At 19th Street House, flooring installation began in the entry parlor with tongue-and-groove bamboo coated with a tough, non-offgassing clear finish. It satisfied the architonic and health requirements and also, at least for the short term, the dollar requirements of the pyramid. It may be good, too, for the environmental piece. In fact, bamboo, a rapidly renewing resource, has gained nearly iconic status as a green building material. I am, however, not confident that it represents much of an advance, if any, over other wood flooring.

The early generations of bamboo flooring did not stand up well. It remains to be seen whether the later versions, touted by their vendors as much tougher, do better. Should bamboo floors end up thrashed, trashed, and replaced at high frequencies, they will turn out to be of dubious environmental benefit when one takes into account the impacts not only of growing but of harvesting, processing, and transporting the material, typically across China and then the Pacific Ocean. For it is very heavy stuff. A question arises: if flooring made from a slow-growing oak tree (like the planking in my living room, which is in excellent shape after seventy years of service) will last five to ten times as long, does the bamboo product really offer environmental benefit? Any certain answer would be found in the murky depths of an involved life cycle cost analysis. But I would place my intuitive bet on the oak.

Moving from the entry parlor through the archway and into the kitchen and dining space, I installed flooring of uncontestable durability: tile. Properly laid, tile can hold up for many decades. Tile can be pricey, but it can also be had for a modest cost. In fact, installed costs for the various flooring choices at 19ᵗʰ Street House—tile, bamboo, and a third choice yet to come—were all in the same moderate range, roughly five dollars per square foot. Over the long haul, all tile needs for maintenance is sweeping, wet mopping, and maybe once a decade or so, a bit of grout touch-up. Tile is consistent, as well, with the maintenance of healthy indoor air. Low toxicity backer boards and mortars are available for tile installation. But even if standard substrates and mortars

are employed, with proper installation of the tile the off-gasses can be largely sealed off. And, of course, while there is a lot of bland looking product on the market, tiles available at smaller supply houses can be uncommonly beautiful.

For 19ᵗʰ Street House, Sandra and I chose a floor tile that was predominantly a muted red in color, but with a strong marbling of creamy yellow that tied it nicely to the caramelized blond of the bamboo. Partly for the sake of continuing our softened craftsman look, we used tile for countertops as well, selecting a large tile of complementary color. Notwithstanding its tremendous durability, beauty, and potentially low cost, tile has fallen out of favor for countertops. It has been pushed aside by cheap granite, attractive plastic laminates, concrete, tops made of recycled glass or even paper, wood, or stainless steel.

The main objection to tile countertops seems to be that cleaning the grout joints is a hassle. At 19th Street House, we were able to eliminate the difficulty. Using a very large tile, laying it diagonally and with only one-eighth inch grout lines, we kept the grout down to around 1 percent of the total area. The result is a surface that is easy to clean. And, I don't mind bragging, it has been a big hit with certain of the neighbor ladies who have visited the house. They seem to find it much more appealing than yet another glossy granite slab. As one architectural critic notes, granite has become the ultimate cliché, with cheap stone glued atop the cabinets in every jerrybuilt, so-called "luxury" condo complex. Installation included, the tile countertop cost me roughly the same as I would have paid for high-quality plastic laminate, but it will outlast a plastic top by many decades.

For the stairway and for the flooring at the upper level, I chose carpet. A brown Berber flecked with tan and gold that ties it visually to both the bamboo and the tile, the carpet is the most controversial of

any material used at 19th Street House. Standard broadloom carpet, the stuff that arrives at a house in huge rolls, has architonic strengths. It can be pleasing visually, to the touch (people like padding around on the plush pile), and auditorily, for it quiets the sound of footsteps. But at every other point of the pyramid,

broadloom earns "Fs." Though recently some headway has been made at recycling the petroleum-based synthetics (of which standard broadloom is made) into new carpet, tile backer board, and even exterior wall sheathing among other things, it largely goes into the landfill, and at a staggering rate. In apartment buildings, carpet gets pulled, dumped, and replaced on average around every three years. Even in occupant owned houses, carpet is removed and replaced roughly every eight years on average. It is estimated that in the United States we throw away enough each year to carpet over an area greater than that of New York City.

Once installed in homes, carpet, even wool carpet, often touted as healthy because it off-gasses less than synthetics, becomes a silent, severe health hazard. Carpet, as John Bower nicely puts it in *The Healthy House*, "stores a huge quantity of filth" including mold, dust mites, and all manner of nasty stuff trafficked in from the yard and street. Attempts to clean the carpet can just make matters worse. Wet cleaning can stimulate mold growth. Dry cleaning can pump in additional unhealthy dust. Vacuuming with standard equipment simply pulls the toxic materials from the carpet and exhausts the finer particles right back into the air. When children play on the carpet, they stir up and immerse themselves in a cloud of pollutants.

Even as it stores and breeds toxics, standard broadloom carpet and the padding over which it is typically installed steadily releases a variety of deadly volatile organic compounds (VOCs) to the indoor air. When I was researching carpet I obtained a small sample of carpet pad, held it to my face and breathed in deeply. Immediately I was hit with a sharp headache.

And yet I chose carpet for the stairway, upper circulation area, and bedrooms at 19th Street House. I had a good reason. I felt the compact house needed the quieter floor surface. I did not want footsteps of people padding around upstairs to be heard below. Fortunately, I was able to get the quieting effect of carpet without building in the environment and health problems inherent in broadloom carpet, for in recent years a new form of carpet has become available for residential use. That is carpet manufactured not in huge rolls but in tiles, each about three square feet in size.

Though substantially more costly than the lowest grades of broadloom, carpet tile is comparable in price to other decent quality flooring products and has promising environmental and health characteristics. Carpet tile is available that (if the manufacturer's claims are to be believed) releases virtually no VOCs. With little effort it can be recycled entirely into new carpet. One manufacturer even provides preaddressed mailing labels so that you can send worn-out tiles back to the factory. Carpet tiles need no pad but are applied directly to the subfloor, whether wood or concrete, with a water-based and benign (if the manufacturer's claims are true) adhesive that becomes tacky but never fully dries. If you spill coffee on a tile, you pull it up, rinse it, let it dry, and pop it back into place. The adhesive will both release and re-adhere the tile. If a few tiles become stained or worn out, you simply swap them out for others.

Carpet tile is far less prone to harbor toxics than standard carpet with a pad. Each tile consists of a layer of fabric applied over a dense rubberlike backing, which is adhered directly to the floor. Stopped by the backing, dirt cannot penetrate deeply into the carpet, and is more easily pulled out by a vacuum. At 19th Street House, dirt that does accumulate in the Berber weave will be sucked up and expelled outside the house by the powerful central vacuum cleaner for which we had run pipe during infrastructure installation. In fact, my decision to install carpet was made together with the decision to install the central vac. Without it, I would have chosen another flooring, fearful that even carpet tile might have adverse health effects on children who came to live in the house.

As always, alas, there's no free lunch here. Even with carpet tile, there is a downside that accompanies the benefits. Mostly it is architonic. Not everyone likes the feel or look of carpet tile, for while the tiles blend together, some seams do show. Jim, who shot the photos of finish work for this book, also helped install the carpet tile at 19th Street House. Like me, he feels good that two old-time carpenters, using our framing hammers and flat bars to nudge tiles tightly together, were able to do a respectable job of the installation. But he absolutely will not consider carpet tile for replacing the worn-out broadloom in his own place, though I urge him to consider the health benefits. He likes to pad around on the plusher stuff, and to hell with the clouds of poisonous particulates his feet might stir up.

An architect friend sniffs at the sight of the 19th Street House carpet tiles, "that trailer trash rug." Sandra does not like the look, either. "Too commercial," she says, and she is not moved by the fact that Martha Stewart, the doyenne of domesticity, promotes a line of carpet tiles. In the past, products initially used in commercial and industrial buildings— metal windows, steel roofs, commercial stoves—have made their way onto the accepted palette for residential construction. Designers into greening their projects are now specifying carpet tile for houses. Perhaps one day carpet tile, too, will strike people not as commercial but as just another of

the many residential alternatives.

For the painting of the interior, the third of the large opportunities to protect health, Sandra chose a lovely color, aptly named "Calm Cream." Available in a formulation touted as producing virtually no off-gasses, it nicely extended the softened craftsman finishes. I had imagined painting selected walls with contrast colors. In San Pablo, a festivity of reds, yellows, avocado and sage greens, blues, lavender, peach, and even orange sherbet has spread across building exteriors. The color relieves drabness on foggy days and adds to the cheer of sunlit days. I had imagined extending strong color to the interior of my house. Yet I ended up with no contrast walls. As I installed cabinet knobs, door handles, and towel bars, and otherwise puttered along at the last of the completion work, I came to favor the uninterrupted Calm Cream. I liked the way it unified the house, flowing across walls and through doorways from room to room. It is, well, calming. It enhances the peace of mind that settles in when you near the completion of a house and neighbors are coming over to look and saying "real nice," and you are feeling you did okay.

Contraption connection and the combi-system

Now, with 19th Street House nearly ready for occupancy, it was time to connect the array of contraptions (the *"contrivances, gadgets, devices (you) don't quite understand,"* Webster's) with which we Americans outfit our homes. With contraption connection comes a chance to capitalize on and extend the possibilities for energy efficiency built into infrastructure. Good dishwashers operated properly—namely when they are full, not containing just two coffee cups and a cereal bowl or even just a half load—can be remarkably efficient. Only persons with the greatest motivation and talent for conserving resources will be able to hand wash dishes, utensils, and cookware using less water and energy than an efficient dishwasher, even taking into account the energy embedded in the machine in the course of material extraction, manufacture, transport, and installation. Yes, the question has been researched. Building scientists have pitted teams of hand washers and machine washers against one another. The machine washers win. It's like computers playing chess blowing away all the opposition other than the grandmasters, and even they struggle.

With clothes washers the opportunities get better yet. Front loading clothes washers reduce water and energy use by a whopping two-thirds relative to the earlier generation of top loaders. They use so little soap, claims Alex Wilson, the respected researcher of "green" products, that savings on soap alone, over the life of the machine, makes up a large fraction of the extra cost of a front loader relative to a top loader. As a bonus, because they gently tumble rather than bash away at clothes with big rubber paddles as top loaders do, front loaders are far easier on fabrics. If you wash your clothes in a front loader, they will last much longer. Assuming no costly maintenance and good durability—a somewhat worrisome assumption since front loaders have computers on board and more complex gaskets and seals—they are strong at both the environment consideration and dollar wisdom points of the pyramid. Though it may be a taste peculiar to a builder who finds beauty in well-designed tools and machines, I find them handsome as well. I installed a high-quality front loader in the laundry room and left it visible rather than curtaining it off with a bifold door.

With the choice of heating devices I came to another high-value opportunity, though I was led to it by an unexpected circumstance. The conventional choice for a heating system at a house like 19th Street, built for a modest budget, would have been a forced air furnace with a natural gas or oil burner. But as it turned out, even the smallest forced air furnace available, given 19th Street House's strong thermal boundary and its capacity for gathering warmth from the sun through its south-facing windows, would put out several times more heat than the house required.

Purchase and installation of an oversized forced air furnace would have wasted dollars and needlessly impacted the environment. In addition to costing more and incorporating more material and embedded energy than necessary, it would wear out more quickly than an appropriately sized smaller unit. Forced air furnaces are most durable and also most efficient when they run at steady rates for prolonged periods—just as a car is most fuel efficient when driven along at a steady speed rather than stopping and starting constantly. Oversized forced air furnaces tend to heat houses with powerful but short blasts of air, shut off, then blast away again, wearing themselves out, wasting fuel, and irritating the people living in the house. George Nesbitt, 19th Street's resident house-is-a-system master, proposed a different solution. Take advantage of the house's low need for heat, he suggested, by going to a different technology—one that will give you a smaller and more appropriately sized heater and do double duty as a space and water heater—in short, a "combi-system." Because combination space/water heating systems were just beginning to be manufactured and marketed and were still very costly if purchased off the shelf, George designed and built a low-cost combi-system right on site. George's system combines two simple contraptions: an efficient (though at my insistence not an ultraefficient and ultraexpensive) tank-type water heater and a metal box that at a glance looks very much like a conventional forced air space heater. The metal box, however, while it houses a fan, contains no gas burner. In place of the burner is a coil of copper pipe that is connected to a supply line from the water heater.

On cold, overcast mornings when there is not enough sun coming through the south-facing windows to warm the house, a thermostat at the second-story landing signals a need for heat. A valve between the water heater and space heater responds to the signal and opens. Hot water flows from the water heater and through the coil inside the air handler. The fan activates, pushing air across the coil so that (Second Law of Thermodynamics at work again) heat is transferred from the hot water to the cooler air, warming it before the fan pushes it out through a system of ducts to the rooms.

Our combi-system supports energy efficiency in a number of ways. It uses a modest-sized water heater, one with fifty gallons of capacity, a choice that entailed a dicey ethical decision on my part. By choosing the fifty gallon unit over a sixty to eighty gallon tank, I took it on myself to deliberately limit the amount of hot water the inhabitants of the house could consume, thereby limiting the amount of damage they could inflict on the environment and on their pocketbooks. With the small tank I selected, if family members take very long showers, they may deprive others of their showers. They may even make it impossible to heat the house for an hour or two until the tank heats a new supply of water. Who am I to impose that choice on them? I have yet to come up with an answer that would make me look good in print (reader suggestions are welcome).

Additionally, because our combi-system is not oversized (or not by much; even the smallest combi-system components available still had more capacity for space heating than 19th Street House actually requires), and because the fan is programmed to operate at a low speed, the air handler side of the combi-system operates at a steady rate rather than cycling on and off. It is also likely that because it does not incorporate a burner of its own, the air handler side of the system will enjoy a long life. In my experience with standard forced air furnaces, it is the burners that go first. When the burners fail, the whole contraption gets tossed, though the controls, fan, and metal box may have much useful life left in them. Lacking a burner, the 19th Street House air handler has a shot at serving for a very long time—especially because the air handler, as we shall see, is called upon to do precious little work each winter. It offers an architonic benefit as well. As a small unit functioning at low fan speed, it is very quiet. Inside the rooms you must listen carefully to know it is operating, so gently does air flow from the registers.

Contraptions not constructed and why

Three years after I had first conceived the idea of crafting a considerate house and writing a book about the journey, and seven months of work from the day Bull's Eye drilled our pier holes, we were closing in on final completion at 19th Street House. Low-flow plumbing fixtures were set. Efficient lighting systems were connected to the wiring, and efficient light sources screwed or clipped into the systems. To the extent I was able, I had made it impossible for occupants to leave lights on when they were not needed. In the bedroom closets and the kitchen pantry, timers rather than standard flip switches controlled the lights. Turn a timer's dial, the light comes on. Select your clothing, or a can of soup, and the timer switches the light off. In the kitchen, the switches incorporate motion sensors. You switch the light on, but if you leave the kitchen or stand motionless as a statue for a few minutes, the sensor—sensing that no further activity is taking place in its space—douses the light.

Motion sensors likewise control the bathroom light and fan. Both shut off automatically when you leave the bathroom—unless humidity levels are high. Then a device called a humidistat set alongside the fan overrides the motion sensor and keeps the fan running until the humidity level in the bathroom is reduced to acceptable levels. If you take a shower, then leave the bathroom and absent mindedly switch off the fan though the room is still choked with steam, the humidistat will turn the fan back on. It will keep the fan running until damp air has been exhausted to below the level at which it would foster the growth of mold or damage finish surfaces.

Certain devices are notable not for their contribution to resource efficiency at 19th Street House, but for their *absence* from the project, to the surprise of certain friends. When I had first begun to conceptualize my considerate house and to tell people about it, no one ever suggested a small footprint, compact interior volumes with strictly limited circulation areas, south-facing windows, pier and grade beam foundations, frugal framing, structured plumbing®, double duty lighting sources, a high-quality thermal boundary, tight ductwork and an appropriately sized heat source, ceramic and carpet tile surfaces, or other green simple and dollarwise strategies I actually used. Rather, they would nod in recognition of my intentions and tell me that I would be employing green roofs, hay bales, tankless (on demand) water heaters, and photovoltaic panels (PV) to generate electricity atop the roof.

Just as hay bales and rooftop gardens play no role at 19th Street House, neither do on-demand water heaters and PV panels. In the public's sensibility, these contraptions (and other elaborate devices like them) have come to be heavily associated with so-called green house building. They should not be. If anything, their popularity and prestige suggest the unfortunate degree to which we have become diverted from astute, frugal (not wasteful) use of our dollars for maximal resource conservation and efficiency to a shopping spree for expensive, cool gadgetry. Taking a hard look at those gadgets might help us resist a drift into green consumerism and the squandering of our wealth that goes with it.

To begin with on-demand water heaters: they do offer one benefit. Roughly the size of an orange crate, they occupy less space than tank heaters and can be mounted on the exterior of a house as well as on the interior, freeing up space for a closet, as in the drawing on the following page. Saving a bit of space can save the material, labor, and energy used to construct and maintain it. The claim of on-demand heaters to green status rests primarily, however, not on the space saving possibility but on the way they use energy. First, they do not store hot water in a tank where it is constantly losing heat and energy into the surrounding air.

Second, unlike tank heaters, they do not have a pilot light. They burn fuel only when hot water is called for by the opening of a hot water faucet.

Sounds good, right? But a closer look at on-demand water heaters reveals enthusiasm for them to be an instance of that single column accounting we so often commit in our quest for green solutions. In our delighted acceptance of the pluses—pushed at us hard by the manufacturers and by plumbers in the business of selling and installing the contraptions—we have forgotten to ask about the minus column.

Minuses there are. On-demand gas units—which for the sake of brevity I will focus on here, leaving the electric units aside—require larger gas lines from the street to the house. They require their own electrical circuit; tank heaters require none. They use electricity not only when they are heating water, but on a 24/7 standby basis. The consumption of that electricity is left out of the figures that manufacturers use to pitch the efficiency of on-demand units.

Also questionable, the durability of the on-demand heaters. The high frequency with which they are turned on and off, and that is

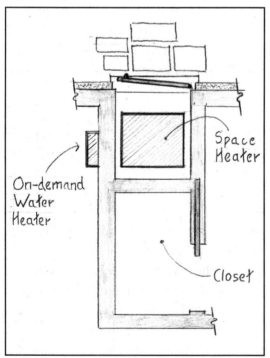

every time that hot water is required, subjects their metal components to repeated expansion and contraction and the risk of fatigue and failure. Unlike tank units, which will survive without the simple maintenance they ideally will receive, on-demand water heaters require costly expert maintenance, and will fail without it in half a dozen years. When an on-demand unit first fires up, cold water is running through it. That cold water, along with the energy used to gather it and deliver it to the tap and take it away, is wasted before the on-demand unit raises the water temperature to a satisfactory level. Even with this long list, I do not cover all the ways these machines peddled to us as green can waste resources and damage the environment. Readers eager to explore their technical deficiencies more exhaustively will find what they crave in Gary Klein's articles (see Resources.)

Here I will mention an additional problem: on-demand water heaters do not exist in a separate reality of their own. As with all technologies, their impact derives from the way humans actually use them. And there's the rub. While the on-demand contraptions don't start using gas until a person wanting to wash up or shower opens a tap, they also do not turn *off* until that person closes the tap. As a result, they can increase rather than lower energy consumption. The endless supply of hot water they will produce (in contrast to a tank heater, which simply empties of hot water, fills up with cold, and takes a long time to heat it) can tempt us into prodigious use.

Some years back as I was making my first naive attempts to raise the level of environment consideration in my building work, I fell for my plumber's pitch for on-demand water heaters and installed one in a client's home. Immediately, to my horror, her energy bill shot up. Why? *Why?* A bit of detective work turned up the answer. My client's son and his girlfriend had arrived home from college for spring vacation soon after the installation of the on-demand device. Each morning, my client headed off to work. Arising later, the young lovers popped into the shower. And there they discovered that at Mom's house, unlike in their dorm back at the college, hot water never ran out. Delighted, they stayed in the shower a long while. By my best guesstimate, they stayed in the shower until about lunchtime, probably a very late lunchtime. I have heard other such accounts about families with good intentions retrofitting their houses with on-demand heaters, typically at a cost of several thousand dollars and much environmental impact, only to find that their energy bills went up, not down as a result.

Photovoltaic fantasy?

Even more than on-demand water heaters, the generation of electrical power from sunlight finds favor in the "green" building movement, and for good reason—up to a point. Installing sun power plants atop big-box stores, apartment buildings, and office towers appears to have more pluses than minuses. It probably makes sense to gather sun power with rooftop photovoltaic panels (PV) at a single family home that also houses an electricity hungry business, such as that of my neighbor who turns out wood products in his basement. It might make sense for single family homes in general in those areas of the United States that experience a much hotter climate than we do in the Bay Area. (My best guess is that it will not when other options are weighed, but serious number crunching on a case-by-case basis is necessary—and I won't attempt it here).

But at 19th Street House and single family houses built in similar mild climates, PV does not compute. There are better ways to spend our money, both for environmental and financial return, than on the elaborate PV panels and the even more elaborate controls, typically installed in the garage, which they require. Green simple proves out over Hummer green—again! Reducing consumption of resources while maintaining comfort trumps the adding on of yet more maintenance-demanding contraptions.

Need numbers? Please consider the case of Berkeley, California, a town eager to prove its "greenness," located a few miles from San Pablo and the 19th Street House. Berkeley has proposed granting twenty year loans to citizens willing to install PV at their homes. The combined cost of the loans, planned taxpayer subsidies of the program, and maintenance of the PV systems after they are installed will run to roughly $250 per month. With minor changes in homeowner behavior and installation of energy efficient devices and fixtures, however, electricity costs can be reduced to a small fraction of the $250. And that raises the question: why spend $300 a month of a homeowner's and the taxpayers' money when, with a far smaller investment, you can reduce bills to much less?

How much less can it be? In our home, located between San Pablo and Berkeley, my wife and I have shaved our electrical use to less than two kilowatt-hours a day per person, or fourteen dollars a month for the two of us in a state where electrical rates are about one-third above the national average. Of course, when it comes to minimizing electricity cost, we do have an advantage over friends in other areas of the country who, either because of climate conditions or because they have not retrofitted their homes for efficiency, require air conditioners, dehumidifiers, electrical stoves, or other electricity gobblers.

Still, we have taken no heroic measures. We are not into self-abnegation or suffering for the sake of the planet. We have more or less the usual array of contraptions from a refrigerator to computers, a DVD player, and a host of appliances. To lower consumption without compromising comfort, we have simply pecked away at it, lowering our use of electricity one small increment at a time. When an appliance or other device wears out, we replace it with a more efficient one. Our new washing machine is an energy sipping front loader. Our light sources are nearly all CFLs. While we don't yet have motion sensors and timers, we have gotten ourselves in the habit of turning off lights, computers, and other electrical contraptions when they are not in use.

A neighbor, even more ardent a frugalista than I, has reduced his family electricity bill to even less per person. As we shall see, the family who now lives in 19th Street House, with virtually no special efforts, turns in a roughly similar performance. Under a program like Berkeley's, if Sandra and I were to install PV, the monthly cost for our electricity would be roughly eighteen times what we are spending now—$250 instead of fourteen dollars. The numbers would be similar for our neighbor and the 19th Street family. Of course, our fellow citizens (taxpayers like you) would be picking up part of the tab via government subsidies for PV. Personally, however, I don't feel any less uneasy about wasting our collective wealth than wasting my own.

To add insult to injury, during its lifespan, optimistically projected to be twenty-five years, PV panels installed at our house, our neighbors', or 19th Street House will steadily degrade until they are producing about one-half as much electricity as at the outset. By the end of the twenty-five years, the panels, likely even the controls, will be worn out and/or obsolete and on their way to the dump—unless someone figures out how to recycle them. Assuming historical rates of inflation, replacing the entire system of panels and controls will then cost in the range of $50,000 to $60,000. Meanwhile, chances are good that the development of even more efficient devices, such as LED light sources, will make possible even further reduction of electrical use without compromising comfort.

Facing such unpleasant math, advocates for perching PV panels atop single family homes mount counterarguments. Among them: Electricity costs will continue to rise more rapidly than the general rate of inflation so that the rooftop sun power systems will look ever more attractive, financially speaking. Sunlight is free; we are foolish to use fossil fuels when so much sun energy is pouring down from the sky. Having your "own" power plant makes you independent of the bad old utility companies. And so on.

Well, no, no, no, and no again. To begin with, predicting economic trends is a hazardous game, and it is worth noting that one major utility, Mid-American Energy, by bringing large amounts of wind power on line, is on track to hold electricity prices stable for its customers for a fifteen year period. As for sunlight, it is no more free than any other energy source. Water, wind, and fossil fuels are "free" too. Harvesting them is where the costs come in. That's where they come in with sunlight as well. And personally, I would rather do business with my power company than maintain my very own power plant on my rooftop. My house demands too much attention as it is.

The arguments can go back and forth for a very long time. I will hold off a complete recounting and mention only that in a final defense of PV, certain of its aficionados hold that even when it is not financially sound, it is a good and generous environmental deed. After all, it saves the use of fossil fuels and thereby slows global warming, they say. However, even putting aside the fact that the PV systems are likely made using energy derived from fossil fuel, dollar stupid and environment considerate do not generally go hand in hand. If you are spending significantly more money for an allegedly "greener" alternative, you are likely wasting not only dollars but also losing an opportunity to create the environmental benefits the money could have been spent on instead. In other words, as the economists say, there's an "opportunity cost" along with the financial one.

For the $25,000 a PV system gobbles up, homeowners can avail themselves, instead, of huge opportunities to make their homes more efficient and environment considerate. The opportunities to decrease electrical use by upgrading devices and fixtures, along with improving habits, is just the beginning. To use Sandra's and my house as an example again, for a third the cost of a PV system, we could upgrade the thermal boundary of our home to the point that our consumption of gas for space heat was as low or lower than our electricity consumption. And that thermal boundary would be at work for decades after the PV system had worn out and been tossed in the dump.

When construction at 19th Street House was completed, and the first family to make the house their home moved in, the consequences of deploying relatively few dollars to reduce resource consumption, rather than lots of dollars for resource harvesting, began to emerge. Together, the family and I monitored the house's performance. We recorded numbers. We exchanged observations. We learned a lot, sometimes groaned, sometimes smiled, and sometimes tossed our hats in the air.

CHAPTER EIGHT

LIVING IN THE CONSIDERATE HOUSE

We are arriving at the end of our story. Looking back, we can appreciate again how much we have come to demand of our houses. We require that they be pleasing to all our senses, stuffed with infrastructure catering to our every need and want, frugal with our dollars, and "green" as well. As we have ramped up our demands, we have also brought new vocabulary on line. Most of the new terms are optimistic. We have "environmentally friendly." We have "advanced energy efficient framing" and "indoor air quality" and "healthy house." We have "sustainably harvested." Another new term that has come into use is, however, not so optimistic. The term is "slippage." Though not familiar to the general public, it is a term well known to people who build homes. "Slippage" describes the tendency of houses to perform below, sometimes far below, the expectations for efficiency encoded in the drawings and specifications.

Commissioning

Seeking to reduce slippage, the construction industry has inaugurated new kinds of inspections carried out by a new breed of specialists known as HERS (Home Energy Rating Systems) inspectors. HERS inspectors use a new array of tools—duct blasters to check duct work,

193

blower doors to check the entire thermal boundary of a house, infrared guns to peer inside walls for damp or improperly installed insulation—that enable them to pinpoint the source of leakage in a building.

Once a house has passed inspection, it is considered "Commissioned," rather like a young lieutenant who has received her or his bars upon graduating West Point. At 19th Street House, commissioning revealed the ducts to leak only half as much air as allowed by a stringent new standard for California heating contractors—or about one-tenth as much as typical ducts from the days before the new standards were established. Overall tightness of the house, its tendency to leak air, was, however, not quite so impressive. The house was not only shy of the standard set by so-called "passive houses," those thermos bottle homes described in Chapter 6, "Infrastructure," that need hardly more heat than generated by a teenager's hair dryer. It was also shy of the tightness of certain town homes recently flung up nearby to replace the decrepit World War II era housing inhabited by University of California graduate students. Even so, after testing, George Nesbitt pronounced 19th Street House "good

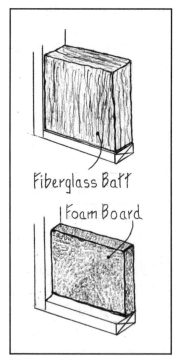

Fiberglass Batt

Foam Board

enough." The house was not at the top of its class, but it still got its bars. The results of commissioning worried me, though. Did the merely "good enough" portend unduly high energy use for heating and, therefore, failure to meet the environment considerate requirement of the pyramid? I would find out only after 19th Street House had been occupied for a year.

George was quite certain he knew where 19th Street's leakage was occurring: behind the bathtubs. I had deliberately eliminated insulation there, knowing from my experience tearing apart and rebuilding rotted bathroom walls that if water penetrated the tub surround, fiberglass insulation placed behind it would hold the moisture and amplify mold growth and decay. Only after the tubs were installed and the walls closed up did I realize I could have used foam board rather than fiberglass insulation, continuing the thermal boundary, but also allowing space for moisture to dry away.

To pinpoint any smaller sources of leakage, George and I could have scanned the interior surfaces of the house with an infrared gun. But a fat lot of good it would have done us, for there is a problem with the commissioning process. Much of it comes too late to be of immediate help. It is done after the house is too far along toward completion. While you might at reasonable cost stop a bit of leakage with a gasket here, a bit of foam there, the defects that commissioning turns up can often be remedied only at unacceptable expense. What do you do if commissioning indicates that your ducts and thermal boundary are performing poorly? Do you tear out the drywall and other finish work to correct weaknesses in your duct sealing or thermal boundary? Probably not. Fixing problems uncovered by commissioning is often prohibitively destructive and expensive. At 19th Street House, I certainly was not going to tear out the tiled tub surround and the tub itself to insert a few additional square feet of insulation.

So why commission in the first place? The answer is that, though it may come too late for the particular house, commissioning offers a great benefit. It shows up weaknesses in your work. It highlights mistakes you can learn from. If you are willing to push yourself up a steep learning curve, you can rapidly improve the efficiency of the houses you build. One "home performance contractor" (yet another new term, this one describing the new category of contractors who specialize in improving home energy efficiency) reports that by carefully commissioning his first four jobs he was able by the fifth to produce first-rate, optimally performing thermal boundaries and ductwork. At 19th Street House, commissioning prompted me to figure out a way of insulating behind the tubs without raising the risk of mold growth, and I stored away the idea for use in my next considerate house.

Those of us who craft houses should have been commissioning each one all along—and not just for energy efficiency at the end of construction but also after a house has been inhabited for a period of time for livability, functionality, durability, impact on neighbors, even for aesthetics. We should have been testing the quality of the spaces we have dreamed up at our desktops once they are actually filled with people and furniture and kids battling for turf rights and time on the Xbox. We should have been asking ourselves to what extent did we realize our hopes and intentions, and to what extent did our projects fall prey to slippage. In my experience, however, other than stopping over for a celebratory glass of wine with clients settling into a new place, architects and other building designers rarely make it back to their projects, much less for the systematic inspections and interviews that would deeply inform them about the performance of their buildings. The architect of the single family residence celebrated in *House*, the perspicacious account by Tracy Kidder of the crafting of a house in Northampton, Massachusetts, did spend a night there just after the owners moved in; and he describes the experience as a rare privilege for folks in his profession.

It's sad that the people who spend months designing the homes their clients will live in for years seldom return to experience those homes even for a day and a night after they are inhabited. They do not see them tested by the stresses and strains of family life; they never commission them. We builders are just as bad. We tend to get back to our completed projects only to fix something that went wrong, or to keep alive a cordial connection with the clients in order to foster referrals to other work. For both designers and builders, completed projects have much to teach about our strengths and deficiencies at our craft. But we tend to view them largely as photo ops for our portfolios or as marketing opportunities, and do not much capitalize on them as learning opportunities.

I have been guilty myself of neglecting the instruction offered by past projects. I have never spent a night in one of the homes I have built. With a few exceptions, I have not visited them for more than an hour at a time. But at 19th Street House I wanted to change course. Though it blends into its neighborhood of gable-roofed bungalows, it is a whole new breed of house. From its void-formed foundation, frugal framing, cement board siding, fiberglass insulated windows, and rain diverters in place of gutters, its combination space and water heating system and its supply-side and central vac based indoor air quality protection system, all the way through to its giant-sized tile countertops, bamboo and carpet tile flooring, flat-pak cabinetry, and timer controlled lights—in all those ways and quite a few others, it is radically different from the surrounding houses and from anything I had ever built before. I wanted to monitor its performance for several years. I wanted to glean from the house every lesson it had to teach me. I wanted to see how it actually worked out for the people who came to live in it. Even while a little anxious about what I would find out, I wanted to see exactly how energy efficient it was or—heaven forbid—was not. And most certainly I did not want to hand it over to new owners until I felt confident it worked. To learn from the house, I needed to find a reliable and alert family who would like to rent it, would treat it with care, and would be willing to share their experience and observations with me. As I had so often been before, as with the hiring of Ryan and Grant and Morris, I got lucky when it was time to find a family to make 19th Street House their home.

At home with Chris and Dean

After he had snugged down the kitchen faucet and hooked up the dishwasher supply line, Dean Fukawa backed out of the sink cabinet, looked over at me, and said, "Dave, would you mind if I brought Chris over to see the house?" Of course not, I told him. I had played Saturday afternoon basketball with Dean for thirty years. Invariably good humored even while intensely competitive, Dean possessed a deadly set shot and superb judgment as a point guard, moving the ball exactly where it needed to go. To his vocation, home maintenance and plumbing, Dean brings the same friendly nature and deft precision he brought to our basketball games. I always call on him when I have small plumbing jobs. I was flattered that he liked 19th Street House so much that he wanted to show it to his wife.

Until Chris Kelley showed up for a second visit, this time with a tape measure in hand to check whether her furniture would fit, I had not quite understood that she and Dean were looking for a new place. With measuring done, Chris pronounced the house "lovely." The three of us signed a lease, and Chris and Dean soon were discovering ways of using the house that were much different from those I had imagined. The landscaping berm, fashioned from the earth Bull's Eye had dropped in the backyard during foundation pier drilling, became the bunker for a pitch-and-putt golf course complete with a flag fluttering on a pole above the hole. The second story became a work/live space, with two of the four bedrooms serving as home offices for the couple, the third as a library/guest room, and the largest as the master bedroom.

But in other ways, Chris and Dean occupied the house just as I had imagined. Dean built boxes for raised-bed gardening in the backyard, and Chris's niece Cassie, who also moved in, filled the boxes with soil and planted vegetables. Chris and I collaborated in the planting of half a dozen cedars, a live oak, a lemon tree in front of the entry porch, a fig tree in the far corner of the backyard, and a lovely Japanese maple along the fence bordering Morris' yard. Two chairs and a table appeared on the front porch. Neighbors and friends stopped off to chat. Chris propped two large pillows in the corner of the stair landing below the bay window, making the space an inviting spot to kick back with a book. The entry parlor was set up to do double duty as a social and TV room.

At parties the couple's friends grouped themselves in all the social spaces—front porch, entry parlor, stair landing, dining table, back deck, and yard—enjoying their glasses of wine and talking.

During their first two years in their new home, Chris and Dean developed a keen sense of what worked in the house—and of what did not. In occasional conversations and in a long interview one spring afternoon in 2009, they shared their thoughts with me. Chris noted that the windowsills should be a couple of inches higher so that a desk could slip under them. Much more importantly, she emphasized, we really did need to bring natural light into the upper bathrooms. When she stepped from the bright sunlight of the upper landing into the sudden darkness of a bathroom, she found herself groping for the light switch. As I listened, my mind flew back to the stand off between me and my architect friend, he arguing for a window in the bathroom tub wall to capture the view, me adamantly resisting it for reasons of cost and risk of moisture penetration into the wall. Locked in disagreement, we had missed a good idea that Chris now proposed: interior windows between each bathroom and the landing to admit the sunlight that poured down the solar tube from the roof. With interior windows in place, Chris predicted, you would never need to switch on a bathroom light in the daytime.

Before our interview, Chris had listed Dean's and her own observations of the house and divided them into two columns. The first was titled "needs improvement." Almost all those items had to do with a single issue: a certain tightness of space that the couple experienced in four areas of the house, beginning with the rear deck. There, I shared their concern. I had goofed up. As Ryan and I constructed that deck, I had focused entirely on the dollar and environmental points of my builder's pyramid. I had been so seized with determination not to buy a single additional stick of lumber and to frame the deck entirely with leftover beams and boards, I had forgotten to pay attention to the architonic quality of the thing I was building. As my architect friend pointed out, I was thinking like an "assembler" and not a "form maker," or even a competent "place maker." As a result, I created a back "deck" that was really just a glorified landing with barely enough room for a chair at either side of the rear door. Instead of functioning as an inviting outdoor place and gracefully connecting the

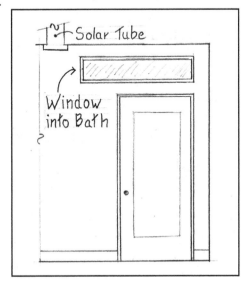

kitchen/dining space to the rear yard, it was a boring box clumsily protruding from the back of the house.

But even as Chris, Dean, and I talked about the problem, a solution to it popped up. Rather than throw away my too frugal deck/landing, we would treat it as the first phase in the construction of a bi-level deck, one that would nicely cascade from the back doorway down into the yard and be comfortable for socializing. The case of the deck, it seemed, might be an exception that proved a rule taught to me by one of my first mentors in the builder's craft: *never, ever build on a mistake!* In this case, the mistake could be transformed into the beginning of a success.

As we turned our attention to the interior, Chris and Dean directed my attention to three areas where they felt the house needed to be larger. Upstairs, they thought, the two smaller bedrooms were too small. Chris pointed out that those spaces, as I had crafted them, allowed furniture to be arranged in one configuration only. Downstairs, she said, the entry parlor was too snug, so that the space worked as a TV room, but not for socializing. It could host only the smallest groups. Finally, Chris emphasized, the downstairs closet space was inadequate, woefully so.

The couple's critique had a powerful effect on my thinking about the house. I found myself returning to their recommendations over and over, calculating the material and labor it would have taken to upsize the house by the requested amount and envisioning the impact the expansion would have on window placement, on plumbing and heating, on the size

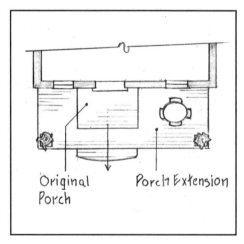

Original Porch   Porch Extension

of structural components, and on the proportions of exterior details. I saw that the increase, if I were to build the house again, could be accomplished for relatively modest environmental and financial cost. All told, the expansion Dean and Chris urged would enlarge the house by a modest fifteen percent. It required only that the house be increased in both length and width by two feet. I concluded that such an expansion was likely to be supported by many of the people who came to visit the house if I were to poll them. I worried about the marketplace consequences of my insistence on building such a compact place at 19th Street. Would people want it?

But when all was said and done I found myself—as I had been during similar dialogues at the time I was drawing the house—resistant to urgings to enlarge it. I was not willing to shrink outdoor space by expanding the house. I was committed to developing small homes, to pulling back as hard against the American tendency to supersize houses as financial realities would allow. And I knew from my earlier experience building small homes that, yes, many potential renters and purchasers, even those attracted by the quality of the house, would turn away from its compactness. But at the same time I knew there would be others who would be attracted by that very compactness, or who would at least accept the trade-offs—smaller place but strong architonic qualities, high-grade construction, low maintenance and operating costs. I knew, also, from studying other Bay Area homes that aimed to be affordable to people of moderate means, that 19th Street House was relatively generous in the functionality it offered.

For all my insistence on holding my ground, however, Chris and Dean's perspective and critique propelled my thinking forward, stimulating me to look for ways to address their concerns and increase functionality, if not by expanding the house then by making better use of the structure as it was. At the smaller bedrooms I did not succeed. I could only fall back on my belief, grounded in my desire to use financial and environmental resources frugally, that they were fine for optional uses such as study or guest room and more than adequate—with their ample closets, desk nooks, and space for a bed and a dresser—to the needs of kids. In fact, as I saw things, kids who might come to live in the bedrooms were fortunate by any realistic measure.

Downstairs closets were another matter, however. They *were* parsimonious for a modern household, I had to admit. But, aha, there was a way to remedy the problem with two adjustments. At the hall closet I could move the vacuum further under the stairway, freeing up the front of the closet for coats and storage. At the service core, I could add a new floor-to-ceiling cabinet for storage of miscellaneous items and thereby free up the closet for linens.

For the entry parlor I had a simpler solution: replace Chris and Dean's bulky older TV with a wall-hung model and thereby make space for two additional captain's chairs where the old TV now sat atop a cabinet. Chris did not like the idea at all. She contemplated the possibility of coming home with groceries and having to walk between Dean and his TV as he was engrossed in a basketball game. The vision genuinely jarred her sense of kinesthetic harmony. I got her point, but again I found myself coming down on the side of the more compact house. My sense of dollar wisdom and insistence on restraining environmental impact was colliding with Chris's architonic sensibility. We had to agree to respectfully disagree.

Because Chris and Dean were so candid and thoughtful in their criticisms of the house, I gave equal credence to the other half of Chris's list, generously titled "Best Features." They told me that passersby often called out "nice place," that when certain close friends came visiting the wife said to the husband, "I want you to build me a house just like this one," and that they themselves loved the house. Chris's list of specific

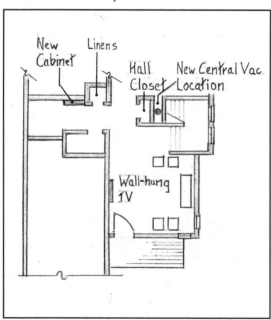

"best" features is long. The thermal boundary, even while it holds down heating bills, muffles the sound of passing trains at night so that sleep is not disturbed. The kitchen countertop tile, with its minimal and narrow joints, has proved easy to clean. Both the countertop and the floor tile are "pleasingly warm," the kitchen pantry "wonderful," the traditional styles of the doors "lovely." Chris finds the central vac so easy to use and efficient, she thinks central vacs should be standard equipment in every home. Dean likes the carpet tile so much he has begun installing it for clients. He enjoys watching the rain diverters break up the sheet of water flowing off the roof into a shower of droplets. Chris likes the softened craftsman detailing of the wall corners, woodwork, archway, and bath tile.

But what they respond to most is the open but not *too* open quality of the interior space. They are pleased that Chris can work in the kitchen and Dean watch a ball game on TV in the parlor without their disturbing one another, even though the two spaces are joined by the archway below the stairs. They like the way the stair landing and bay window extend the volume of the parlor; and the three-quarter height walls of the upstairs foyers create a sense of private entry to the master bedroom and Chris's office, yet allow for the landing area to be experienced as a single flowing space rather than a chopped-up one. They like the long view into the rear yard through the glass panel of the back door; the distinction and variety that the nooks and offsets give to each of the bedrooms; the enhanced sense of spaciousness that the absence of upper cabinets contribute to the kitchen. And they love their abundant sunlight.

They exult (it's not too strong a word) over the sunshine coming into the house from all directions. Sunlight floods through the south-facing windows into the kitchen and dining area. It pours down the solar tube across the upper landing and comes through the bay windows, illuminating the stairwell. Sunlight warms the bedrooms and lights nearly every room from several sides. Chris and Dean love the sunlight for the pleasure it gives them. And they doubly appreciate it because the illumination and warmth the sunlight provides has helped them to operate their home for remarkably little cost.

Energy

Home energy efficiency depends on three main contributors: Advances in technology. Astute selection of the technology by builders who understand its benefits to the planet and their competitive position in the construction industry. And occupants who will not casually override it but rather capitalize on the potential benefits the technology offers to the environment and to their finances. At 19th Street House, I attended to the builder's piece by installing a core plumbing system with short wait times for hot water and an appropriately sized combination water and space heating system. I put in CFLs (compact fluorescent lamps), low-flow showerheads and faucets, efficient appliances, and motion sensors and timers to control lights. No

home efficiency measures are capable, however, of overcoming wasteful users. They can easily undermine efficiency by substituting incandescent bulbs for CFLs, loading the house with entertainment devices and computers and leaving them on 24/7, taking very long showers and letting faucets drip, operating the dishwasher or washing machine with partial loads, leaving windows open while at the same time heating the house, and in myriad other ways.

Chris and Dean capitalized on the efficiency potential built into 19th Street House. The story of their attentive use of energy unfolds in a spreadsheet (displayed on the next page) that Chris compiled for their first two years in the house. As you can see in the table on the following page, they got off to a slow start during the turmoil of moving into a new home, using almost a third more energy in July 2007 than they would a year later. In August, performance improved, but largely, Chris observed with dry wit, because she and Dean went on vacation. Then in September, it went to hell in a handbasket as the utility bill doubled. Dean discovered one reason. The motion sensor in an outdoor security light had failed and the lamp was on around the clock.

With the defective light replaced—but likely more for other reasons that I am not quite able to pinpoint, perhaps simply because Chris and Dean were getting the hang of operating the house—energy use began to decline until lower temperatures in the fall and winter required use of the heating system. Chris and Dean, however, kept heating cost down by slipping on sweaters when the house became a bit cool. By the end of the heating season, their efforts had produced great news. Nineteenth Street's thermal boundary, in combination with its strong exposure to southern sun and the heat storing capacity of its tile floors, plus Chris and Dean's attentiveness, had virtually eliminated fuel consumption for artificial space heating. As can be figured from the record of costs in the spreadsheet, their bills for gas for space heat from November through May totaled approximately sixty dollars, with a very small additional amount being spent for electricity to power the fan in the air handler.

Then Chris and Dean made another substantial improvement. They replaced their old computers with more efficient ones and got into the habit of turning them off when not in use. Their electrical consumption and the accompanying utility charges dropped from the same months of the preceding year. The good news kept right on coming. During their second heating season, their use of gas for space heating dropped yet lower. And for their entire second year in the house, from May 2008 through April 2009, Dean and Chris used $648.43 worth of energy. That's $1.80 a day including taxes—about the taxed cost of a medium-sized cup of coffee at the Starbucks just up San Pablo Avenue from 19th Street.

The combination of the built-in efficiency and Chris and Dean's attentive use held down water consumption as well. Dean did briefly experiment with a gusher of a showerhead, a handsome fixture he had brought home from work one day. When I first saw it I groaned inwardly but held my tongue, not wanting to be demoted from appreciated builder to overbearing landlord. On a subsequent stop by the house, I was relieved to see that the gusher was gone. It had been replaced by a model that could be adjusted, I was told, from 1.5 to 2.5 gallons per minute. Good! I thought. Over time the difference in consumption that results from using a three gallon a minute showerhead rather than a gallon and a half per minute head is huge. If two people are each taking a ten minute shower daily under a three gallon gusher, they will use 11,000 gallons more water (enough to fill a row of one gallon milk jugs over a mile in length) during a one year occupancy of their home. Since much of the increase is heated water, energy consumption is shoved upward as well.

MONTH	GAS (Therms a Day)	ELECTRIC (KWH a Day)	COST ($$$ a Month)
June 2007	.5	6.1	28.23
July	.6	10.1	64.77
August	.4	8.5	44.91
September	.6	13.1	82.41
October	.6	10.9	63.98
November	.5	10.4	59.22
December	.9	10.2	76.61
January	1.2	9.5	78.49
February	1.2	8.8	76.58
March	.7	6.9	59.84
April	.7	8.3	58.28
May	.6	7.7	54.50
June 2008	.5	7.4	55.33
July	.4	7.2	49.45
August	.4	6.1	42.59
September	.4	7.6	48.43
October	.4	7.6	41.95
November	.6	8.8	53.21
December	.9	9.2	68.36
January	1.2	9.2	71.91
February	.8	8.8	61.30
March	.9	8.9	55.48
April	.6	7.9	45.92

During the first years Chris and Dean lived in the house, California experienced a drought. Householders were required to hold their water consumption within tight limits or face severe penalties. Chris and Dean stayed fifteen to twenty percent beneath their allowance, even with some water being used to irrigate the young saplings in the yard. Paradoxically, their very success at capitalizing on the efficiencies built into 19ᵗʰ Street and containing their energy use left me with the toughest challenge to do better—tougher even than ferreting out room for more downstairs closet space— that I had yet faced.

I had spent approximately $7,000 for the space heating side of the house's combination space and water heating system. When I installed the system, it seemed to me a great advance on the conventional oversized forced air alternatives. And it is a substantial advance, but now I saw that even so I had put in an awful big machine for delivering such a small volume of service. It was as if I had bought a pickup truck to haul a few sacks of topsoil and fertilizer home from the garden store a few times a year, and counted my purchase as dollar wisdom because I had not bought a ten wheel dump truck.

As I thought about ways to improve on the 19ᵗʰ Street House, I began searching about for an alternative. Given the need to ventilate and filtrate as well as heat a thermally tight house, however, coming up with a more dollar smart and environment friendly option is proving remarkably difficult, as we will see in a few pages in "Better Yet?" Meanwhile, I will continue to enjoy bragging about 19ᵗʰ Street House's picayune heating costs. "Sixty bucks a month for gas, that's pretty good compared with the bill I get," people reply, misunderstanding me. "No," I clarify, "that's sixty bucks *per year.*" They grope for an explanation. Solar? Hay bale walls? Some kind of new technology? "None of that," I love to answer, launching into my pitch for "green simple" over "gadget-and-glamour green," and expounding on frugal framing, thermal boundaries, passive heating via south-facing windows, and house-is-a-system thinking until their eyes glaze over or they glance at their watches and flee, calling back over their shoulders that they have a pressing doctor's appointment.

What did the house cost?

Often, when I brag about the heating bill, I get back questions. How much did it cost to construct a house with such low operating costs? And, by the way, how badly did you get burned by the steep, long slide in real estate prices that began during the construction of 19ᵗʰ Street

House? I'll begin with the construction cost question, but want to give a warning first. When we get into the subject of construction costs, we are stepping into treacherous territory. Even building professionals, never mind owners from outside the construction world, are often startled at how much the actual costs exceed expectations. As Barry LePatner says in the title to his thought-provoking book (see Resources), we are plagued not only with "Broken Buildings" but with "Busted Budgets."

Unrealistic expectations are fed from several directions. Designers, desirous of commissions and eager to build projects, understate the costs going into a project. Sometimes they do so from naiveté, sometimes wishfully. Now and again, their optimistic projections are willfully manipulative. An architect once told me that he would never get a job if he told clients at the outset what their project was really going to cost them.

Newspapers and magazines regularly report construction costs so low they strike building professionals as preposterous. As best I can figure, the low numbers make it into print because the gatekeepers, the editors who decide what will get published and what will not, simply do not understand construction costs or are not interested in them. They lack either the ability or the motivation to evaluate the numbers given to them by their sources. In one typical instance of strikingly low reported cost I recently came across, the home appears to have been built by its architects as a labor of love. They had worked for compensation much less than usually enjoyed by skilled tradesmen, but that possibility was hardly visible in the article.

Book authors occasionally present numbers just as dicey as those reported in the press. Some years back, for example, I attended a book reading by a young writer who had put together a charming collection of stories about architecturally enticing yet affordable homes. In some cases the costs reported were so low they amounted to less than what I would have had to pay for materials alone. After the reading, I asked about the costs for those homes. It turned out they had been built largely by their owners. One had been crafted by a young man who had painstakingly salvaged much of his material from other buildings and worked on his place full time, nonstop for four years, with his father pitching in nearly every weekend. In the costs that the author enthusiastically related to the people at the reading, the young man's labor and his dad's had been valued at zero—in other words, left out of the cost figures altogether—and the extravagant amount of effort needed to make use of salvaged material not mentioned at all. Readers without the background necessary to evaluate such stripped-down figures could easily conclude that they will be able to have a project built at a price point well below what is possible in the normal marketplace.

Along with architects and journalists, builders feed the optimistic expectations around construction cost. Often we are asked to provide free preliminary cost estimates. (In my own practice, I generally decline to provide free estimates, offering preconstruction services for a fee instead. But that is another story. It is told in my book, *Running a Successful Construction Company*; see Resources.) Many builders accede to the request for free preliminary estimates, viewing them as loss leaders for the construction contract they hope to sign. Unfortunately, they cannot anticipate everything the project will require from the sketchy drawings available for preliminary estimates. Major costs get left out of their estimates.

Builders often do recognize that their preliminary numbers are going to prove very low compared with the eventual actual costs of the project. But the free bid system in which they are working all but forces them to keep that information to themselves. They've learned the same lesson as the architect who believes he would not get a job if he told the client the truth about likely costs. They know if they break the bad news too early, they may be crossed off the list of builders being considered for the project. Once, when I did accede to the request of a designer and gave a free estimate, I was ordered off the client's property. "You're a crook," she told me when she looked at my estimate. She did not call to apologize when it proved just slightly lower than the amount she ended up paying for her addition.

I know ethical builders troubled by the prospect of owners being ambushed by a huge difference between preliminary and actual costs. They have tried submitting estimates that include a contingency for items not shown in preliminary drawings. As a result, they repeatedly find themselves scratched off the list of candidates for the projects and end up doing a great deal of estimating work without reward, relearning the old axiom that bearers of bad news are not welcomed.

In the ultra hardball world of large-scale construction, builders go a huge step farther in the opposite direction. They submit final as well as preliminary bids they know to be low, having closely calculated 1) by how much the bids are low, 2) how much they will be able to charge for the additional work not anticipated in the architect's drawings that will inevitably crop up as construction proceeds, and 3) how much profit they will earn on the project as a result of the "change orders" they will write up for the extra work. Occasionally, hardball operators make their way into the world of custom home building and remodeling, driving up their earnings by working their "change order artistry" on hapless homeowners.

"Outrageous," you may be thinking. How do they get away with it? Barry LePatner offers an insightful explanation. During bidding, builders are operating in a highly competitive environment. But once a contract has been signed and construction is under way, the winning builder moves to the position of monopolist. He's got a lock on the job. With the project rising up out of the ground, the client can turn back toward other possible builders only at considerable legal and financial risk. In fact, the client, and even the client's designer (for designers, including architects, are typically not skilled at construction cost estimating), will have difficulty even in mounting a coherent challenge to the builder's change order charges. The client and designer simply do not have enough information to challenge the charges successfully. They must accede to them or risk their project coming to a halt.

Even if cost estimates and reports from architects, other designers, building journals, and builders were reliable at the moment given, they would still be of limited use. They go rapidly out of date. Costs experienced on one project may have little relevance to those that will be experienced on a subsequent one. Construction costs, especially on the material side, are highly volatile. Between the time I began drawing 19th Street House and took delivery of 2x6s and plywood at the jobsite, lumber prices dropped by roughly a third. By the time I finished construction, they had dropped further still as the housing industry cycled from a giddy boom to bust. Had I been building during another point in the business cycle, lumber prices might have risen steeply instead.

Adding to the difficulty of using cost data from past projects for estimating future projects are the great differences in construction costs between regions of the country or even locales within a state. Drive two hours north from the San Francisco Bay Area, where costs are similar to other major metropolitan areas, and you will find that the wages commanded by an experienced carpenter drop by a third. Drive four hours farther north and wages drop to half of what a Bay Area carpenter makes. Similarly, according to a widely published book of cost data, construction labor costs 60 percent less in Kansas than in the Bay Area (and materials about 10 percent less). If you take your cues on cost from Northern California or Kansas for a project in a major U.S. city, you are in for a shock when the bills start coming in.

Even the cost to build two apparently similar projects in the same locale can be markedly different. During the same period I was drawing and building 19th Street House, a young general contractor of my acquaintance got his start adding second-story additions to small bungalows in a town a few miles south of San Pablo. On the first few, his carefully figured estimates proved accurate. He grew confident that he could precisely project the cost of similar looking jobs merely by reviewing the plans, figuring square footage differences, and adjusting from his costs for the earlier additions. For a few projects his relaxed method worked. On the next, his costs soared above his projection. As he put it, using the technical language favored by construction professionals, "I lost my ass." On the surface, his new project looked to entail the same scope of work as the earlier ones. Beneath its skin, however, it required complex and costly framing details absent from the earlier projects. The young builder's estimating failed to take the differences into account.

All this is to say that while it's natural to ask the question, "How much did it cost you, David Gerstel, to build 19th Street House," the answers I will give—*like all construction cost data*—should be used guardedly, especially if you are thinking of building a considerate house yourself.

My figures will not substitute for a skilled estimate based on detailed plans for your particular project in your particular locale. Nothing ever does.

My total *cash outlay* for building the 19th Street House including the lot was $306,353. Of that total, $80,000 went for the lot, and $68,490 for permits and other services—expenses largely locked in before a single stick of lumber was ever delivered to the jobsite. Professional builders operating in urban areas will not be surprised at the permit and service costs. They pile up and typically are a high percentage of total building costs. In the case of 19th Street House, $4,000 went for engineering (soils plus structural) even though I produced the structural drawings myself, relying on an engineer only for review and an official stamp of approval to placate the building department. Nine thousand went for plan checking and building permits, five grand to the school district, then many more thousands to the sewer district and the utility company and for course-of-construction insurance.

The direct construction costs, those incurred right at the jobsite for material and labor, seemed unbelievably low to my Bay Area builder friends. At $157,863, my direct cash costs came to about ninety-two dollars per square foot including the garage and front porch (both more costly to build per square foot than the bedrooms). Ninety-two bucks a square foot was, at most, about a third of the going rate for remodels and new homes comparable in quality to 19th Street House at the time I was building it. My friends were right to be disbelieving, for I was not a miracle worker.

Out-of-Pocket Costs to Build 19th Street House	
Lot	$80,000
Preconstruction	$68,490
Labor & Material	$157,863
Not Included: Drawing, hands-on construction, and project management by David Gerstel. Overhead. Profit.	

The figure represented merely my *out-of-pocket* cash expenditures for direct labor and material costs. It did not include the value of my own labor as project manager, lead carpenter, and sometime helper. Nor did it include overhead or profit such as builders necessarily charge when building for clients. Additionally, I held out-of-pocket costs down in three other ways: I took several months more to build the house than I would have had I been working for a client, which enabled me to do more of the work personally rather than hiring additional help. Together with Ryan, I worked alongside the skilled tradespeople and subcontractors that I hired to perform the most costly specialty trades—namely mechanical, plumbing, and electrical. And, I used a gambit similar to that employed by the builder who pays his student workers with educational opportunity. I explained to several key workers that, given my tight budget, I could offer them wages at the going rate, but no additional compensation such as medical benefits. In the place of such benefits, what I offered was a chance to learn how to build in accordance with house-is-a-system and green simple principles. They accepted the trade-off.

In sum, ninety-two dollars a square foot is the out-of-pocket direct construction cost achieved during a construction bust, when material was cheap, by a builder (me) with decades of experience, good carpentry skills, strong management skills, the time to do much of the work himself, and workers willing to take educational opportunity in lieu of dollar benefits.

A different person in a different locale and with a different skill set might have a very different cost experience. The lot might be cheaper or more costly. The permit and service costs might vary, though in any urban area they are likely to be painfully high. Direct material and labor costs could be lower or higher. During a severe recession with construction deflated, direct costs may be less; during a robust economy, much higher. Another builder might not have such good luck at finding workers as I did. He might elect to craft fewer labor-intensive details such as the fir and copper stair rails and the tile walls, countertops, and floors that I installed at 19th Street House. He might be a slower and less capable carpenter than I am, or a faster one—though it is not likely that he will be better at project organization or superior at wielding a broom during cleanup time. I am an ace at that stuff.

Whatever his or her skills and choices, forecasting and controlling labor cost will be the greatest challenge. Labor cost varies enormously in response to the complexity of the building, the makeup of the crew, the site, and weather conditions. Over the years, I have found it invaluable to record labor costs from each project I complete. (See *Running a Successful Construction Company*, described in Resources, for efficient methods.) I have built up a thick notebook of costs from past jobs, and rely on it when generating estimates for new ones. The cost records are highly detailed. They record hours per unit to install, for example, a wall frame or a particular kind of window under particular circumstances ("steep site, difficult access, tantrum throwing owner who distracted and demoralized crew," or "level lot, easy access, owner supported high crew morale with daily serving of chocolate chip cookies and regular admiration for their work").

But I also record hours by much larger units, the major divisions of a project such as framing or plumbing, and even by whole projects as I have done here for 19th Street House. They help me gauge whether new estimates of labor hours for phases of work or whole projects are at least very roughly within range of actual costs. The figures I have presented here *may* help you evaluate your estimate of labor hours for a project of your own so long as it is substantially similar to 19th Street House. *One last time: be careful if you apply my figures to your project.*

Phase of Work	Skilled Labor Hrs.	Apprentice. Labor Hrs.
Site Prep & Mainten.	47	68
Foundation & Conc.	155	147
Frame	611	338
Infrastructure	270	359
Skin & Ext. Detail	589	276
Interior Finish	364	299
Drywall Subcontractor	100 +/-	
Tile Subcontractor	160 +/-	
Carpet	20 +/-	60+/-
Stucco Subcontractor	80 +/-	
Paint Subcontractor	160 +/-	
TOTALS	2,556	1,547
TOTAL LABOR: 4,103 HOURS		

Building $ense

Building for yourself or for a client entails estimating risk; if you don't project the costs correctly, you may find yourself in a deep hole. Building "on spec," as I did at 19th Street House, for a customer you do not yet know brings yet other risks. I have several friends who for a time have enjoyed financial success as developers, building on the speculation that they would find buyers for their completed projects. A few built fortunes along with sound and appealing homes. Most eventually lost their life savings when market prices plunged or mortgage rates soared just before they were ready to sell their completed projects.

When I began the drawings for 19th Street House, I knew I faced a dicey market. Real estate prices, which began ballooning in the Bay Area during the high-tech boom of the 1990s, were rapidly becoming untethered from such economic realities as the wage levels of potential buyers. I had watched housing prices blossom and wilt before, and had been expecting them to drop by a third or so this time around. In fact, they dropped far more, especially in modest towns like San Pablo. Had 19th Street House been completed the day I began drawing, it could have fetched $650,000. During the time I was building the house, its potential sales price was dropping by nearly a thousand bucks per working day, or $160,000 in total by the time it was completed. At the time I am writing these lines, it has dropped at least another $120,000. It may go lower yet, dragged down by fire sale prices on nearby foreclosed homes, and eventually descend to the level of my out-of-pocket costs, maybe lower.

Even so, I am relieved to report, 19th Street House has thus far proved a financial success, thanks to my abiding by the principles laid out in *The Intelligent Investor* by Ben Graham, mentor to the Nebraska billionaire Warren Buffett. Graham's book is built around a single profound yet straightforward idea: invest *only* with a wide *margin of safety*. Investing, or for that matter undertaking any business enterprise with a margin of safety means operating so that you can ride out the toughest of times that capitalism offers up. The harsh recessions of 1972 and 1982, never mind the mild ones that followed in the 1990s and at the end of the twentieth century, were not the toughest of times. The depressions of the 1930s and the 1870s were. As I write these lines in 2009, it remains to be seen whether the current economic unraveling intensifies to the extent experienced in those worst of periods.

To establish financial margin of safety in the vulnerable marketplace of 2006 when I began crafting 19th Street House, I relied on three primary measures. They are measures worth the consideration of anyone who intends to build on spec—even if you are building in part for the joy of it and as research for a book, as I was.

Use private capital, not a bank loan. Relying on bank loans for real estate development is too risky. Build either from your own funds or in limited partnerships with investors who are putting in their own money in the hope of a good return while allowing you to remain in control. Then you cannot be forced by a bank's demand for payment to sell at fire sale prices during a down market. You can hold out for a better opportunity. In the event you do not have the capability to acquire sufficient capital—the opportunity and discipline to save it out of your earnings, family patrons, limited partners who want to trust you with their money, whatever—other than by borrowing from banks, then my advice is to stay out of speculative building. Go to Las Vegas or Monaco and have some fun losing your money.

If you do have access to private capital, then establish a sensible budget, one that allows you to build a very good house that is, however, not extravagant for the neighborhood, and stick to that budget. If you are building in a giddy market, don't allow yourself to be infected with the giddiness. If you overspend on your project, you greatly reduce your chances of a decent return—just as you can by underspending and building a crummy place. At 19th Street House, I stuck to my budget, anticipating that in a bad-case scenario, if I did have to sell soon after completing construction, I would have a reasonable chance of recouping my cash outlay and receiving modest pay for my work. In a better scenario, I would be able to sell at a price that would return my capital and pay me well for my work.

Maintain renting or leasing as an option to selling. In the event you complete your project during a down market, you can then avoid selling for an anemic return or at a loss. At 19th Street House, I calculated that in a good scenario, leasing would provide a solid return on my investment of capital; in the worse case, it would at least cover my insurance and taxes and provide a small free cash flow. Be prepared to lease for a long time. Down markets can last many years.

All in all, maintaining a margin of safety by working with your own money or that of financial partners, by sticking to a realistic budget, and by preserving options other than selling will greatly increase the chances of a satisfactory financial result from your investment of time and money. Even more critical, you greatly reduce your chances of taking a loss. That's the irreducible minimum goal of investing with margin of safety: contain the risk of losing your shirt in one of the frequent implosions that beset capitalist economies.

With 19th Street House, I had always intended to lease rather than sell immediately as I wanted to monitor its performance closely for a few years. With prices still dropping rapidly as I completed the house, leasing seemed also the best option from the financial point of view. It has worked out well. In fact, even though I hold the rent to a moderate level, leasing has been producing a yield on my cash investment many times better than I would have enjoyed had the funds invested in 19th Street House remained in the money market account from which I pulled them. As for pay for my work on the house, I will have to wait patiently until prices rise again. Someday they may. Meanwhile, I feel awfully good about 19th Street House. I had a lot of fun crafting it alongside some great folks. It is home to friends who love it. It taught me an enormous amount about house-is-a-system thinking, about green simple, and about the connections between the four points of the builder's pyramid. All in all, not a bad gig, this architekton deal. I'm ready for another round.

EPILOGUE: BETTER YET?

Along with deflating 19th Street House's market value, the crash in real estate prices of 2007 through 2009 has brought new opportunity in San Pablo. Lots that had been going for $200,000 during the market frenzy of 2006 now can be had for 85 percent less. I have begun looking around for a likely parcel; I want to craft a second edition of the considerate house to improve upon both the process of creating it and the final product. I even intend to try a new approach to conceptualizing the volumes and mass of the house, relying less—at least at the outset—on the pattern language approach that I favored for Considerate House One.

John "Mac" McLean, an architect with whom I often discuss design and building issues, admires Christopher Alexander's *Pattern Language*. But he also points out its limitations. Pattern language, Mac says, amounts to a "kit of parts," and as such can constrict residential design. Take, for example, the pattern "porch," he suggests. "When one uses the word 'porch,' a particular image of something comes to mind. That image has certain design components that can be manipulated," but only up to a point without destroying the idea of "porch." To escape this limitation, Mac prefers to think abstractly, to envision a "zone of space" between the private space inside one's home and public space outside it. Mac feels that the more abstract notion of a zone frees him up to imagine all kinds of building assemblies that might occupy the space "in order to come up with something fresh and interesting."

With Mac's critique in mind, as I begin imagining my new considerate house, I will try to stay loose at the outset, playing with ideas for the shaping, arranging, illuminating, servicing, and detailing of spaces from the most private to the less so. Bathrooms? Perhaps not three boxes outfitted, as at 19th Street House, with tubs and showers, water closets, and vanities in the conventional way. Perhaps instead a larger six sided or eight or ten sided bathing space, or even one constructed with sensuously curving walls punctured along several planes to allow in sunlight and provide outlook. And then, backed up to that bathing zone, a couple of completely separate and compact toilet rooms, perhaps with miniature libraries housed in wall nooks. Bedrooms? Maybe a sleeping area with moveable partition walls that can accommodate an evolving, now growing, now shrinking family. Entry parlor? Maybe none at all, but instead, an outdoor-indoor space that serves as a transition to a gathering place for dining and visiting; and off to one side a cozy media nook—or two.

My guess is, however, that after some playful conceptualizing and free drawing, I will move along to a tried and true pattern language. I have in mind a form and details for the house inspired by the barns I worked on decades ago at the beginning of my carpentry career. It is a bit taller than 19th Street House, more emphatically vertical, with tall windows and vertically arrayed, barn style, plank siding. I want to build it.

Whatever forms and patterns I settle on, as I draw them, I may make more use of sections, along with floor plans and elevations. "A floor plan demonstrates the organizational logic of a building; a section embodies its emotional experience," suggests a useful little book titled *101 Things I Learned in Architecture School*. Perhaps so. The author is not certain himself; he calls his comment about sections a "random unsubstantiated hypothesis." It's worth a try. One thing is sure: by drawing sections you can verify that your spaces are properly connected and actually buildable.

As I craft Considerate House Two, I will continue looking for ways to reduce environmental impacts and to deploy dollars more wisely. Likely

Bull's Eye will be back, drilling shafts into the ground for a pier and grade beam foundation—still the most resource efficient option I can come up with for our earthquake threatened Bay Area. I will, however, pare away a pier or two at the gable-end walls. With the side walls carrying the weight of floors and roofs the gable-end walls do not require quite as beefy a foundation. Likewise, as I move into the framing, I hope to achieve improvements in resource efficiency by combining the new frugal (i.e., advanced energy efficient) framing with a very old style of framing. That is the "balloon framing" that I first learned about when remodeling Victorian houses in San Francisco. With a balloon frame, rather than shorter studs being used for each floor as at 19th Street House, very long studs are run from the foundation to the roof trusses, and the floor framing is hung from the studs rather than sitting atop them.

With a balloon frame, lumber will be saved. No sills or plates will be needed other than at the mudsill and for a single plate beneath the rafters. The thermal boundary will be improved. Wall insulation will not be interrupted by floor framing. Instead it will run continuously right past the floor framing. When it comes time to build, I will have to do some exacting number crunching and decide whether to give my balloon framing ideas a go, or retreat to the frugal version of platform framing. But I am intrigued by the idea as I have sketched it here, and think it may help us site builders get another leg up on the factory builders.

Balloon framed or not, Considerate House Two will almost certainly be cubic, or nearly so. No other form can provide as much functionality per unit of material and labor, or offer as complete a home within reach of people with moderate incomes. This time around, there will be two cubes. I will find a parcel big enough so that the San Pablo authorities will approve, as state law

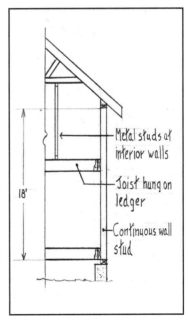

requires, a grandparents' unit at the front of the lot. As the new cubes rise, they will, like 19th Street House, be oriented to take in southern sun for heating, lighting, and nourishment of the soul; will be sheltered by a broad eave; and the interior will be shaped so that a minimum of square footage is consumed by circulation-only space. Those are patterns I hold dear for their efficient use of resources and architonic appeal.

I hope also to correct a shortcoming of 19th Street House beyond those that Chris, Dean, and I discussed. With its various stairways—up to the front door, down to the backyard, up to the bedrooms—it is not a house that comfortably serves people who have difficulty getting about, as is the case for almost all of us as we age, and for a fair number of us earlier. By installing ramps and including a downstairs bedroom, I hope to build a home suitable for a lifetime and for people of any physical ability.

Can all that be achieved without incurring intolerable additional cost? I hope so. It is critical not to increase the costs of building the considerate house. Unfortunately, though I hope to pare away a bit of cost at the foundation and frame, as I come to the crafting of the infrastructure, I fear I will not find much opportunity for reduction. The plumbing, though it can be structured more exactingly to reduce use of water and the energy embedded in it to a level even lower than at 19th Street House, will cost about the same to install; likewise for the wiring and lighting.

Similarly, as things look now, I will run into obstacles when I consider how I might reduce costs for those highly interdependent components: thermal boundary, heating, and ventilation. To provide the tiny bit of heating required each winter by the 19th Street House with its high-qaulity thermal boundary, I spent roughly $7,000 on the space heating side of the combination water and space heating system. It will be over a century till the cost of the fuel used to heat the house equals the cost of the device that distributes the heat.

Looking for a way past that awful allocation of financial resources, I have explored an alternative popular with "green" builders. It begins with intensifying the thermal boundary even further, to the level of the thermos-like construction favored by *Passivhaus* builders described in Chapter Six, then eliminating the space heating side of the combi-system used at 19th Street altogether and installing a heat-recovery ventilator (HRV). Picture a metal box and inside of it a motor, fan, and intertwined ducts, one to exhaust dirty air, the other to bring in fresh air. Running twenty-four hours a day, the HRV would pull dirty air from the bathrooms and kitchen and pump clean air into the other rooms. It would recover heat in the outgoing air and transfer it to fresh incoming air. On those rare occasions when the house needed more heat than given off by its appliances, lights, other electrical devices, human residents, and their pets, a small electrical backup heater integrated into the HRV's ductwork would fire up and inject additional warmth into the incoming air.

The HRV solution has a certain elegance. Several devices, the space heating side of the combi-system and its fresh air supply duct along with several bath fans, would be replaced with just the HRV and its electric booster heater. Appealing though it may be, however, the HRV plus the upgraded thermal boundary solution appears to generate negligible if any installation savings over the systems it replaces. Deciding whether or not operating and maintaining it would save money is at best a crapshoot. It may cost significantly more. An HRV must run continuously. Likely, therefore, it will require more maintenance and more frequent replacement of parts than the

Cost comparison of a heat recovery ventilation system to the combi-system used at the 19th Street House		
Installation costs	Combi-system	HRV
Basic system	$7,000	$4,000
Electric booster heater	$0	$1,500
Bath fans (3)	$800	$0
Added thermal boundary	$0	$2,000
TOTAL INSTALLED COST	**$7,800**	**$7,500**
Annual operating costs	$80	$300
Yearly maintenance	$20	$50
TOTAL ANNUAL OPERATING COST	**$100**	**$350**

COMMENTS: The estimated installed costs of the two options are nearly a wash. Over the course of ten years, operation of the HRV system may run about $2,500 more.

combi-system used at 19th Street House. Additionally, the electrical booster the HRV relies on to add warmth when needed is brutally expensive to operate, as are electrical heating devices in general. If it consumes more in parts and fuel than a combi-system, chances are the "green" HRV system will also impose greater environmental impact.

And there is something else, too. HRV-dependent houses worry me a bit. I have seen too many new building technologies, exciting to begin with, turn catastrophic, engendering horrible financial, environmental, and health costs as they fail. What happens when the HRVs break down? Suppose the homeowners delay repair and maintenance, as homeowners so often do with their house systems. What then? Will toxics build up in the house, damaging the respiratory systems of the occupants, especially young children?

I continue to scratch around for a heating ventilation solution that will reduce financial and environmental costs. But for the moment I am stuck. I may have reached the limits of my own inventiveness and must wait on further evolution of technology. For the moment, as I dream ahead to Considerate House Two, I find myself inclined to stick with the 19th Street House infrastructure systems and to settle for whatever incremental improvements I can turn up. Margin-of-safety thinking is kicking in. Building a house on spec is risky enough. Why then switch to systems with unknown costs? If you have a strategy that is working, why exchange it for an uncertain alternative you have never used before?

Before giving up hope of making any substantial improvement over Considerate House One infrastructure, however, I push aside my inclination toward frugality and force myself to take a long look at a last possibility, one straight from the world of glamour green. It is a possibility that involves, of all things, the rooftop photovoltaic (PV) panels for generating electricity that I so emphatically rejected for Considerate House One. In fact, the new possibility I consider includes, as well, a second set of rooftop panels, a so-called "solar thermal" system, to heat water. It even includes an electricity producing wind turbine. It is an all-electric house, with natural gas powered appliances eliminated altogether, that features a thermos-like thermal boundary and has a charging station for an electric car at the garage.

This house is, in the language of the green building movement, a "net zero" or even a "net plus" house—one that uses no power beyond what it produces right on site. Or even more beguiling, in the net plus version, produces more power than it consumes and uses the surplus to charge a vehicle or feeds it into the electrical grid for consumption at other buildings. It does have a certain futuristic allure, this net zero house.

Unhappily, just as with the PV systems discussed in the final section of Chapter Seven, net zero turns out to be a mirage when the financial realities are brought into focus. When the numbers are crunched, all the net zero add-ons increase the construction budget for my considerate house by roughly one-third, or by close to half if the cost of an around-town electric car is figured in. And just what operating expenses are displaced by this huge outlay of capital? The cost of a cup of coffee for utilities each day; and each year, about four trash cans' worth of liquid fuel for the kind of high-mileage, around-town cars that are coming on the market in increasing abundance and variety. (The math, in case you are interested: 8,000 around-town miles divided by forty miles per gallon equals 200 gallons, or four fifty-gallon trash cans' worth of fuel.)

Joe Lstiburek, the sardonic building science guru, has dismissed net zero as "boutique technology." I agree. Net zero is, for the moment, nothing more than a fashion statement. It's for people with money to toss around on cool gadgets intended to show off their greenness to friends and neighbors, or maybe a fun project for techno-nerds.

With the vanishing of the net zero vision, I conclude that it is not likely I will achieve any big breakthrough in cost reduction at Considerate House Two. I will chip away where I can during the production of the foundation, frame, and exterior skin, and during interior completion. But I know I will not be able to chip away much unless I become willing to descend from dollarwise construction to the "affordable" construction that generally turns out to be merely crummy, soon crumbling.

I will not be willing. To offer the house at a lower price point, I may have to offer a less complete house, a house with, for example, only one finished bathroom and with the other potential bathroom spaces only rough plumbed and wired, available as storage spaces until the owners are able to complete them. It may turn out that for people of modest means to afford my considerate house, some of its comforts may have to arrive as Christmas presents in future years. These folks will, I console myself, be able to save for those presents to themselves by maximizing the energy sipping possibilities of their new home. They will have to pony up for the gifts, but at least I will be able to leave them with the box and a ribbon.

Though I will continue searching for improvements, the strategies for Considerate House Two will, it seems, remain much the same as for One. I won't be firing off any big silver bullet, just hoping to forge a few more silver B-Bs. I will aim to go green by designing in efficiency, not by glamorous gadgetization. I will stick with green simple over Hummer green. And I will stay with the pyramid of values that guided the construction of 19ᵗʰ Street House: Healthy. Environment Considerate. Dollarwise. Architonic. That, as best I can figure, is what a house should be.

GLOSSARY

Air hammer—A synonym for air handler (see below).

Air handler—A term used by heating and air conditioning professionals. Typically an air handler is a metal box containing a fan that moves air across a burner or coil to warm or cool it, then pushes the air into the building through a system of ducts.

Architekton—Chief carpenter, derived from the Greek roots "archos" (chief) and "tekton" (carpenter). As used in *Considerate House*, "architekton" refers to a person who practices the work of imagining, drawing, and constructing buildings as a unified process rather than working exclusively on one side or the other of the current designer/ builder divide.

Architonic—The quality possessed by buildings that satisfy all our senses, not only the visual (with which the term "architecture" is so heavily associated).

Big "A" architecture—A term used by certain architects to laud buildings that possess unique and memorable form, space, and detail.

Budget—The funds available for crafting a house from start to completion, including conceptualization of alternative schemes, drawing, engineering, permits, construction, and recycling of waste.

Building scientist—A person who applies scientific methods of observation and controlled experimentation to determining the relative performance of alternative building systems.

Change order—An order for additional work beyond that covered by the initial contract for construction of a project.

Chase—A passageway built into or along the face of a wall, ceiling, or floors to carry ducts, pipe, or wires.

Compact fluorescent lamp (CFL)—A small fluorescent lamp with its tube formed into a tight coil.

Crafting—In *Considerate House*, "crafting" is given a broad meaning suggested by Webster's (1968 Second College Edition) first definition: exercise of a "special skill, art, or dexterity," and not the narrower definition indicating only manual capability. Thus, "crafting" is used to suggest a unified process for the making of buildings, as opposed to a process divided into design and construction practiced by separate (often antagonistic) professions.

Direct costs of construction—The on-site costs of the labor, material, and services required by a construction project.

Dollar wisdom—Thoughtful and frugal allocation of financial resources so as to maximize environmental, health, and architonic benefits and to reduce waste in the crafting of a house.

DWV—An abbreviation for "drain, waste, and vent," the three types of plumbing lines that work in combination to remove water and waste from a building.

Elevation—A drawing that gives a straight-on view of interior or exterior walls.

Embedded or embodied energy—The energy used in creating a building product. The author prefers "embedded" to the more widely adopted "embodied" because we put, or embed, energy into products in the course of creating or using them. They do not embody the energy in and of themselves prior to our intervention.

Environment considerate building—Building that seeks to minimize negative impacts on the habitat of living things—including plants, animals, neighbors, and the wider human community.

Fenestration—The arrangement of the windows and doors within a building.

First costs—The costs of constructing a building, as opposed to heating, cooling, lighting, and otherwise operating and maintaining it.

Flashing—Elements of a building skin intended to direct liquid water away from the frame and interior.

Frugal—Not wasteful.

Frugalista—An affectionate term describing a person who practices frugality with religious feeling.

Gerstel corner—Aa corner in a house frame that uses strips of scrap plywood rather than whole pieces of lumber to provide backing for drywall.

Green simple—Environment considerate building that emphasizes low-cost, consumption reducing measures rather than adding on costly devices.

Greenwashing—A marketing strategy that emphasizes an allegedly "green" aspect of a product while hiding or glossing over its environment damaging aspects.

Healthy houses—Houses in which the use of toxic materials for construction and operation is minimized and good indoor air quality is maintained.

Heat recovery ventilator (HRV)—A device that transfers heat from the stale air it is moving out of a house to the (hopefully) fresher air it is pulling in.

House-as-system and House is a system—Terms emphasizing that the performance of a house, especially with respect to its use of energy for operation and maintenance and its durability, depends on the relationship of its subsystems (such as framing and insulation), not simply on each system taken separately.

House wrap—Sheet material wrapped around a building frame to protect it against moisture.

Hummer green—A term coined by Harold Newman, MD, to describe huge houses festooned with highly visible, allegedly "green" devices in order to lay claim to environmental awards or prestige.

HVAC—An abbreviation for heating, ventilation, and air conditioning.

IAQ—An abbreviation for indoor air quality.

Joists—The lumber, typically 2x8s, 2x10s, 2x12s, or TJIs (see below), used to frame floors.

Life cycle cost assessment (LCA)—A calculation of the environmental impacts or costs, particularly in terms of energy inputs and toxic outputs, from the beginning to the end of a product's life.

Mudsill—The sticks of lumber attached to a house foundation that bear the weight of the other elements of the house frame.

Nominal dollars—Dollar figures that have not yet been adjusted for inflation.

Oriented strand board (OSB)—Panels made from flakes of wood and glue that have supplanted plywood in recent years.

Overhead—The costs of construction (such as expenditures for office computers and supplies) beyond those of the labor, materials, and services consumed at a job site.

Panel goods—Plywood, oriented strand board (see above), or other sheet goods, typically measuring four feet by eight feet, used especially for sheathing of walls and roofs and for subfloors.

Precautionary principle—An idea put forward by ethicists mandating, with respect to building, that 1) if the safety, long-term cost, or environmental impact of a product or method is in doubt, you should hold off using it; and 2) lack of evidence that the product is harmful should not be considered adequate assurance that it is okay. In short, better safe than sorry.

Real dollars—Dollar figures that have been adjusted for inflation.

Rise and run—The vertical and horizontal distance traveled by a stairway or by its individual steps, i.e., its risers and treads.

Section—A drawing that portrays a slice through a building.

Slippage—The tendency of buildings to perform less well than forecast during conceptualization and drawing.

Structured plumbing®—Plumbing supply lines carefully sized, laid out, and installed to minimize the waste of water and energy, particularly in supplying hot water from the water heater to a tap.

Studs—The vertical pieces of lumber, typically 2x4s or 2x6s spaced sixteen or twenty-four inches apart, in a wall frame.

TJIs—A modern, engineered form of lumber made up of thin strips and flakes of wood and resin. TJIs are used in place of the large pieces of solid lumber traditionally installed to support floors.

Two feet on-center framing—Framing for which the joists, studs, and roof trusses or rafters are placed so that their center lines are two feet from the center lines of the adjacent sticks. Thus, the distance from the center line of one stud will measure two feet to the center line of the next.

Working drawings—The detailed drawings of building components used as a guide for construction in the field.

RESOURCES

So much to learn, so little time! For that reason I have described here only the resources—among a multitude of useful books, magazines, and Web sites related to building—that I have found especially valuable.

Books:

Between Silence and Light: Spirit in the Architecture of Louis I. Kahn by Louis Kahn and John Lobell—A concise exposition of Kahn's approach to capturing and excluding light in order to enhance our experience of built form and space. Yes, a bit highfalutin at times, but illuminating, too.

Biomimicry: Innovation Inspired by Nature by Janine M. Benyus— If you love building but worry about the impact of the work on our planet, *Biomimicry* can fill you with hope for the future. Benyus is criticized for not getting all the technical details right as she covers a wide range of scientific subjects armed merely with a master's degree. But even those who try to take her down admit that Benyus is making an important subject more accessible to lay readers. By imitating nature (biomimicking), she reports, we can convert our economic processes—design and construction among them—so that they merge with rather than poison and disrupt the organic cycle. Anyone up for a house paint whose pigments are modeled on the chloroplasts in plants and that would produce the power for the building that the paint is applied to? Now that might be real "green" building, not merely environment considerate.

Broken Buildings, Busted Budgets: How to Fix America's Trillion-Dollar Construction Industry by Barry B. LePatner—Rightly criticized for being overly redundant and for a lawyer's bias toward his clients (owners as opposed to builders and designers), LePatner's book is, nevertheless, an exceptionally vigorous exposition of the ailments of and possible cures for the construction industry.

Builder's Guide to Mixed Climates: Details for Design and Construction by Joseph W. Lstiburek—While *Mixed Climates* is appropriate to construction in my part of the world, Lstiburek also publishes guides for building in cold and humid climates. His books are invaluable for their clear illustrations and explanations of such critical components of new buildings as framing systems, thermal boundaries, and vapor management.

Building an Affordable House: Trade Secrets to High-Value, Low-Cost Construction by Fernando Pagés Ruiz—Mr. Ruiz, a builder of small housing tracts for people of modest incomes in New Mexico, relentlessly searches for ways to trim construction cost while maintaining durability and energy efficiency in his homes. Even builders who may judge it dollarwise to initially spend more for the sake of greater architonic, health, and environmental benefits and reduction of long-term maintenance and operating costs will find his book full of thought- provoking and immediately useful ideas.

The Healthy House: How to Buy One, How to Build One, How to Cure a Sick One by John Bower—A comprehensive guide, based both on experience and research, by one of the pioneers in the healthy house field, Bower's book is enormously helpful if you are building, remodeling, or renovating a house. If you are unfamiliar with healthy house principles and living in a home that was built or renovated without regard for them, you might prefer your ignorance to the fear the book may create. On the other hand, when it comes time to repair, renovate, or improve your home, Bower's book will give you a better shot at doing it without further threatening the health of you and your family.

Home: A Short History of an Idea by Witold Rybczynski—Amidst architects' commentaries on their craft, too often impenetrable or breathtakingly arrogant, Professor Rybczynski's book stands out as a down-to-earth vision of priorities. The point of drawing and constructing a house, Rybczynski reminds his fellow architects and the rest of us, is so that a family can make a comfortable home within. Rybczynski is a good storyteller. He entertains as he educates us about the history of our concern with such matters as privacy, air quality, efficiency, light, and intimacy in our homes.

A Pattern Language: Towns–Buildings–Construction by Christopher Alexander, Sara Ishikawa, and Murray Silverstein with Max Jacobson, Ingrid Fiksdahl-King, and Shlomo Angel—Professor Alexander's title smacks a bit of pretentiousness. Why not just *Patterns for Building*? That is what the book contains, a series of 253 patterns for building that, in the view of Alexander and his coauthors, have proved their worth over the centuries. The numbered patterns are ordered from the largest to the smallest in scope, for example: #2 The Distribution of Towns; #21 Four-Story Limit; #159 Light on Two Sides of Every Room; #236 Windows Which Open Wide.

Whether by accident or from hubris, with its paper cover removed, the book could be mistaken for a bible. But the fact is, in the world of building, it comes as deservedly close to bible status as any book I know of. It is a profoundly humane work, rooted in anthropology, sociology, and progressive social thought as much as in a love for the sensory pleasures provided by well-wrought buildings. Illustrated with the simplest of pencil sketches and black and white photographs, it is concerned not with producing art-trophy houses for the wealthy and privileged but with enriching everyday experience for us all.

Readers who don't feel quite ready for Alexander's bible can approach it through two simplified versions. *Patterns of Home: The Ten Essentials of Enduring Design*, by Max Jacobs, Murray Silverstein, and Barbara Winslow, features large glossy photos of costly homes and is markedly less humanistic than the original work, but does an excellent job of successfully distilling out patterns of central concern in house design. Sarah Susanka's popular *Not So Big House* series also offers simplified, clear, and helpful access to building pattern language.

Residential Energy: Cost Savings and Comfort for Existing Buildings by John T. Krigger and Chris Dorsi—A clear and comprehensive guide to the fundamental principles and practices of energy conservation in house construction, the book gets you well on your way to understanding "house as a system" thinking. Visit Krigger and Dorsi at Saturn Resource Management (srmi.biz) to learn about their prodigious experience in the field of energy efficiency, their other books, and the online training courses they offer.

Running a Successful Construction Company by David Gerstel— With some hesitation, I will mention a book of my own. For the fact is, I regularly hear from readers who express the kind of appreciation for it that I have expressed here for other books. If you have found *Crafting a Considerate House* useful and feel it would be helpful to understand more about the management side of construction (alternatives to competitive bidding, estimates, overhead, profit, contracts, sequencing phases of work during a project, and so on), my earlier book may be worth a look. See for yourself; both the strengths and limitations of *Running a Successful Construction Company* are well articulated in reviews posted at online bookstores.

Why Buildings Stand Up: The Strength of Architecture by Mario Salvadori, together with ***Why Buildings Fall Down: How Structures Fail*** by Matthys Levy, Mario Salvadori, and Kevin Woest (even more gripping a read, of course), provide an accessible and fascinating introduction to the principles of structural engineering.

Wood: Detailing for Wood Performance by William Dost and Elmer Botsai—Dost's book is a superb and clearly illustrated guide to building durable wood houses. The entire book is available online, free. Just Google the title and you will locate a PDF of the book at the Web site of Contra Costa County, University of California Cooperative Extension.

Magazines and Articles:

Atlantic Monthly—If you are an architekton, independently crafting buildings and master of your immediate universe, a cover-to-cover reading of the *Monthly* is an efficient and stimulating way to keep track of emerging forces in the larger world that will inevitably buffet your own.

Ecostructure—Not surprisingly, given that the magazine is free (to building professionals), the editorial content can be a bit uneven. Mostly, however, *Ecostructure* is accessible and informative. The projects it presents are inspiring both architonically and environmentally. Its analyses of the challenges inherent in "green" building are penetrating, a powerful antidote to the glib prescriptions often offered elsewhere. I read it cover to cover every month.

Fine Homebuilding—For decades, *Fine Homebuilding* has produced carefully crafted information. It has been rightly criticized as too focused on homes for the economically privileged, for a tendency to honor lavish houses as "green," and for naivete about construction costs. But the magazine is fueled by love for the work of crafting homes and infused with respect for the men and women who do it. The writing and editing is generally excellent and often moving. At finehomebuilding.com you can download over a thousand of the magazine's articles, including many that offer clear how-to information about such tasks as frugal framing, thermal boundaries, and flat-pak cabinets that are part and parcel of building a considerate house.

Saving Water and Energy in Residential Hot Water Distribution Systems by Gary Klein—Klein's illuminating articles on structured plumbing®, are available at www.allianceforwaterefficiency.org

Seminar:

Pacific Energy Center—The Energy Center offers superb, free, all-day seminars on energy efficiency at a variety of locations in California. The presenters come from all over the United States and even from Canada and the education they offer is helpful in many climate zones, not only in the West. Increasingly, the seminars are available online.

Bookstore:

Builders Booksource—Located in Berkeley, California, the Booksource is much beloved locally and is a destination for building professionals visiting the San Francisco Bay Area. The knowledgeable staff can guide you to a useful book or magazine on every aspect of crafting houses. Books may also be ordered online at <u>buildersbooksource.com.</u>

INDEX

CPSIA information can be obtained
at www.ICGtesting.com
Printed in the USA
BVHW041431261218
536437BV00022B/1099/P